FACILITATING
CAREER DEVELOPMENT

FACILITATING
CAREER DEVELOPMENT

STRATEGIES FOR
COUNSELORS

Edited by

ROBERT C. REARDON, Ph.D.

Associate Professor
Counseling Psychologist
Florida State University
Tallahassee, Florida

and

HARMAN D. BURCK, Ph.D.

Associate Professor
Florida State University
Tallahassee, Florida

With a Foreword by

Harold F. Cottingham, Ed.D.

Professor
Florida State University
Tallahassee, Florida

CHARLES C THOMAS · PUBLISHER

Springfield · Illinois · U.S.A.

Published and Distributed Throughout the World by
CHARLES C THOMAS • PUBLISHER
BANNERSTONE HOUSE
301-327 East Lawrence Avenue, Springfield, Illinois, U.S.A.

© *1975, by* CHARLES C THOMAS • PUBLISHER
ISBN 0-398-03359-5 (paper)
0-398-03360-9 (cloth)
Library of Congress Catalog Card Number: 74-23880

With THOMAS BOOKS *careful attention is given to all details of manufacturing and design. It is the Publisher's desire to present books that are satisfactory as to their physical qualities and artistic possibilities and appropriate for their particular use.* THOMAS BOOKS *will be true to those laws of quality that assure a good name and good will.*

Printed in the United States of America
N-1

Library of Congress Cataloging in Publication Data

Reardon, Robert C.
    Facilitating career development.

    Includes index.
    1. Vocational guidance—Addresses, essays, lectures. I. Burck, Harman D., joint author. II. Title.
HF5381.R338   331.7'02   74-23880
ISBN 0-398-03360-9
ISBN 0-398-03359-5 pbk.

CONTRIBUTORS

ELLEN S. AMATEA, Ph.D.
Assistant Professor
University of Florida
Gainesville, Florida

JOHN R. BONAR, Ph.D.
Director, Academic and Career Advising Services
Florida State, University
Tallahassee, Florida

DONALD A. BROWN, Ph.D.
Director, Counseling Center
University of Michigan, Dearborn
Dearborn, Michigan

HARMAN D. BURCK, Ph.D.
Associate Professor
Florida State University
Tallahassee, Florida

MARY Q. BURKHART, Ph.D.
Office of Continuing Education
Auburn University
Auburn, Alabama

DONALD J. COCHRAN, Ph.D.
Counseling Psychologist
Illinois State University
Normal, Illinois

MICHAEL J. GIMMESTAD, Ph.D.
Assistant Professor
Florida State University
Tallahassee, Florida

S. DAVID HOFFMAN, Ph.D.
Counseling Psychologist
Illinois State University
Normal, Illinois

ROBERT MacALEESE, Ph.D.
Assistant Professor
Boston University
Boston, Massachusetts

CAROLE W. MINOR, M.S.
Career Development Specialist
Florida State University
Tallahassee, Florida

DAN MONTGOMERY, Ph.D.
Counseling Psychologist
Florida State University
Tallahassee, Florida

WILLIAM L. OLIVER, M.S.
Director, Cooperative Education Program
Florida State University
Tallahassee, Florida

GARY W. PETERSON, Ph.D.
Research Associate
Florida State University
Tallahassee, Florida

ROBERT C. REARDON, Ph.D.
Associate Professor
Florida State University
Tallahassee, Florida

WINIFRED O. STONE, Ph.D.
Assistant Dean and
Director of Graduate Admissions
Bowling Green State University
Bowling Green, Ohio

PATRICK SWEENEY, Ph.D.
Research Associate
Florida State University
Tallahassee, Florida

FOREWORD

THERE IS NO SHORTAGE of publications in the counseling and guidance area today. There is however, a deficiency of titles which have both substance, practicality, and relevance. This book meets these criteria. In addition, it offers a transition between the more theoretical aspects of career development and the needs of counselors in the field.

One of the problems facing the career development movement is the limited material on programs and practices which has immediate personal or institutional application. While theories exist, supported by both longitudinal and choice-point research, the greater concern voiced by many is for methods and practices which can be used directly by those who help adolescents face vocational decisions. Hence, the availability of a volume such as this can serve a genuine purpose in complementing those existing publications which focus less on the application and more on the conceptualizing of significant factors in career counseling. Yet, a published collection of practices can also have a valuable reciprocal effect on the theorizing process, since as practices are executed, prior theories may be validated or implicit assumptions may become new theoretical constructs. It is certainly a sound premise that vocational decision-making continues in many settings, despite lack of confirmed roots in explicit theory. As methods such as those illustrated in this book are shared among practitioners, the seeds for even more useful research and concept building can be sown.

A number of distinctive features characterize this volume. It obviously reflects some of the newer educational trends, applicable to career development. The value of more individualized approaches as well as program designs for preventive assistance are both clearly recognized. The mere breadth of suggested strategies offers a rich grouping of resources for the counselor seeking a more dynamic or innovative means of vocational guidance interventions. This scope is easily illustrated by material dealing with special populations, group process, simulation methods, or contractual schemes. An awareness that career planning is not the exclusive domain of the professional counselor, but an opportunity for other educators or settings, is seen in an emphasis on curricular offerings as well as community and self-help resource services. The central thrust of career education with its stress on element identification, outcome qualities and self-actualization is evident in the writings of many of the contributors. Although the primary focus of the suggested strategies is on the process of helping the individual find himself through his work, the broader role of the educational system in career development is not overlooked. In summary, this book is a welcome addition to the career development literature.

The writer takes pride in the fact that most of the contributing authors were at one time among his students at Florida State University. This factor may be more coincidental than significant. However, it has currently accentuated his personal involvement in this project.

HAROLD F. COTTINGHAM

PREFACE

THIS BOOK IS ABOUT THE facilitation and promotion of career development. It differs from most books in psychology and counseling because it attempts to emphasize growth and development in the vocational sphere of a person's life. This is certainly one of the most fundamental and challenging areas of professional activity for helping persons. The book focuses on many different intervening strategies and delivery systems which a counselor might use to facilitate career development.

In this book, "career" is viewed as a time-extended working out of a purposeful life pattern through work undertaken by the person. Career development, in turn, refers to the total constellation of psychological, sociological, educational, physical, economic, and chance factors that combine to shape the career of any given individual. Work is seen as a basic component of one's life style, and the way in which one attempts to satisfy his very basic needs. Work may be defined as effort expended to create something of value to self or others, which includes leisure or other nonpaid activity. These definitions are taken primarily from the National Vocational Guidance Association—American Vocational Association joint position paper on career development and career guidance.

It should be noted that we have intentionally avoided extensive reference to career education in this book. This is not meant as any negation of the career education movement currently flourishing in many sections of the country. It is, however, based on our belief that career development is a broader concept than career education which is often viewed primarily as an educational delivery system; that counselors have a legacy and mandate to promote individual career development which preceeds the present emphasis on career education; and that counselors can facilitate individual career development either in spite of or in concert with career education.

The book emphasizes practice. Practice is defined as those activities and strategies which persons in helping professions, particularly counselors, can implement to help a variety of clientele in becoming more effective, adaptive, and maneuverable in their careers. Most other books in this area have addressed themselves to describing theories of career development, collating scattered and segmented readings in the general area of vocational development, reporting techniques for the acquisition and dissemination of occupational information, and describing *either* counseling *or* programmatic ways of intervening in career guidance. Our primary aim is to present to the practitioner those media, techniques, strategies, and delivery systems which will be of immediate assistance when he is confronted by either the young person who is struggling with the question, "What will I do with my life?" or the school wanting to improve the quality of the career plans of its students.

The chapter authors were deliberately selected because of their academic interest and professional commitment to the facilitation of career development. They have presented extended descriptions of practical techniques for intervening with individuals, groups, or larger social systems to promote career development. Each of the chapters has been carefully edited to reflect the central purpose of the book, and the chapters have been written from a common format. It is suggested that the reader begin by reading Chapters 1 and 2, and the brief introductions to Parts II and III. In this way, an overview of the scope, content, format, and the unique contributions of each chapter can be quickly grasped.

We have endeavored to prepare this book for practitioners in the helping professions, especially vocational counselors; secondary level counselors; counselors in post secondary settings, e.g. vocational-technical and community colleges, colleges and universities; employment counselors; academic advisors; placement officers; cooperative education directors; and psychologists working in a wide variety of settings. Likewise, the book would be of use for students enrolled in undergraduate and graduate programs such as psychology, counselor education, student personnel work, vocational rehabilitation, social work, or where there is an emphasis on the practice of facilitating career development. Of course, the primary clientele to be affected by this book are youth from sixteen to twenty-two years of age.

We would like to express thanks and appreciation to many people, including Charles C Thomas, Publisher. They have been very supportive, helpful, and encouraged us to do this book the way we wanted. The thirteen chapter authors put up with our deadlines and requests for additional drafts for a year, and we appreciate their commitment, mutual encouragement and continuing interest. We also acknowledge the special contribution of the career development model prepared by Camille Ashcraft which is included in Appendix A. A special word of thanks also goes to Ann Benson, Sandy Cole, and Debra Martin who have helped us with typing and other parts of the project along the way.

R.C.R.
H.D.B.

CONTENTS

Page

Contributors v

Foreword vii

Preface ix

PART I BACKGROUND AND ASSUMPTIONS

Chapter

1 FACILITATING CAREER DEVELOPMENT: PAST EVENTS AND THE
CURRENT SCENE 5

2 CONTRIBUTIONS OF CAREER DEVELOPMENT THEORIES 17

PART II COUNSELING STRATEGIES

3 USING INFORMATION IN CAREER COUNSELING 37

4 THE ROLE OF ASSESSMENT IN CAREER COUNSELING 52

5 SIMULATION TECHNIQUES IN CAREER COUNSELING 70

6 A SHORT TERM CONTRACTUAL APPROACH TO CAREER COUNSELING 85

7 GROUPS IN CAREER COUNSELING 100

PART III PROGRAM STRATEGIES

8 DEVELOPING AN EDUCATIONAL/CAREER GUIDANCE PROGRAM ... 130

9 CURRICULAR APPROACHES AND SELF-HELP TECHNIQUES FOR
CAREER DEVELOPMENT 152

10 DEVELOPING A CAREER RESOURCE CENTER 178

11 USING COMMUNITY RESOURCES 197

12 CAREER DEVELOPMENT FOR WOMEN 213

13 CAREER COUNSELING FOR THE HOMOSEXUAL 234

14 CAREER DEVELOPMENT FOR ETHNIC MINORITIES 248

15 ACCOUNTABILITY IN PROGRAM EVALUATION: A HYPOTHETICAL
CASE STUDY 268

Page

APPENDIX A A CAREER DEVELOPMENT MODEL IN A UNIVERSITY
          SETTING 283

Author Index 309
Subject Index 313

FACILITATING
CAREER DEVELOPMENT

Part I

BACKGROUND AND ASSUMPTIONS

Chapter One

FACILITATING CAREER DEVELOPMENT: PAST EVENTS AND THE CURRENT SCENE

HARMAN D. BURCK

"I WANT TO GO INTO COUNSELING, but I'm not interested in doing vocational guidance."

This statement reflects the attitudes of many counselors in training and on the job. Career counseling, generally, is low in prestige among professional counselors, and seems to be acceptable to many only as a stepchild of personal and social counseling. In many settings it has been relegated to a separate, but not equal, status. Generally, there is little emphasis on the career counseling process in most counselor education programs. Why has the important task of assisting youth plan for their future been looked upon with dislike and disinterest by counselors and counselor educators, especially at a time when contemporary youth experience bewilderment, confusion and conflict in the process? The purpose of this chapter is to attempt to answer this question by (a) pointing out some of the past and current events and attitudes affecting vocational guidance, and (b) indicating the complexity of the task of facilitating career development by looking at the contemporary adolescent and his environment.

VOCATIONAL GUIDANCE: THE PAST AND CURRENT SCENE

Whereas the writings of great pioneers in the field such as Frank Parsons, John Brewer, Jesse Davis and others (who were, incidentally, social reformers rather than counselors) have always reflected complex and comprehensive theoretical notions about the task of vocational guidance; history indicates an emphasis on the imparting of occupational information and the use of testing as primary tools. This trait-and-factor approach, revolutionary and imaginative in its time, has persisted as the most popular way to go about helping youth. Essentially this approach consists of giving the client a battery of aptitude tests and interest inventories, and interpreting the results by matching the individual profile with particular sets of job requirements. Such an approach has met with very little success in today's world, largely because it is limited in helping with immediate, specific decisions, is more descriptive than explanatory, and is unable to incorporate rapidly changing facts and trends in the labor market. Yet, many counselors still continue to operate exclusively from this model—the test profile in one hand, and the occupational brief in the other.

In the late 1940's, as if to leave behind all that had been accomplished from theory and research, a sharp trend developed in which the major emphasis was to explore the dynamics and motivations of the client with an eye to assisting and enhancing his self-concept. This resulted in the application of psychodynamic therapeutic theories (psychoanalytic, client-centered, etc.) to vocational concerns. In theory, at least, testing became a no-no, and occupational information became much less important. Theoretically and practically, this trend made a very important contribution; yet, attempts to help youth with their career planning exclusively from this theoretical point of view has not been particularly productive because a. these therapeutic models are too far removed from the career confusion the client may be experiencing; b. they usually have singular goals for all clients; and c. they lack important elements like occupational information, labor forecasts and trends, and the relevance of cognitive processes.

So, the use of outmoded theoretical models and the frequent and overzealous adaptation of inappropriate therapy and personality change theories are partly responsible for the current sad state of affairs. At least three other factors have also contributed to the present situation of disinterest in career guidance: the notion that vocational counseling is routine and simple, resulting in a low prestige factor; the lack of academic excitement about the topic and lack of vocational guidance practice in most counselor education/training programs; and a singularity of approach in dealing with clients presenting vocational concerns.

First, helping a youth with vocational concerns is viewed by many professionals as uninteresting, routine, simple, and a service anyone with little training (particularly if they have work experience!) or imagination can perform. Because of professional pettiness and narrowness we have made vocational counseling routine in practice, but that does not make it easy. Helping a confused student start thinking about what he will do in life vocationally, is as difficult, intricate and challenging a task as working with a sexually deviant client or a drug addict. In fact, when we look at the complexity of the task, we might find that it is more intricate and difficult than much so called personal-social counseling. Perhaps it may be that a greater diversity of skills and competencies are needed. Historically, the counseling and guidance professionals have been charged with the vocational and occupational guidance of youth. Yet, ample evidence suggests that the profession has not delivered well in this area. Ginzberg (1971) concluded that the "60-year-old school guidance movement has failed to reach its goals," and that counselors generally do not play "a decisive role in the career plans" of students. But the need for services exists. Based on a study sample of 32,000 eighth, ninth and eleventh graders at two hundred public and parochial schools, the American College Testing Program (Prediger, 1973) reports that 56 percent of the eleventh graders indicated they "had received little or no help with career planning via discussions with counselors." Consider also, the results of a national profile report prepared by the College Board (1974) and which involved over one million high school seniors: "though the . . . profile of college-bound students indicates that large numbers are, by their own account, seasoned and successful at academic work and ambitious for advanced placement and advanced degrees, approximately 70 percent also indicate a strong need for college counseling about educational and vocational plans and opportunities."

Today, counselors are involved in a myriad of other activities which they feel should consume their time: drug abuse, human relations, affective education, parent effectiveness training, crisis intervention, out-reach programs, and routine administrative duties. No doubt these interests and activities are very important and worthwhile endeavors, but it leaves precious little time in the life of the professional who has a concern for assisting youth with their career development.

The above situation has helped shape a set of professional attitudes which has to do with the prestige and status afforded career counseling. Within the counseling profession there is no doubt that there is low prestige for the counselor whose main interest is facilitating career development. This is best exemplified in an article by Putsell (1965; also see Burck, 1966), in which the organization and structure of a unified counseling center is described. Putsell states, "His (vocational counselor) concentration on the vocational counseling frees the clinical psychologist to spend more time with students having emotional problems," and concludes ". . . a clinical or counseling psychologist trained at the doctoral level is apt to become dissatisfied if circumstances require him to spend most of his time doing routine vocational counseling which is uncomplicated by psychological difficulties" (1965, p. 172).

All too often, vocational clients are referred to beginning practicum students and interns, and other junior staff members in order that senior staff may work with the so-called "real" counseling cases. Much too often, we attempt to clearly separate vocational concerns from personal-emotional ones, although this is impossible to do, which the following example demonstrates. A first year student who had studied for years and had set her sights on being a concert pianist, was suddenly but bluntly told by her piano professor that she would never make it and that she ought to think of entering another vocational field. She was reported to be a vocational client by a beginning clinician. Obviously, she had a vocational problem, but a counselor would not get far until he thoroughly explored the emotional aspects of the situation. Career counseling and programs must be reinstated into our work priorities, and they must be afforded greater status and prestige.

Secondly, an event which has occurred in the academic prepartion of counselors has been most distressing and contributory to the present situation; namely, the de-emphasis of vocational counseling and the rather unconcerned fashion in which students have been introduced to it. A survey of most Master's counseling programs would reveal just one course in this area, and it is often referred to as Occupational Information, although it might occasionally encompass a superficial introduction to several career development theories. Frequently, these courses are dull and taught by junior faculty who have little interest, limited knowledge, and even less skill in the facilitation of career development. Consequently, many students complete counselor education programs where they have acquired few skills or competencies which will assist them on their jobs, and where they have been exposed to little excitement about career counseling as an activity.

Finally, in practice it is noted that most counselors, whatever their theoretical counseling point of view, generally approach the task of career counseling in a singular sort of fashion. These same counselors commence the vocational counseling process in a rigid, standardized sort of way; yet, when dealing with client concerns of a more delineated personal/emotional nature, they usually try to start the counseling process where the client is in his emotional development. Seldom does it seem that the vocational maturity level of the student is taken seriously into consideration. For example, the client whose main immediate concern is difficulty with authority (manifested by trouble with his father) somehow is treated in a similar sort of way as the student who is much more vocationally mature and who is trying to decide whether to major in medicine or biophysics.

THE CONTEMPORARY ADOLESCENT

Today's youth find themselves living in one of the most complex, affluent, technocratic and turbulent societies ever known to man; a society which is undergoing very rapid and extensive change in all segments.

As a result, youth today, more than ever before, find the problem of career planning and choosing a vocation a confusing and intricate one. They are confronted with a seemingly ever-increasing array of opportunities from which they might choose, yet find themselves with little, if any, information and knowledge about the general nature of the work world, much less with comprehensive knowledge of specific job areas or the career planning process. Yet, high school students across the nation seem to be aware of their need for help in this area of their life. For example, the ACT study referred to previously (1973) showed that "more than three-fourths of the nation's high school juniors and nearly as many eighth and ninth graders would like help with career planning." In a study in the state of Montana (*Guidepost,* 1973) it was found that students, parents and teachers felt counselors should provide more vocational services to students. A survey of 1,244 students by Daniel Yankelovich, Inc. (1971) revealed that four out of five students surveyed believe that "commitment to a meaningful career is a very important part of a person's life." In addition, these students were more concerned and serious about studying and more fearful about being able to get a job in the future than a group surveyed in 1968 and 1969.

In addition to the above confusion, contemporary youth seem to know little about themselves as people, their feelings or fears, their prejudices or preferences, or an understanding of their behavior. They desperately want to understand and become aware of these personal characteristics and attributes, sort them out in meaningful ways, and relate them to their career progression. Career planning and choosing has not always been as complicated as it is presently. In bygone times, the son taking over his father's farm had a very firm idea of what his job would consist of—indeed, he had been involved in his future occupation for many years. He probably had been able to establish a pretty accurate assessment of how well he might perform such a job. Also, he lived in a rural society whose values and behavior preferences were clearly spelled out and rather static. Today's young person is far more distant from the eventual locus of work—in fact, he probably could render few accurate facts about what his father does at work and is likely not to have even physically visited the work site. His own eventual choice may be in an occupational area of which his family is totally unfamiliar.

The ways in which theorists have conceptualized the dynamics of human behavior and personality change in relation to career development have increased immensely in recent years. Theorists like Holland, Roe, Super, Tiedeman and others have provided rich theoretical explanations of the crucial importance of certain personality constructs and dimensions as influencers of career development. Such constructs include: self-concept, self-understanding, attitudes, values, perceptual processes, life-stages, developmental tasks, identity formation, to name only a few. These considerations must be taken into account along with more traditional notions of career determinants, like interests, aptitudes, abilities and work experiences. This reconceptualization of who a person is, how they get the way they are, how they behave, and how we should go about changing them, has dramatic implications for changing the ways in which we attempt to facilitate career development. Some examples of this importance follow. Today, we must realize that people have as much, if not more, capacity to create problems for themselves and others than to solve problems, that they can very effectively sabotage huge business ventures or massive social programs in innocent and unintentional sorts of ways, and that they can become very different kinds of people if only they desire it. As observers of human behavior, it is interesting to note how frequently parents psychologically harm their children; how employees sabotage their supervisors' pet project, and in a burst of activity reduce productivity; and how committee members, under the guise of cooperation, divert the group's tasks, and hopelessly stymie progress. People are not static—they can modify old traits and acquire new ones. Their potential for change is virtually unlimited. The implication of these examples is that extensive knowledge and deep understandings of human behavior are needed by the counselor as he works with his clientele and their career motivations and aspirations.

YOUTH'S ENVIRONMENT

Contemporary youth will find a vast array of inconsistencies and ironies in their environment. Living in "America the Beautiful," youth will find that they live in a society which, in terms of sex habits, is one of the most liberated in the world, yet there is less intimacy and sensitivity in interpersonal relations than in most countries. They will not give much thought to the fact that they will probably see their next door neighbors more frequently at the local shopping mall than from their own homes. Even more disconcerting might be the fact that while the unemployment rate might be rather high (like 6.5 percent) there will be no need for well-educated engineers, but a great need for practical nurses or plumber's helpers. They will not be much aware that society has changed drastically since the second world war, but might notice that the change is so pervasive and occurs at such a rapid rate it taxes the coping behavior of the most healthy functioning person. The change affects every facet of life: education, government, family, religion, peer groups, and business and industry to name a few. All of this change, and the dynamics of it, have serious implications for counselors as they approach the task of attempting to facilitate the career development of youth.

Present day youth will find that they will spend much more of their life in formal and informal educational settings. This will occur at both the preschool and at the post-secondary level. In most situations, after twelve to sixteen years of formal schooling, they will be in apprentice or training programs, whether in business, industry or the military. Not only in the amount of time, but also in content and methods of delivery are vast changes taking place in education (e.g. individualized instruction, relating academic content to the work world, affective education, sex education, modular scheduling). Youth in school today witness, and are a part of, a swiftly changing educational process.

In their dealings with government at all levels, they will find that their life becomes more and more shaped by decisions made by governmental agencies. They may discover that the local government has all the problems, the states have all the rights, and the federal government has all the money. The youth will come to depend more and more on government for the satisfaction of various needs, will realize that their national government can make wise or devastating decisions in dealing with other nations, and that, more and more, nations become greatly inter-dependent on each other to satisfy their basic human needs. Indeed, they may begin to wonder if a representative type of government has the flexibility, adaptability and speed to adequately deal with the social problems they see around them.

They will see vast changes taking place in their own family. In their lifetime, they may have witnessed the decline of the extended family, and seen the family unit relying more on interpersonal closeness and security rather than living together for economic reasons alone (see Blocher, 1973). They will certainly become aware of the obscuring of fixed sex roles between parents, siblings and relatives. In all probability, their mother may well be actively pursuing a career of her own which will be quite different from the father's career but no less rewarding, intense, demanding or as personally important. In terms of their own career confusions and planning, youth will find few resources, skills or knowledge to assist them from the family, although there may be real pressures for them to pursue one profession over another.

Within their own religious sphere they will be a part of a dynamic philosophical questioning and searching, if indeed, they are participants or observers of organized religion at all. Their religious leaders and others will be attempting to inculcate certain moral values or challenging them to explore their own sense of morality, which may seem to conflict with their own feelings and behavior they observe in the everyday world.

As our youth grow older, there will be one group with whom they will identify more, and by whom they will be most influenced—their peers. Many old values that they have will be challenged by this group, and peers will be most influential in shaping certain behaviors—from hair style, clothes and automobile preferences to work values and post-seconday vocational plans. The older youth become, the more this peer group will be the satisfiers of their psychological and physical needs, and shapers of their career aspirations.

The female youth will have some special developmental tasks to master. Because of a legal mandate, and hopefully a growing recognition that women should have the same career opportunities as men, the female adolescent will need to carefully consider how she would like to dovetail her desires for motherhood with her career aspirations, or whether she even wants to. Occupational information and working role-models will be incomplete or non-existent in many job areas. If she is interested in vigorously pursuing an active and demanding career, her mate (if she chooses to have one) must be carefully selected in order for her to have an understanding and cooperative husband rather than one who might be "old fashioned" in his views and expectations about women and motherhood.

And when, finally, our imagined youth begin to learn about business and industry, they will find that this segment becomes more complex, organizationally, and ever changing. They will find that more and more a worker's sophistication at interpersonal skills is as equally important as specific job-related skills and competencies. Generally, they will find the following trends which have implications for their own career planning and preparation:

1. The productivity is rising rapidly and continues to rise; Gross National Product per capita has tripled since 1900.

2. A growing proportion of workers now enter the job market as employees of large corporations instead of as independent workers.

3. The baby boom of the 1940's is now being reflected in approximately one million new workers per year than was the case before 1964 and earlier.

4. There is a rising proportion of women workers with attendant changes in ego concepts and educational needs.

5. Jobs are steadily shifting from the unskilled, semiskilled, and goods-producing type to technical, professional, and service-type occupations.

6. There is a paradoxical change in the length of the work week. Laborers and hourly workers are working less hours per week, while professional and managers generally are working more hours per week (Bernard and Fullmer, 1969, p. 282).

The adolescent will soon learn that something seems to be wrong with the quality of life in the eyes of most Americans. In one way or another discontent seems to surface and be expressed in the nature of complaints and dissatisfaction with work. Our imagined youth will be confused about this and realize that the problem is big, obscure and certainly very complex. Here are parts of a social view he will observe from parents, teachers, peers, television and other sources:

1. Many workers see their job as dull, repetitive, meaningless, and offering little challenge or autonomy.
2. Productivity of the worker is low—as measured by absenteeism, turnover rates, wildcat strikes, sabotage, poor-quality products, and a reluctance by workers to commit themselves to their work tasks.
3. Blue-collar blues is manifested as a result of blocked mobility and occupational rigidity.
4. Most young workers view the workplace as authoritarian.
5. Dull and demeaning work, work over which the worker has little or no control, as well as other poor features of work, contribute to an assortment of mental health problems.
6. As work problems increase, there may be a consequent decline in physical and mental health, family stability, community participation and cohesiveness, and balanced sociopolitical attitudes, while there is an increase in drug and alcohol addiction, aggression and delinquency.
7. Whereas most Americans have received great increments in pay and fringe benefits, dissatisfaction and discontent with work continues to spread across the country like a disease (*Work in America,* 1973) .

SUMMARY

This then is part of the current scene. Career development is a very complex and intricate process. Facilitating that process requires highly imaginative, innovative and dynamic delivery systems. Since it is so complicated, it will become an endeavor, which if done properly and effectively, demands prestige from our colleagues and the public, and will be afforded proper status. If, indeed, career counseling is now being given inadequate attention because it requires increasing knowledge and skill, and this is certainly part of the explanation, the future will see the task grow more difficult, not less. For the task of working with bewildered adolescents in a rapidly changing society and world, in order to help them plan what they want to be experiencing fifteen years hence, in a world which is now largely unpredictable, is one of the most exciting and challenging tasks a professional can accomplish. Our final goal in this endeavor is to deliver the programs and experiences which will make youth become more adaptable, maneuverable, responsive and self-directed, with greater tolerances for ambiguity and the unknown.

BIBLIOGRAPHY

Bernard, H.W. and Fullmer, D.W. *Principles of Guidance: A Basic Text.* Scranton, Pennsylvania: Intext, 1969.

Blocher, D. Social change and the future of vocational guidance. In Borow, H. (Ed.), *Career Guidance for a New Age.* Boston: Houghton-Mifflin, 1973.

Burck, H.D. Putsell's unified college counseling center: A reply. *Journal of College Student Personnel,* 1966, 7, 3-4.

The College Board News. New York: College Board, Vol. 2, No. 2, January 1974.

Ginzberg, E. *Career Guidance: Who Needs It, Who Provides It, Who Can Improve It.* New York: McGraw-Hill, 1971.

Guidepost. Washington, D.C.: American Personnel and Guidance Association, Vol. 15, No. 18, June 1, 1973. P. 4.

Prediger, D., et al. A Nationwide Study of Student Career Development: Summary of Results. Research Report No. 61. Iowa City, Iowa: American College Testing Program, 1973.

Putsell, T.E. A unified college counseling center. *The Journal of College Student Personnel,* 1965, 6, 171-174.

Work in America. Report of a Special Task Force of the Secretary of Health, Education, and Welfare. Cambridge, Massachusetts: M.I.T. Press, 1973.

Yankelovich, D. *The Changing Values on Campus: Political and Personal Attitudes of Today's College Students.* New York: Washington Square Press, 1971.

Chapter Two

CONTRIBUTIONS OF CAREER
DEVELOPMENT THEORIES

Ellen S. Amatea

THE NEED FOR WELL DEVELOPED career guidance strategies is vividly apparent. All too frequently young people function ineffectively in dealing with career development, and increasingly, counselors are recognizing that the needs for career guidance are quite diverse. Not only do individuals need assistance at significant choice points, such as the entry to high school and college, they also need to experience career guidance as a long-term educative process. The students described below reflect such needs:

> Chuck, a senior at an inner city high school, is "turned off" by academia and education as he has seen it. He is recognized as a leader in the school who can always be counted on to get things done and people organized. Chuck keeps ducking his friends' question: "What are you going to do when you graduate?" He probably will never seek out a counselor for assistance in answering this question.
>
> Kitty, a bright, verbal honor student, is a college sophomore who has begun to question her parents assertions that she strive for a career which is "convenient for a woman to have." Talented in arts and academia, she seems to suffer the problem of "overchoice."
>
> And then there is Mike, a high school sophomore, who sees school lying out before him like some vast desert. Confronted by failure, both in and out of school, he feels unsure of what he can do or wants to do, but considers the world of work too far away to really think about seriously.

Obviously, these three young people represent different points on the career development and decision-making continuum. How does the counselor determine which career guidance strategy will be most effective for each of them? That is the basic question, and the focus of this chapter.

In order to function effectively in designing career guidance interventions, the counselor must examine his own assumptions regarding the nature of career development. He needs to ask himself: What is the nature of the career choice process? When do people decide on careers? Just what is meant by a career decision? When should certain decisions be made? How are career decisions made by individuals who do not seek (and feel they do not need to seek) assistance?

Answers to these questions should form the basis for the development and selection of career guidance strategies, and an effective resource for potential answers is career development theory. Career development theory should assist in both describing what *should* happen in career development and explaining what actually *does* happen. Thus such theories can provide information about the purposes of guidance; that is, *who* should receive *what* kinds of strategies for which purpose *(why)*.

This chapter will examine selected theories and research efforts which have implications for the practice of career guidance. Although it is not possible in one short chapter to thoroughly acquaint the reader with the major theories of career development, the highlights of several of these theories will be presented along with a description of the implications each has for counseling practice.

CAREER CHOICE: A POINT-IN-TIME EVENT OR A DEVELOPMENTAL PROCESS?

Most of the major theories of career development can be categorized in terms of two perspectives: (1) those theories which emphasize the specification of factors or processes at work during the time of the career choice event, or (2) those theories which emphasize the lifelong nature of a cumulative career choice process. In essence they provide two very different answers to the question: What is the nature of the career choice process?

Trait-factor theorists, Anne Roe, and John Holland have conceptualized the career choice process largely as an *event* which occurs sometime during late adolescence. Their theories are concerned primarily with predicting the direction of this choice through the analysis of relationships between a variety of factors. In contrast to this perspective, theorists such as Eli Ginzberg, Donald Super, and Peter Blau and associates, conceptualize the career choice process as a long term *sequence* of events influenced by factors which operate over the lifetime of the individual. Such a difference in persepective has very direct implications for the analysis of the career choice problem as well as the solution proposed for that problem. A brief review of these theories and their implied suggestions for career guidance practice will illustrate the broad and varying implications these theories hold for career guidance practices and programs.

Trait-and-Factor Theories of Occupational Choice

Probably the most venerable theory regarding career choice-making is that of trait-and-factor. Viewing the career choice process as largely a point-in-time event, trait-factor theorists assume that a straightforward matching of an individual's abilities and interests with the world's vocational opportunities can be accomplished. More importantly, once such a matching is accomplished, an individual's vocational choice problems are solved. Thus a matching of objective data about the individual with objective data about the requirements of the job world is the central characteristic of this approach (Hewer, 1963).

From this perspective a number of interesting relationships between specific variables and occupational choice-making have been examined.

Abilities: Obviously, a person's level of intelligence (or aptitude) significantly influences the relative *level* of employment he is able to attain. However, in most studies relating intelligence to specific occupational categories, researchers have found that there is no differential distribution of general ability across different kinds of occupations (Zytowski, 1970).

Interests: The most frequent way that researchers have denoted motivation for particular occupational fields has been through the concepts of interests, and many researchers view the construct of interests as external demonstration of psychological needs. In studying the development of occupational interests and their relative role in career development, Tyler and Ellis (1968) noted that unlike earlier assumptions that occupational preferences were formed by the development of interests, it now appears that preferences are formed just as much by the development of dislikes as by likes.

Values: There appears to be a significant body of evidence corroborating the assumption that what an individual values both in work and in its rewards has a significant effect upon his vocational development and decision-making. Furthermore, there appear to be clear discriminations between the values and personalities of different occupational groups. Although it is certainly not clearly established that occupations are homogeneous in their potential to provide such satisfactions, values do appear to play a significant part in the career decision-making process (Herr and Cramer, 1972).

Family Factors: Family factors, such as family socioeconomic status and child-rearing practices, have been investigated extensively in relationship to occupational choice. Lipsett (1962) identified a host of social factors which influence the vocational development process: social class, parental and family interactions, the school environment and culture, and specific community and pressure groups.

The counselor working from the trait-and-factor perspective would typically arrange opportunities for his client to explore a variety of different occupational positions. Typically he would do this using a sequence of several techniques. First, he would introduce procedures designed to enable his client to clarify details concerning himself. A battery of tests would be administered for this purpose. Second, the counselor would also attempt to clarify various career patterns, either specifically in terms of positions or more generally in terms of career titles. Procedures such as reading occupational literature, visiting plants, offices and professional establishments, and hearing discussions and lectures on careers by practitioners would be utilized to implement this step. Following these two steps, information about the client would be matched with career information, and a career direction would be selected. Thus, from the client's viewpoint, career guidance would largely consist of a process of information collecting and information giving, rather than clarification of goals or self-concept. Personality factors or processes other than those reflected indirectly in interest and value assessment would not be considered in this process.

Roe's Personality Theory of Career Choice

Unlike the trait-and-factor approach which characterized career choice-making as a cognitive and conscious process, Roe's (1956) theory of career choice-making emphasizes the personality determinants which influence the career choice event. In specifying the factors and conditions at work in the career choice process, Roe employed an analysis of psychological needs and personality traits in describing the career choice process. Analyzing the vocational development of eminent physical and social scientists, Roe concluded that vocational direction was related to personality development and that this development resulted from early parent-child interactions. Roe hypothesized that the varying propensities individuals possess for dealing with people or dealing with things determine the types of occupations to which they are attracted. Such propensities for dealing with people or with things result from the need structure which the individual develops during early parent-child interactions. For example, an individual raised in a warm and accepting family climate is attracted toward occupational fields in which contact with people is frequent since his needs for affection and belongingness are high. Conversely, the individual who is reared by cold and/or rejecting parents develops the propensity for avoiding people and chooses work in which his contacts with people are minimal. Roe hypothesizes that this individual would be operating at a lower need level at which safety and security needs preempt higher order needs. Roe based her need hierarchy upon the work of Maslow (1954) who arranged human needs along a continuum in which higher level needs would emerge only as lower order, or more primitive, needs were satisfied.

The relationships between parent-child interactions, resulting need structures, and ensuing orientation toward or away from people were translated by Roe into a classification of occupations by field (or group) and level. Occupations were organized into two major categories, those which were person-oriented (such as service, business contact, organization, general culture, and the arts and entertainment) and those which were nonperson-oriented (such as technology, outdoor, and science groupings). For each of the subcategories with this schema, occupational levels were specified which represented progressively higher levels of job responsibility. While the selection of the field (or subcategory) was dependent upon an individual's need structure, Roe contended that selection of a level within that field was more dependent upon the individual's relative level of ability.

Since Roe's entire schema of career choice-making rests upon the assumption that the need structure of the individual is directly related to his vocational choice, counseling from this perspective would logically be aimed at helping the individual effectively clarify and understand his need structure. Using an interview procedure and assessment instruments designed to provide information about the client's early family interactions and his resulting need structure, a hierarchy of preeminent needs would be determined. This needs hierarchy would then be matched with those offered by various occupations. (Thus it would be necessary for the counselor to have at his disposal a classification of a wide range of occupations catalogued in terms of their resulting needs structure.)

If, in assessing the client's family background, the counselor discovered that certain circumstances had thwarted the development of a normal need structure, two choices would be open to the counselor. He could either provide counseling aimed at changing the client's need structure (in which the client would be led to understand the shunting of his needs, develop higher order needs, and acquire techniques for satisfying such needs), or merely assist the client in evaluating the potential of various fields for the satisfaction of his current need structure.

Recent revision of Roe's theory has resulted in less emphasis upon the relationship of needs to occupational choice, and more emphasis upon providing the client with information regarding the interrelatedness of occupational fields. Psychological attributes are still considered to be a major determinant of career choice.

Holland's Theory of Occupational Types and Environments

In many ways Holland's theory of occupational types and environments represents a viewpoint very similar to Roe's in its emphasis upon the development of personality typology by which occupational choices can be predicted. However, Holland (1966) considers personality style (rather than psychological need structure) to be the major determinant of vocational decision-making and development. Holland proposed that at the time of occupational choice, the person and his personality result from the interaction of environmental and genetic factors. From this interaction the individual develops a preferred personal *style* for dealing with his environment. Such a personal style, or "modal personal orientation" as Holland calls it, can be classified in terms of six different personality types: Realistic, Intellectual, Social, Conventional, Enterprising, and Artistic. Figure 2.I shows a description of these types.

According to Holland, the individual chooses a work environment which satisfies his particular personality style. Work environments can be classified into categories similar to their requirements to the six personality orientations. Figure 2-1 also contains a description of the corresponding work environments. Since successful performance in each work environment rests upon specific abilities, values, and attitudes, a direct relationship between personality style and work environment is specified in Holland's theory. In addition, a hierarchy of job levels within each occupational environment is developed in which level of intelligence and individual self-evaluation are the determinants.

Thus the counselor operating from Holland's theoretical perspective, would have at hand a data bank containing information about a wide variety of occupations classified in terms of modal work environments. Within the context of this occupational classification system, the counselor would utilize several techniques for identifying the major personal style of the individual client (e.g. use of assessment instruments such as the *Vocational Preference Inventory* and the *Self-Directed Search,* and rankings of descriptions of characteristics of the six personality orientations). After clarify-

	Personality Types	*Environmental Models*
Type	*Description*	*Typical Occupations in Which This Type is Found*
Realistic	Persons oriented toward this role are characterized by aggressive behavior, interest in activities requiring motor coordination, skill and physical strength, and masculinity. They prefer concrete rather than abstract problem situations, and typically avoid tasks which involve interpersonal and verbal skills.	Laborers, machine operators, aviators, farmers, truck drivers, carpenters, etc.
Intellectual	Persons oriented toward this role are characterized by thinking rather than acting and emphasize organizing and understanding the world rather than dominating or persuading. They tend to avoid close interpersonal contact.	Physicist, anthropologist, chemist, mathematician, biologist, etc.
Social	Persons characterized by this role seek close personal relationships and are adept in these relationships. They avoid situations where they might be required to engage in intellectual problem solving or use of extensive physical skills.	Clinical psychologist, counselor, foreign missionary, teacher, etc.
Conventional	Persons orinted toward this style are typified by a great concern for rules and regulations, great self-control, and a strong identification with power and status. Since this person prefers structure and order he seeks interpersonal and work situations in which structures are readily apparent.	Cashier, statistician, bookkeeper, administrative assistant, post office clerk, etc.

Enterprising	Persons characterizing this role are verbally skilled but uses these skills for manipulative and persuasive purposes, rather than for supportive purposes. They are concerned about power and status and they work very hard to acquire it.	Car salesman, auctioneer, politician, master of ceremonies, buyer, etc.
Artistic	Persons oriented toward this style are characterized by strong manifestations toward self expression particularly through the arts media. Such people dislike structure, show their emotions much more easily and demonstrate relatively little self-control. They tend to be relatively introceptive and asocial.	Poet, novelist, musician, sculptor, playwright, composer, stage director, etc.

Figure 2-1. Holland's Schema of Corresponding Personality Styles and Occupational Environments.

ing the specific loadings of the individual client in regards to the six personality orientations, the counselor would assist the client in identifying the particular occupational environments that seem most relevant, and locating the level in that environment which seems most suitable for him.

Although, in many regards, this approach sounds much like the prior description of the traditional trait-and-factor theorists, there is an additional psychological dimension to Holland's theory introduced by the moderator variables of *self-knowledge* and *self-evaluation*. Holland emphasizes the importance of self-knowledge (which he defines as the amount and accuracy of information the individual has about himself) and self-evaluation (which he defines as the worth the individual attributes to himself). He considers them important sources of data to collect about the individual who is experiencing vocational problems. For example, an individual may experience vocational choice problems in determining the *level* of choice because of an inconsistent or inappropriate self-evaluation. Thus these two sources of information about the individual are important factors to examine in the vocational counseling process.

Although Holland's theory has a great deal to say about factors to be considered, examined, and evaluated in the process of assisting the individual concerned with making a vocational choice, it has the same limitation as all the career choice as-a-point-in-time conceptualizations. The problem is that it fails to address either the fact that people can (and will) change both themselves and their environments over time, or that a lot of important things happen to the person before he is ready to make a career choice. Thus while these three theories can provide some definite direction to the counselor engaged in assisting a youngster who considers himself in need of career guidance (which most young people identify as a need), they have much less to contribute in the way of suggestions for long term developmental programs which are preventative in nature.

The developmental theorists are much more concerned with the longitudinal expressions of vocational behavior. Their formulations are described in the following pages.

Ginzberg's General Theory of Occupational Choice

Ginzberg and his associates (1951) were the first to publish a theory which emphasized the developmental nature of the career choice process. After studying the types of occupational choices made by middle and upper income male high school and college students, they concluded that occupational choice was a developmental process occurring over a period of six to ten years (or more) and characterized by major distinctions in the occupational behaviors of different age levels.

In Ginzerg's original formulations, this developmental process was viewed as largely irreversible, meaning that choices could not be repeated and that each choice would limit subsequent choices. However, as Ginzberg and his associates have continued to study the vocational development of various groups, such as women and the disadvantaged, they have made several refinements in their original theory. They now propose that although early choices *do* have an effect on subsequent choices, they are not irreversible. In fact, the career choice process which Ginzberg originally saw as ending in the late teens or early twenties is now viewed as one which "remains open as long as one makes a definitive occupational commitment" (Ginzberg, 1972).

How would a counselor utilize Ginzberg's theory in his guidance practice? Since this theory spells out the kinds of tasks and potential problems that might be encountered by clients at predictable stages of development, this theory is readily adaptable to designing programmatic strategies for developing preventative programs. The theory is somewhat less applicable in designing specific procedures for working with individual clients with specific career guidance problems. Super and his associates (1953) have been much more concrete in specifying the nature of counseling interventions and the developmental tasks required at different stages of the career development process.

Super's Developmental Self-Concept Theory

Building upon the work of Buehler (1933) and the Ginzberg group (1951), Super and his associates attempted to bring both a developmental and a phenomelogical perspective to the staging and determination of career patterns. They combined many diverse elements from a broad range of academic areas and research, such as the concepts of individual differences, multipotentiality, occupational ability patterns, identification with role models, and differential and developmental psychology. Super and his associates attempted to formulate a theory which would "explain the process through which interest, capacities, values, and opportunities are compromised" (Super, 1953).

Super attempted to clarify his theorizing via a longitudinal research project, the Career Pattern Study, which he undertook with others in 1951. The purposes of this study were: to develop methods for monitoring the career progression of individuals rather than just predict initial occupational entry; to describe the nature of vocational exploration which leads to the making of prevocational and vocational choices; and to analyze the relationship between certain life stages and those behaviors which one manifests at each stage in dealing with particular vocational tasks.

By far the most central and crucial characteristic of Super's theory is the role he ascribes to the self-concept. In essence, Super sought to provide an explicit and detailed explanation of vocational development by describing how the self-concept is formed and implemented occupationally (Osipow, 1968). While corroborating much of Ginzberg's approach, Super expanded (1) the focus of examination by emphasizing the need to examine the career patern of the individual versus the initial occupational selection of the individual, and (2) the range of factors affecting the developmental process, e.g. the self-concept.

Probably more than any theory previously described, Super's theory seems adaptable for use in both programmatic and individual intervention efforts. Super contended that environmental factors, such as social and economic conditions, and genetic factors influence the development of the self-concept. Since the implementation if the self-concept vocationally is considered the very essence of the vocational choice process, and the self-concept is open to outside influence during the formative years, counselors can be particularly effective in planning strategies which will affect the career choice process.

Assessment would and could be made of the client's relative level of vocational maturity since data regarding the skills, attitudes, and level of knowledge characterizing each developmental period have been collected by Super and his associates. After ascertaining the level of vocational maturity at which the client was functioning, the counselor would identify the next vocationally relevant tasks to be accomplished. If the client was vocationally immature, specific steps could be taken to make the client aware of the stage related behaviors he had yet to acquire and suggest potential ways for acquiring these behaviors. For example, if it was determined that a ninth grader was operating at a vocationally immature level by demonstrating little knowledge about the choice he needed to make and by having difficulty even posing vocationally relevant questions, then the client would not be, according to Super, in a position to make a sound career decision. Therefore the goal of counseling would be to assist the client in developing a sense of the need for careful planning rather than emphasize the development of a specific career plan. In counseling such an individual, the counselor would typically focus upon the client's feelings regarding the problem rather than upon his attributes. His counseling efforts would be directed toward creating an interview environment conducive to self-exploration and self-expression. Tests, inventories, and occupational information would be de-emphasized since the counselor would probably conclude that their introduction would inhibit this process of self-discovery and self-expression. As the interview progressed, data would be generated by the client concerning the background to his current indecision, and the counselor would assist the client in helping him to interpret and integrate such background data into his ultimate decision.

When presented with a career guidance problem, the counselor operating from this framework would try to appraise the life stage of his client in order to define relevant counseling goals. He would also seek to help the client clarify his self-concept, and within the context of the particular client life stage, expose him to events which would help him move toward a greater clarification of that self-concept. Experiences both inside and outside the counselor's office would be used in this clarification process.

A Conceptual Framework of Occupational Choice

Unlike any of the theorists described previously, the "conceptual framework" of Blau, Gustad, Jessor, Parnes and Wilcock (1956) represents a two-pronged effort at describing and explaining the nature of the career development process. Not only is the vocational choice process detailed, but the occupational selection process as well. According to Blau and his associates (1956) the concurrent operation of *both* of these processes result in the occupational entry and subsequent progression of the individual through the work world. Thus an examination of the factors at work in these two processes is necessary in order to effectively assist individuals in this process. These theorists, who bring a heavy sociological flavor to the description of occupational behavior, describe the process of *vocational choice* (i.e. the individual's choice of a preferred occupation) as a compromise between the individual's hierarchy of preferences and his hierarchy of expectations. That is, while the individual may prefer some occupations over others, he may realize that he has little chance of entering them. As a result, he compromises and settles for something less than he may optimally prefer. This process of vocational choice interacts with the process of *occupational selection* (i.e. the process by which the job market is developed) and is also characterized by a compromise between hierarchies of market preferences and expectations.

These two processes form a double chain of events which determine occupational entry. The vocational choice chain, which is based upon individual characteristics, includes biological and psychological factors. The occupational selection chain reflects the conditions which affect the economic opportunities open to the individual, such as available social resources, geography, opportunities for mobility, and variations in the potential rewards of various jobs.

This theoretical approach is by far the most difficult from which to extrapolate individual counseling techniques since it is primarily group oriented in its view of occupational behavior and its influencing variables. However, its impact upon the design of developmentally based programs could be substantial. Psychologically-based interpretations of career development have focused almost exclusively upon the individual. (Holland is the only other theorist who attempts to identify specific situational variables.) The sociology of the work setting and the dynamics of the work place have not typically been examined as closely. Yet such factors as the interaction of persons in a work setting, the particular relationships toward authority encountered in the work setting, and the requirements for psychological distancing required to enhance job mobility are all significant areas of information which young people need in order to develop skills for coping with the world of work. Thus, sociologically-based theories of career development such as that proposed by Blau and his associates provide major sources of information for the identification of skills and information needed to cope with and adapt to a career pattern.

SUMMARY

The career development theories presented in this chapter have not been described in exhaustive detail nor have all of the more significant theories been presented. The theories discussed, however, have been used to illustrate the broad array of different approaches they represent for practicing career guidance.

Theorists in the area of career development have typically viewed the career choice process from two very different perspectives. Either they have tended to look at the career choice process as an event which can be analyzed in terms of the personal and situational determinants which precede it, or they have viewed the actual choice of a career direction as but one event in a long chain of events which comprises a developmental pattern. Although most experts in the field now recognize the validity of the latter conceptualization, point-in-time emphases upon career choice-making hold some major implications for the practice of individual career counseling. Trait-factor theory, Roe's personality theory, and Holland's theory all specify certain processes or factors at work in forming the career choice. Their research and theory building is quite useful to the counselor in identifying sources of information about the client which must be considered in career choice-making, and in systematically organizing information about the world of work into readily understandable patterns.

Developmental theorists, such as Ginzberg, Super and their associates have described a characteristic sequence of developmental tasks and stages which provides definite direction to the counselor committed to long-term developmental programs. Persons concerned with developing career education programs, for example, can glean information regarding the specific competencies and sequencing of those competencies from the developmental theorists. In emphasizing both the nature of the work place and the work world, Blau and his associates provide an additional base of information relevant to a developmental program.

BIBLIOGRAPHY

Blau, P.M., Gustad, J.W., Jessor, R., Parnes, H.S., and Wilcock, R.S. Occupational choice: A conceptual framework. *Industrial Labor Relations Review,* 1956, *9,* 531-543.

Buehler, Charlotte. *Der Menshliche Lebenslauf als Psycholisches Problem.* Leipzig: Hirzel, 1933.

Ginzberg, E., Ginsburg, S.W., Axelrad, S., and Herma, J.L. *Occupational Choice: An Approach to a General Theory.* New York: Columbia University Press, 1951.

Ginzberg, E. Toward a theory of occupational choice: A restatement. *Vocational Guidance Quarterly,* 1972, *20,* 169-176.

Herr, E.L., and Cramer, S.H. *Vocational Guidance and Career Development in the Schools: Toward a Systems Approach.* Boston: Houghton-Mifflin, 1972.

Hewer, V. What do theories of vocational choice mean to a counselor? *Journal of Counseling Psychology,* 1963, *10,* 118-125.

Holland, J. *The Psychology of Vocational Choice.* Waltham, Mass.: Blaisdell, 1966.

Lippset, L. Social factors in vocational development. *Personnel and Guidance Journal,* 1962, *40,* 432-437.

Maslow, A.H. *Motivation and Personality.* New York: Harper & Row, 1954.

Osipow, S.H. *Theories of Career Development.* New York: Appleton-Century Crofts, 1968.

Roe, A. *The Psychology of Occupations.* New York: Wiley, 1956.

Roe, A. Perspectives on vocational development. In J.M. Whiteley and A. Resnikoff (Eds.), *Perspectives on Vocational Development.* Washington, D.C.: American Personnel and Guidance Association, 1972. Pp. 61-82.

Super, D.E. A theory of vocational development. *American Psychologist,* 1953, *8,* 185-190.

Tyler, L., and Ellis, R.A. *Planned and Unplanned Aspects of Occupational Choice: Toward a Morphology of Occupational Choice.* Unpublished research report. Eugene, Oregon: University of Oregon, 1968.

Zytowski, D.G. *Psychological Influences on Vocational Development.* Guidance Monograph Series IV. Boston: Houghton-Mifflin, 1970.

Part II

COUNSELING STRATEGIES

Chapters Three through Seven present something old and something new for professionals concerned with vocational guidance and career counseling.

Chapter Three presents an old, familiar friend and tool in guidance, information services. Most professional writing about information and its use in vocational counseling discusses, almost exclusively, the different kinds of information and how it should be presented to counselees. Reardon, in this chapter, takes a more complex and aggressive stance in discussing the use of information in counseling. He presents not only the problems and purposes, but also the acquisition and actual use of information in the decision-making process. Finally, he ends with some very practical comments and suggestions for the counselor using information in facilitating career development.

Assessment, in one form or another, has been discussed and mentioned as an indispensible process in vocational guidance since the days of Parsons. In Chapter Four, MacAleese takes an exciting and critical look at the whole area of assessment as it applies to minorities, women and other groups, and then discusses at length the assessment of aptitudes, achievement, interests, vocational maturity, and values. Specific inventories and tests are briefly analyzed. In discussing creative measurement, he concludes with this note: "Counselors are limited only by their innovativeness, imagination and flexibility within the framework of their training in attempting different ways to interpret and personalize the data obtained from these instruments."

The contents of Chapters Five, Six and Seven usually are not found in books dealing with career development, and in this sense, represent something of a departure. Sweeney's chapter, "Simulation Techniques in Career Counseling," takes a bold swing from the presentation of a sound theoretical rationale for the use of simulation in career counseling to the suggestion of very specific games and simulation techniques the counselor might use. For example, he presents a solid case for the use of simulation and gaming in the crucial areas of modeling and role playing, decision-making, and problem solving, ending with an excellent reference list for locating additional specific resources.

Montgomery's chapter, "A Short Term Contractual Approach to Career Counseling," takes a straightforward, no-nonsense behavioral approach to the use of contracts. He gives an excellent presentation of the advantages and characteristics of this technique, along with a step-by-step description of how the counselor should negotiate and execute such a contract. This is all brought to life by his use of a partial transcript of counselor/client interaction.

Finally, in Chapter Seven, Hoffman and Cochran have surveyed the literature and reflected on their own experiences about the proper use of groups in the facilitation of career development. They present a clear rationale and then quickly move to the presentation of five kinds of career development groups: Career Development Group, Vocational Exploration Group, Case Conference Group, Life Planning Workshop, and Future Groups. For each they carefully explain the rationale, purposes, and procedures, and offer a brief critique.

Counseling has been the primary means of helping people with career development problems from the beginning. The five chapters in Part II are designed to provide the practitioner with some familiar, but revitalized counseling techniques and ideas that can be translated into improved professional practice.

Chapter Three

USING INFORMATION IN CAREER COUNSELING

ROBERT C. REARDON

I<small>T'S</small> <small>DIFFICULT TO KNOW WHERE</small> to begin in discussing the use of information in career counseling. While information is logically viewed as one of the basic ingredients in decision-making, much is written about acquiring and displaying information materials, and Frank Parsons described it as the second essential step in vocational counseling, there is precious little in the literature on how to use information in career counseling. Sinick (1956) has observed that although the ability to use occupational information is one of the professional competencies identified as needing professional preparation, there is little written about the topic, and it may remain "one of the weakest links in the counseling process" (Brammer and Shostrum, 1959). The purpose of this chapter is to provide counselors with some ideas which may make this counseling competency a stronger link in professional practice.

This chapter begins with an analysis of some of the problems of using information in career counseling. It then moves to a discussion of the various purposes of using information, information as a part of decision-making, the classification of information methods, and an analysis of counselor needs for information. Finally, the chapter will focus on specific suggestions for the counselor, both in terms of personal attitudes and the acquisition of new skills.

PROBLEMS

There are several problems the counselor is likely to encounter when using occupational information. A major difficulty involves the poor quality of the materials. Samler (1964) and others have written about this problem. Some materials, for example, fail to describe the psycho-social aspects of work, which are often very important for counselee consideration in a choice. Such things as the exercise of personal values and attitudes in the job, the status/position of the worker, the authority relationships involved, the patterns of social interactions among workers or the public, the contribution of the job to a larger social good, and the life style of the worker away from the job are frequently ignored.

Other difficult problems have to do with the counselees themselves. Regardless of the counselee's good intentions, many have trouble motivating themselves to search for and use information. In a sense, their request for information is premature because the motivation problem must be handled first. Other counselees may be unable to choose among competing alternatives which each have similar advantages/disadvantages, or they may have poor job stereotypes based on limited personal work experience, misinformation from friends, parents, and television, or poor social attitudes. But the most difficult kind of counseling problem probably relates to the counselee whose job goals are inappropriate, or who is being pressured into a choice by parents or peers. In this instance, the use of information is an especially delicate matter requiring expert professional counseling skills. (Chapter 6 identifies some useful counseling strategies for the counselor.)

In addition to poor information materials and unmotivated or confused counselees, the counselor may be very ambivalent about the use of occupational information in counseling.

Many are either negligent or intentionally shy away from learning as much as they can about occupational information. Although many counselees come for counseling with specific requests for information, counselors have chosen to duck the responsibility for developing and maintaining their professional expertise in this area. Some of the historical and psychological explanations for this are discussed in Chapter 1.

Goldman (1967) has analyzed this problem as a dilemma which the counselor must face squarely if he is to use information successfully in counseling. Some counselors feel that using objective facts and data disturbs the subjective nature of the counseling relationship. The use of information interferes with the counselor's ability to focus on the client's feelings and attitudes. Moreover, in using information the counselor is likely to play an authoritative role, not unlike a physician. The counselor prescribes the appropriate information as an antidote for the counselee's decision-making ills. Of course, if the counselor is unsure about the prescription, e.g. the reliability and validity of the information materials, he is in a precarious position and vulnerable to the counselee demanding help. As Goldman stated:

> . . . If counselors don't use the most complete and up-to-date appraisal and environmental information possible, they are neglecting to provide their clients with one of the important elements of a good plan or decision. . . . On the other hand, bringing assessment and environmental information into the counseling room seems to disturb the counseling process, by shifting from the internal to the external frame of reference, by shifting from feelings/values/goals to facts, and by evoking from the counselor persuasiveness and defensiveness, rather than acceptance, clarification, interpretation (1967).

In short, problems in the use of occupational information center around: the nature and quality of the information materials themselves, the needs of the counselee, and the counselor's own hang-ups. The following sections of this chapter will focus on ways to overcome these problems.

PURPOSES

The purposes for the use of information in counseling are quite varied. Some purposes, for example, are quite unrealistic given the limitations of the materials, the counselee's readiness, etc.

Samler (1964) observed that information should be used for self-exploration, vicarious role assumption, and self-understanding. Patterson (1964) has noted that occupational information should be used in counseling to help the client clarify the goal he wants to reach and move in the direction he wants to go, assuming the means to the goal are not illegal or injurious to self or others. While Patterson's statement does somewhat calm the fears of client-centered counselors who might not see the place of information in counseling, there are some loose ends. What if the client's goals are inappropriate; how should the counselor use information in such a case?

Rusalem (1954) identified two purposes for using information in counseling. The *exploratory role* of information would help the counselee come to view himself as an adult—to test reality as he reads or listens to information. One may think of a student who is adrift in his decision-making and then finds reassurance in being able to reaffirm his vague perceptions of what he thought a physical therapist did with what being a physical therapist actually involves. The information is thus used as a stimuli to help the counselee elicit, explore, and clarify his needs, values, attitudes, aspirations, and expectations of his work role and self-concept. He can project himself into various occupations and learn more about how and why his perceptions and cognitions function as they do. The *verification role* of information involves the reality test over a period of time. The counselee examines conflicts and inconsistencies between the job and self-concept. The purpose of information here is to help clarify and understand feelings subsequent to a choice.

Isaacson (1971) has surveyed the literature and identified four purposes for the use of information in counseling.

Motivational: Information may be used to stimulate the counselee to identify alternatives or confirm tentative choices. This can sometimes be an exhilerating experience for the counselee, because it is a step in the direction of self-determination and the beginning of career planning.

Instructional: The use of information here involves a more careful, systematic assessment of the counselee's needs in order to design appropriate learning experiences. The focus, unlike (adjustive) below, is on cognitive understanding of a particular occupation or, more broadly, the process of career development. The purpose of information may involve attitude change, increased understanding of the career decision-making process, or other goals. It must be assumed, of course, that the counselor is sufficiently informed himself that he can help the counselee locate, use and evaluate the appropriate materials.

Adjustive: Information can help the client to refocus and accommodate discrepancies between his plans and success in a field. The purpose is to help correct perceptual distortions of self or the environment. As noted earlier, a typical problem involves over and under estimates of self-achievement. Printed or canned information is probably most appropriate here because it enables the counselor to limit his own presentation of information and to focus instead on the counselee's perceptions of the information.

Distributive: The purpose of information in this instance primarily involves placement in, rather than selection of, an occupation. The counselor is primarily involved in helping the counselee locate and use appropriate job information before entering a specific job position.

Thus the purposes of using information in career counseling are quite varied. The role of the counselor in using information depends on the situation, e.g., the location of the counseling agency, and the needs of the counselee. In the case of school counselors, it seems that all four purposes identified by Isaacson would be appropriate. The implications for counselor practice are significant, and will be amplified in later sections of this chapter.

DECISION-MAKING

A bit of reflection suggests that a focal point of most counseling involves planning and decision-making activities. Whether the counselee is concerned about running away from home, marriage, coming out of the closet, or suicide the matter of choice is a central part in counseling.

Apparently all models of decision-making, of which choice may be seen as a part, stress the importance of information. Figure 3-1 graphically depicts the process (Dunphy, 1969).

Step No. 2, Stating Alternatives, basically involves an environmental assessment and information search of the options available for the solution to the problem or the answer to the question identified in Step No. 1. It is apparent that Step No. 2 is an

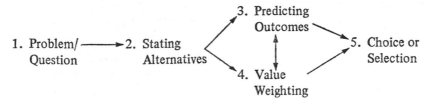

Figure 3-1.

especially critical one in career counseling and also one of the key problem areas noted earlier. For example, it was suggested that: there are basic weaknesses in the quality of the information available; counselees are either unmotivated to locate the needed information or they are looking for inappropriate information; counselors are ignorant and/or conflicted over their role in helping the counselee locate and use information. Thus it is somewhat meaningless for the counselor to focus on Steps 1, 3, and 4, where he is probably most comfortable, because the quality of the choice as an outcome of decision-making (Step 5) can be fatally determined by what happens in Step No. 2, the information-alternative search.

If the counselor is committed to focusing on the client's desired outcomes, then the use of information in counseling fits into the decision-making process by helping the counselee to clearly specify the nature of the problem and/or questions to be answered, to identify and locate all relevant information about the alternatives, and to clarify those alternatives and examine the likelihood for desirable outcomes. From this vantage point, the counselor is simply failing to do his job if he fails to be helpful at Step No. 2. And from the counselee's point of view, this is likely his area of greatest need.

ACQUIRING INFORMATION

One possible reason for the lack of counselor helpfulness in the use of information involves the typically passive approach the counselor utilizes. The strategy or method used in helping the counselee locate information can be quite varied, and must be tailored to suit the person, time and place.

Albert Thompson (Hollis and Hollis, 1969) has classified the methods by which counselees might obtain information. They range from those where the counselee (or counselor) have minimum involvement (passive role) to those where the counselee has maximum involvement (active role). Most counselee use of information would appear to be at the passive, or minimum involvement level.

Classification	*Examples*
1. Prestructured or fixed	a. Publications. b. Audio-visual materials. c. Planned programs, such as visiting speakers, career days, etc.
2. Input controlled by counselee	a. Programmed instruction, such as SRA Job Experience kits. b. Computer Assisted Instruction, such as, SIGI, ILS, ECES. c. Interviews with a worker.
3. Simulation of the situation	a. Role playing or career games. b. Synthetic work environment, such as a hospital room recreated for nurses training.
4. Real situation	a. Direct observation, such as "shadowing" a worker or a field visit. b. Direct exploration, such as volunteer work or participation in cooperative education. c. Actual job experience.

This classification scheme has some special implications for the counselor. At level No. 1 the counselor can simply open a file or flip a switch to provide information for the client. At level No. 4, however, the counselor would have to be more actively involved with the client in using the information. He would have to have first hand knowledge of the referral resources, and maybe even be able to create such information resources especially for the counselee. It is also important to note that as the counselee moves toward information sources where he has maximum control, the impact of the information on feelings, values and attitudes probably increases. While the counselee may not be able to get in touch with feelings about nursing from reading a printed brochure, it will probably be easier following a role play exercise or volunteer work experience. All of this, of course, creates another bind for the counselor who wants to passively focus primarily on Steps 3 and 4 of the decision-making model. Unless he actively helps the counselee locate and use career information in which the counselee has maximum involvement, he is not really helping in the decision-making process.

COUNSELEE NEEDS

Before describing the ways in which the counselor can improve the use of information in career counseling it is important to briefly discuss some of the important needs which counselees may have.

As noted earlier, most counselees probably want help in decision-making and planning. They frequently come for vocational counseling with some fairly well defined information needs. But in addition to the need for information, some authorities have raised the question as to whether or not counseless actually use the information or if they use it appropriately (Biggers, 1971). Teaching the counselee to use information is a creative, often neglected facet of career counseling.

For some clients it is especially important that the information be easily accessible and comprehensible. Norman (1969), Martin (1971), Minor (Chapter 10), and Gimmestad (Chapter 9) have addressed this topic. In these instances, counselor involvement may or may not be required.

Some other counselees are in special need of encouragement

and motivation to move ahead in their planning activities. Others have special needs for reality based experiences in this age of rapid economic change. Possible strategies for helping such counselees are discussed in the next section of this chapter and in most chapters in Part III.

The most difficult counselee problems involve those instances where an inadequate self-concept is influencing the perception of occupational information (Step No. 1 in decision-making). Fear of change, fear of failure, perceived barriers to growth, parental aspirations and other psychological influences can cause perceptual distortions of information which then significantly complicate the decision-making process. Rusalem observed that "it is not what exists in 'reality' in a vocation which enters into occupational thinking, but what comprises the individual's personal perceptions of it" (1954). Self-concept, then, is central to the counselee's perception of information, and the counselor must exercise his professional skills in determining whether or not the counselee's self-image is sufficiently adequate to engage productively and effectively in career decision-making activities.

SUGGESTIONS FOR THE COUNSELOR

While the quality of the materials and the sophistication of counselees may increase, counselors themselves must assume a major responsibility for improving the use of information in career counseling. Unfortunately, there do not seem to be any shortcuts or panaceas for improved practice in this area. Thus, a basic assumption must be that counselors are no longer content to put the use of occupational information in counseling at the bottom of the prestige of practice list—but to view it as an essential function in career counseling worthy of renewed professional attention.

Counselors must learn career information: This first step is absolutely essential to the sound use of information in counseling. The counselor must know what information is available, where it is located, and how it can be best used by the counselee. Indeed, the counselor must know his information resources so well that he can use them without fumbling or stumbling. The *Occupational*

Outlook Handbook, The Dictionary of Occupational Titles, and one or more commercially produced filing systems are minimum resources the counselor should know. The *DOT,* for example, can be useful in showing counselees the scope and depth of various occupational areas, the data-people-things concept, the worker traits notion as it relates to the level of occupation, and the idea of field or occupational groups. By treating information as an important treatment resource, the counselee too will realize the importance and value of the information materials.

Ideally, the counselor would also have available the "covert information" described by Overs (1967). This information is not recorded or filed and usually erratically communicated among counselors. It often modifies, amends, corrects or contradicts the overt (formalized) information. Sources for covert information include present and former clients, informal meetings with administrators, professional contacts, newspapers, observations gathered in field visits, etc. It excludes gossip. The identification and creation of such information requires maximum involvement and participation on the part of the counselor.

Moreover, counselors should stop being defensive and timid about the use of information—they should use everything they know if it will help the counselee in his decision-making. The appropriate safeguard is to inform the counselee of the nature and source of all information transmitted by the counselor. It seems that counselors have copped out of learning and using career information for two bad reasons: the belief that rapid socio-economic change will make much occupational information obsolete in a few years, and the fear that developing and sharing personal bits of information will limit the counselee's freedom of choice. Both reasons offer little help to the counselee caught up in the confusion of a choice which must be made in the next few days or weeks.

Thus, the first prerequisite is for counselors to stop retreating from the task at hand, and to aggressively learn career information in order to be helpful to counselees. This is the only way the counselor can hope to them make the work world real through the use of verbal symbols—to talk about work effectively.

While the counselor must be willing to immerse himself in

information, *he must also attend to the counselee's perceptions.* The counselor must help the counselee evaluate the information available—he must facilitate the use of information in the decision-making process. The counselor must know the client well enough to be able to hypothesize how he will react to or use the information presented to focus on the counselee's feelings and attitudes. When it becomes apparent that the client is unprepared to use information, either because of lack of motivation or a perceived threat in the decision-making outcome, the counselor must be sufficiently flexible to back off from the information per se and attend to the psychological state of the client.

Some authorities (Goldman, 1967) have observed that it might be necessary for an information specialist, perhaps a paraprofessional, to dispense information and for the counselor to attend to the client's feelings, etc. This writer suggests that information mastery is still the responsibility of the counselor. But the professional use of such information involves the exercise of expert, discriminating judgement on the counselor's part. The counselor must be aware of his own biases, so that he will not allow his presentation of information to prejudice the counselee towards or away from certain choices. One of the most powerful criticisms of contemporary career counseling practice concerns the counselor's alleged direction of the career choices of women and Blacks into traditional, stereotyped occupations. It is clear that the professional use of information in career counseling demands the most exacting counseling skills and counselor attitudes.

Principles for using information in career counseling have been identified by several authorities (Patterson, 1964; Isaacson, 1971; Sinick, 1956). These principles are summarized as follows:

a. There is a recognizable client need, sometimes inferred by the counselor, for information. In some cases, the client's request for information may be premature, or the client may not share a perceived need for more information. In either case, the counselor attends to the immediate client needs for learning or decision-making and times the presentation of information accordingly.

b. Information is not generally used in an evaluative way to praise or condemn the client, and it is not usually used to manipulate a client to make a certain choice. Of course, it is not appropriate to be absolute in either case, because there are certain exceptional circumstances where information could be used in just these ways.

c. The counselor should seek to maximize the client's location and use of information materials in order to develop his problem solving skills. The problem here is that too little counselor help can be interpreted as a lack of interest, which it is especially important to avoid. To determine just how much help to provide, the counselor must rely on his experience with the client, his assessment of the client's immediate situation, the amount of motivation the client has for solving the problem, etc. A set approach such as reading the material aloud with the client during the counseling hour, is sterile and likely to fail in most cases. When in doubt, it is probably best to err in the direction of too much help at the beginning of counseling, and in the direction of too little help after a sound relationship has been established. After all, the final responsibility rests with the client, even if that means failure in decision-making activities.

d. The counselor must help the client evaluate and explore the personal meaning of information materials. This is especially true if the purpose for using the information is adjustive or instructive.

e. The selection of the proper means of acquiring the information, maximum vs. minimum client control, is especially crucial, and requires expert judgement from the counselor. Such factors as the stage in the decision-making process, the amount of time available, the variety of resources available, the client's reading level, etc. would all combine to help determine the selection. Poor readers, for example, might prefer sound-filmstrips or audio-tapes, while many college students prefer printed materials which they can skim rapidly. Ideally, the counselor would have a large resource center available and a wide range of materials from which to choose. Stewart (1969) has identified the acquisition of information in terms of six client behaviors: write, observe, read, listen, visit, and talk. It may be helpful for the counselor to discuss the ranges of these behaviors in detail with the client before selecting the means of acquiring information. Shy clients may need special help before they can visit or talk as a means of securing information.

f. The counselor can maximize client readiness for using information materials by reinforcing the client's needs for information and by generally helping to develop good questions for which answers can be sought.

g. The counselor must make sure that all relevant information about an occupation is considered by the counselee. This can be done during the clarification phase after the counselee has gathered some information and is in the process of evaluating it.

h. It is especially important for the counselor to help the client focus on the appropriate next step for him rather than some far distant goal. While the client must view each choice as a step in the career development process, he must also view job and educational alternatives from an entry as well as terminal vantage point.

The use of *modeling* procedures in career counseling has been reported by Stewart (1969), Thoresen, Krumboltz, Varenhorst (1967), and others. Basically the procedure involves creating an audio or video tape where a model counselor reinforces the model client's expressions of a high need for information or questions asked. Information seeking statements include: "I suppose I ought to find out; Can I take a test to find out; What are the requirements for; Maybe I could talk with; Last month I wrote to. . . ." The model counselor uses appropriate verbal and nonverbal reinforcements such as: "Yes, that would be a good thing to know; I'm glad you're wondering about that because such information is certainly important in your decision; Very good; Mm-hmmmm;" nodding, smiling, etc. The model counselor also asks leading questions and helps the client develop a contract as to his appropriate next steps.

Research reports suggest that the use of model tapes in conjunction with 1 to 1 or small group counseling can have a significant effect on the rate of information seeking behaviors with some counselees (Krumboltz and Schroeder, 1965; Thoresen and Krumboltz, 1967). The use of such modeling procedures is especially important for some hard to motivate clients. The creation of such model tapes appropriate for the local situation could be an especially important development for counselors concerned about the use of information in career counseling.

SUMMARY

The use of information in counseling has been plagued by nagging, difficult problems, but this area of professional activity must assume a new, higher priority in counseling practice. The chapter identified some of the purposes for using information and the diverse means for acquiring information materials. It was suggested that information be viewed in terms of the decision-making process.

Although client needs were identified as an important factor in the improved use of information in counseling, the practicing counselor was identified as the target for primary attention. It was suggested that counselors will have to change their attitude toward the use of information in counseling, and generally become more active in developing their expertise and assuming their responsibility in this area. Some of the counselor binds and hang-ups were identified and solutions were proposed. Traditional principles and new strategies for using information were described.

BIBLIOGRAPHY

Biggers, J. The use of information in vocational decision-making. *Vocational Guidance Quarterly*, 1971, *19*, 177-182.

Brammer, L., and Shostrom, E. *Therapeutic Counseling*. Englewood Cliffs, N.J.: Prentice-Hall, 1959.

Dunphy, P.W. (Ed.). *Career Development for the College Student*. Cranston, R.I.: Carroll Press, 1969.

Goldman, L. Information in counseling: A dilemma. *Personnel and Guidance Journal*, 1967, *46*, 42-46.

Hollis, J., and Hollis, L. *Personalizing Information Processes: Educational, Occupational, and Personal-Social.* New York: Macmillan, 1969.

Isaacson, L. *Career Information in Counseling and Teaching.* (2nd Ed.) Boston: Allyn and Bacon, 1971.

Krumboltz, J., and Schroeder, W. Promoting career planning through reinforcement and models. *Personnel and Guidance Journal,* 1965, *44,* 19-26.

Martin, A.: *The Theory/Practice of Communicating Educational and Vocational Information.* Guidance Monograph Series. Boston: Houghton-Mifflin, 1971.

Norman, R.P. The use of preliminary information in vocational counseling. *Personnel and Guidance Journal,* 1969, *46,* 693-697.

Overs, R. Covert occupational information. *Vocational Guidance Quarterly,* 1967, *16,* 7-12.

Patterson, C.H. Counseling: Self-clarification — the helping relationship. In Borow, H. (Ed.), *Man in a World at Work.* Boston: Houghton-Mifflin, 1964. Pp. 434-459.

Rusalem, H. New insights on the role of occupational information in counseling. *Journal of Counseling and Psychology,* 1954, *1,* 84-88.

Samler, J. Occupational exploration in counseling: A proposed reorientation. In Borow, H. (Ed.), *Man in a World at Work.* Boston: Houghton-Mifflin, 1964. Pp. 411-433.

Samler, J. Psycho-social aspects of work. *Personnel and Guidance Journal,* 1961, *39,* 458-465.

Sinick, D. Occupational information in the counseling interview. *Vocational Guidance Quarterly,* 1956, *1,* 115-149.

Stewart, N. Exploring and processing information about educational and vocational opportunities in groups. In Krumboltz, J. and Thoresen, C. (Eds.), *Behavioral Counseling.* New York: Holt, Rinehart, and Winston, 1969. Pp. 211-234.

Thoresen, C., and Krumboltz, J. Relationship of counselor reinforcement of selected responses to external behavior. *Journal of Counseling Psychology,* 1967, *14,* 140-144.

Thoresen, C., Krumboltz, J., and Varenhorst, B. Sex of counselors and models: Effect on client career exploration. *Journal of Counseling Psychology,* 1967, *14,* 503-508.

Chapter Four

THE ROLE OF ASSESSMENT IN CAREER COUNSELING

Robert MacAleese

T HE TASK OF WRITING COMPREHENSIVELY about assessment and its relationship to career counseling is a formidable one, as career counseling has become an increasingly complex field. Career development may be conceptualized in many different ways; it varies with respect to both time and situation, and the meaning of any component in the process of a person's career development is highly dependent on other components and their organization.

Counselors must take a critical look at the assessment procedures they are using. Newer developments may hold great promise in a field where change and innovation is rapid. The key is the counselor's intellectual curiosity, flexibility and creativity in making use of the best possible resources. The counselor's main responsibility is to obtain accurate data, then translate that information so that it will be of use to the counselee in making career decisions. Prediger (1974a, p. 345) states that:

> Both career development theory and career decision-making theory suggest that the role of tests in career guidance is threefold: first, to stimulate, broaden and provide a focus to career exploration; second, to stimulate exploration of self in relation to a career; and third, to provide "what if" information with respect to various career choice options.

Herr and Cramer (1972, p. 250) also speak of the role of assessment as follows:

> . . . we have come to accept the premise that assessment procedures help individuals to understand themselves not only in terms of their talents, but also in terms of their interests, values and personality characteristics. The greater the degree of accurate self-understanding an

individual has, the more likely he is to make realistic, satisfying educational and vocational choices, it is assumed. While accurate self-understanding does not guarantee good decision-making, good decisions probably cannot be made without a realistic picture of one's abilities and interests. Again, assessment devices provide a vehicle that contributes to student self-understanding and accurate appraisal.

CRITICISMS OF ASSESSMENT

Since the testing "boom" began during the 1920's, assessment techniques have been used more and more each year in increasingly diverse types of settings. The purposes of testing have been greatly expanded, and decisions about persons are frequently based at least in part on test results.

The increasing popularity of assessment has also led to frequent criticisms concerning its use. While it would be impossible to enumerate even a majority of points critics have made in this chapter, it is possible to briefly discuss several key areas of concern which may be of particular relevance to the counselor.

The Trait-And-Factor Approach to Assessment

This approach to assessment has a history of extensive use. It is exemplified by the belief that the characteristics of an occupation can be successfully matched with an individual's characteristics to indicate the relative suitability of that profession for the person. Much attention has been given to trait-and-factor theory and its applications to assessment (Cronbach, 1960; Anastasi, 1961). Prediger (1974a, p. 328) makes the point that it is not so much the identification of traits and factors that is undesirable, but the manner in which they are used:

> Unfortunately, the measurement of psychological traits and the study of group distributions on these traits have, for many, become synonymous with "square peg" approaches to career guidance . . . It need not be. "Square-peg" approaches to career guidance are not dictated by trait-and-factor theory. The same persons who believe "marriages are made in heaven" can readily implement a "square-peg, square-hole" approach to career guidance independent of any objective measures or research on the characteristics of occupational groups. The counselor's viewpoint does have a great deal to do with the *effectiveness* of the career guidance he provides, but the existence of trait-

and-factor measures does not force any particular viewpoint on him. Blaming trait-and-factor theory for a mechanistic approach to guidance is somewhat like blaming skin color for racial discrimination.

Prediger further suggests that measurement of personal traits can be beneficial if taken as an additional source of information in helping the individual explore career choice options.

Assessment Techniques With Minorities

One of the primary criticisms of assessment techniques, particularly intelligence tests, is that they have been designed so as to reflect the cultural values of a predominantly white, middle-class society. This has been especially true when test results have been used in a *predictive* rather than an *exploratory* fashion. Minorities are then discouraged from exploring anything other than "safe" probabilities instead of looking at the many alternative possibilities which exist. Prediger (1974a) points out that assessment techniques provide information regarding both *probabilities* and *possibilities,* but the task of changing attractive possibilities into probabilities rests with the counselor as an agent of social change, not with the test. The author would add that one of the advantages to assessment techniques is that they can reveal cultural influences that contribute towards determining which are more or less promising alternatives for the individual. The counselor can then point out remedial steps which can be taken to come to grips with those problems.

Assessment Techniques With Women

One of the major criticisms of assessment techniques used in career guidance (particularly the *Kuder Occupational Interest Survey-Form DD* and the earlier edition of the *Strong Vocational Interest Blank*) has been that they have used sexist language in describing occupations, and have thus implicitly fostered the idea that certain jobs are open exclusively to males. Another criticism has been that separate testing forms have frequently been used for men and women, denying women useful information used by men in making choices. This practice may encourage the counselor to view occupations as being stereotypical of "men" or "women" and reinforce traditional occupational roles (see Chapter 12) .

Influence of Counselor Bias

The author has experienced two main sources of counselor bias with regard to the use of assessment techniques. First, many counselors feel that there is something intrinsically dehumanizing about testing. Testing is thought to necessarily involve the counselor's assuming a superior role, the role of the "all-knowing expert" who knows more about the client than the client knows about himself. The relationship which then results may often be cold and impersonal.

Of course, the counselor should not act in this fashion. If he does, it really is more the fault of the counselor than the test. Tests themselves do not promote a mechanistic approach to assessment. Assessment techniques provide data about the client's future, his strengths, weaknesses and areas of interest. Data by themselves are not cold and impersonal, only informative. When assessment techniques are used in an exploratory fashion, the role of the counselor is not to inform the client of what action he thinks he should take. Rather, it is to interpret the test data to the client so that he may make informed decisions in the process of career development.

The second source of counselor bias the author has frequently encountered is the addiction of counselors to the idea that test results should be communicated to the client through long, personal, one-to-one talks. Otherwise, how can the client be expected to understand them?

Test interpretation has traditionally been *oral*. In other words, while *written* or *visual* communication of test results has been somewhat inadequate, the burden of interpreting the data by word of mouth has fallen on the counselor. However, recent advances in test communications (as the American College Testing Program's *World of Work Map*) have made it possible for data to be communicated much more effectively, either in written form or graphically.

The majority of counselors carry the yoke of heavy caseloads upon their back; improved methods of presenting test data may permit the counselor to lay the groundwork for future discussions with the client by initially being more active in introducing test information. The client may then be given the test data in a form or computer printout which summarizes the findings in easily understandable terms for him to consider outside the counseling session. Subsequent appointments might be scheduled if further clarification of data is necessary, but these appointments would generally be planned in order to explore further career alternatives suggested by the data, not to further sift through it in an attempt at organization. Test results might also be discussed in groups, with individual appointments following, if appropriate.

METHODS OF ASSESSMENT

The major types of assessment techniques used in career counseling are those which measure the factors of aptitude, achievement, interests, vocational maturity and work values. The purpose of this chapter is to describe several instruments which measure these factors, with the emphasis on how they may provide information of practical value to the counselor.

It is not the intention of this chapter to provide a glossary of all possible tests which are available. Nor is it to deal with the more technical terminology surrounding the interpretation of data. Goldman's book (1961) covers the latter topic very thoroughly. The assessment techniques which were selected for inclusion in this chapter met the following criterion: they demonstrate promising and innovative ways of delivering test data which the counselor can use as information. They may either be relatively new and unknown instruments, or widely-used instruments which have been revised in response to new technical knowledge.

ASSESSMENT OF APTITUDES

Aptitude tests imply prediction in that their function is to provide the counselor with some basis for predicting future level of performance. They are often used to predict success in some occupations, to select individuals for admission to training programs, or, in some cases, to make institutional decisions regarding fellowships or scholarships. Rather than emphasizing a strictly predictive function, aptitude tests can also be used in career counseling to help the client discover his *individual* patterns of achievement. This will help him in making choices regarding future career exploration, rather than placing him in a specific vocation.

Several aptitude tests are currently in wide usage, such as the *Flanagan Aptitude Classification Tests* (Science Research Associates), the *General Aptitude Test Battery* (U.S. Employment Service) and the *Differential Aptitude Tests* (Psychological Corporation).

The DAT basically consists of six aptitude tests: *V,* verbal reasoning; *N,* numerical ability; *A,* abstract reasoning; *S,* spatial relations; *M,* mechanical reasoning, and *C,* clerical speed and accuracy. In addition, there are two achievement tests (spelling and grammar). It is principally designed for use with students in grades eight through twelve, although it may be most frequently employed in grade eight where children often face important decisions regarding a future occupation.

Validity data on the DAT were collected from some 50,000 students in forty-three states, and predict high school achievement as well as (to a more limited extent) college achievement. Two follow-up studies have been completed with a large sample of high school students, but the predictive validity of the DAT regarding occupational criteria is questionable, as is the case with most other aptitude tests. The general advantages of the DAT are that extensive data collection supports its educational norms, and that the test has been developed in a highly competent and technical manner. Its main disadvantages are the amount of time required for administration, and its relative lack of occupational norms.

In keeping with the purpose of this chapter, however, the primary concern is not with reviewing the test, but to point out the new innovations that have been developed and how they can be used. The Psychological Corporation has introduced the *DAT Career Planning Program,* consisting of the following: Three forms of the DAT (L, S and T); The Career Planning Questionnaire and answer sheet, and The Career Planning Report. On the Career Planning Questionnaire, the student is asked to list his preferences from among ninety-two school subjects, activities and sports. He is also asked to list his preferences among one-hundred occupations. The time of administration is approximately forty minutes and may be either group or individually administered.

Computerized scoring of the answer sheets is offered, comparing the student's patterns of DAT choices with his occupational preferences and most valued activities. Two copies of the report, including a profile of the client's DAT scores, are returned to the counselor. This report includes descriptions of the aptitudes measured by the DAT, and informs the student whether his choice of career goals seems appropriate considering his aptitudes. It also suggests alternative occupational groups for the student to review.

The accompanying counselor's manual was written by Donald Super in collaboration with the staff of the Psychological Corporation. It presents background information with suggestions for interpretation and use of the report.

How will these additions to the DAT help the practicing counselor? First, the interpretation of test results is now computerized, meaning that the counselor will no longer have to do an extensive amount of calculations and cross-checking to be sure the raw data accurately match the correct norms. Secondly, specific suggestions are available in the manual as an aid in communicating the results to the student. As the interpretation of the results is couched in easily understood terms, the counselor may consequently find it easier to involve the parents in a discussion of the report's implications for the student's career development. New normative data based on a nationwide restandardization are also included.

The test gives the student more information upon which to make decisions about his career choices at a time when it becomes necessary for him to begin eliminating some options. It also clearly points out the areas in which the probability of the student's further success is greater. One of its biggest advantages is that it takes into account the student's future educational plans and choice of school subjects in indicating whether those appear to be congruent with his career goals.

ASSESSMENT OF ACHIEVEMENT

The *Comparative Guidance and Placement Program* of the College Entrance Examination Board (Educational Testing Service) consists of two questionnaires and six tests. It is designed for use with students admitted to two year colleges and vocational-technical institutes. The questionnaires provide biographical data concerning the student as well as measuring his *interest* in various academic and vocational areas. The tests measure the student's *ability* in verbal and mathematical areas, as well as other less traditional special abilities.

The counselor receives a one page student report from ETS. This report includes the test scores given in percentiles, a profile of the student's interest pattern as compared with other students, and a placement forecast of his probable success in specific English and mathematics courses. It also includes a performance forecast showing the student's chances of succeeding in the various curriculums offered by the institution, based on past studies of student performance in those programs where abilities were quite similar.

The performance forecast has the following advantages. First, it provides the counselor with information about the progress of students which he would usually not be expected to know. Secondly, it visually presents information which can be assimilated and understood much more easily than if the counselor attempted to communicate that same information orally. And last, it enables the student to translate the predictive information about possible outcomes into decision-making regarding the alternatives open to him.

ASSESSMENT OF INTERESTS

The *Strong Vocational Interest Blank* (Stanford University Press) is the old standby of interest inventories and is familiar to every counselor. Several changes have recently been made in the Strong, and it has been merged into the *Strong-Campbell Interest Inventory* (SCII, Form T 325) .

Since in the past men and women usually entered different occupations, the SVIB provided separate norms, scales, and profiles for each sex. Now, even though men and women do show substantial differences in the strengths of their interests in some areas, the SCII uses only one booklet and profile (separate normative data are retained for each sex) . Men now respond to items formerly only included in the women's booklet, and vice versa.

Another major change in this edition of the SVIB provides a

profile that arranges the person's scores according to six occupational themes, twenty-three basic interest scales (both based on Holland's six occupational personalities) and 124 occupational scales ordered according to Holland's classification system. This profile provides the counselor with more information, and that information is also more clearly presented than in the earlier forms. Helpful suggestions are also given in the Inventory for interpreting the data and computerized scoring is available.

Along with the *Strong Vocational Interest Blank*, the *Kuder Preference Record-Vocational* (Science Research Associates) is probably the interest inventory with which counselors are the most familiar. The primary disadvantage of the *Kuder Form C* has been that it is impossible to predict occupational choice using it, as there are no accompanying occupational keys.

The *Kuder Preference Record—Occupational Interest Survey (Form DD)* is a new form which has eighty and thirty-six occupational keys, respectively, for men and women. Interpretation of the data is based on the degree of relationship existing between the client's pattern of interests and the interest pattern of the occupational group in question. These occupational groups are specific, as compared to the more general occupational groupings used in the SVIB. Thus, it is possible for a counselor to use the instrument in a very precise fashion. Another advantage in terms of time savings to the counselor is that *Form DD* must be machine-scored.

As Anastasi (1961) has stated, many of the scores for women are obtained with scales developed using male criterion groups in fields where men predominate, but which offer some vocational opportunities to women.

ACT Interest Inventory

The American College Testing Program publishes the *ACT Interest Inventory* as the most recent addition to their Assessment of Career Development Program. It consists of ninety items which measure student interest in six major areas: social service, business contact, business detail, trades, scientific, and artistic. These correspond to Holland's (1973) six types of personal orientation. The time of administration is approximately fifteen minutes, and the student responds to the items on a five-point scale—indicating the degree he would like doing that activity.

The counselor receives a Student Profile Report which indicates how the student's scores compare to other entering college students, and how his scores relate to those college seniors in twenty-four educational majors. This is termed the Educational Major score, and is plotted on the ACT Interest Map. This map is divided into two dimensions. The horizontal one consists of a business-science continuum, and the vertical dimension consists of higher scores plotted in terms of business detail while lower scores fall in the area of creative arts and social services.

The interest map visually demonstrates the student's area of major interest, and allows him to explore new alternatives he may not have previously considered. Prediger (1974b) also suggests that if the field in which the student has scored highest does not seem to attract him, the counselor can suggest "those fields are good possibilities, but . . . there are others which are also possibilities." Again, this helps keep as many options open to the student as possible, but does provide the student with information upon which to make decisions. The counselor may also consider directing the student towards extracurricular guidance materials, such as giving him the DOT codes corresponding to his preferences.

The ACT has also introduced the *World of Work Map for Job Families* (1972), which classifies occupations into two bipolar dimensions: Data and Ideas, and People and Things. The CPP Student Report locates which of the regions on the map the student falls. Prediger (1974b) views the map as analogous to a traveler's map, in that the student is given a start towards finding his way, but must look further for the necessary details. First, the student receives an exploring booklet, which leads him to the realization that he is "on the map." The student is then encouraged to ponder the implication of his preferences for data, people or things. The goal is to provide him with a broader focus for occupational exploration, and to try to place the test results in a larger context.

Non-Sexist Vocational Card Sort

At the University of Florida Psychological and Vocational Counseling Center, an instrument has been developed by Dewey

(1974) termed the *Non-Sexist Vocational Card Sort* (NSVCS).

The NSVCS was conceived as a response to the "traditional" sex-role stereotyping which frequently occurs on such vocational tests as the SVIB and Kuder. It is a process-oriented technique which gives each sex a greater range of vocational choices to explore. In addition, it enables the client to personalize the information in terms of his own values.

The NSVCS was derived from a modified version of the *Tyler Vocational Card Sort* (Dolliver, 1967). Beginning with the combined SVIB and Kuder DD forms, seventy-six occupational categories were chosen and typed on cards. These were then coded according to a modification of Holland's (1966) six personality types, so that conclusions may be drawn regarding the client's choices. On the reverse side of each card, the job duties and responsibilities are summarized according to the *Dictionary of Occupational Titles*.

The theoretical framework of the NSVCS is grounded in Holland's work in classifying vocations. Dewey states that this system was chosen because of its simplicity, the importance it gives vocational choice as an expression of the client's personality, and its grouping of occupations by personality type in a given occupation rather than by occupational status or educational requirements.

Administration of the NSVCS also follows Dolliver's (1967) modification of *Tyler's Card Sort*. The client is asked to sort the set of occupational title cards into three piles: the "Might Choose" group, identified as those occupations the person might choose, or those that have "specific appeal" to him; the "Would Not Choose Group," which are described as those occupations which "don't seem particularily appropriate" for the client; and the "In Question" group, termed those occupations about which the client is "indifferent" or "uncertain."

Following the sorting of the three piles, the client is then asked to talk about why he selected the items in each category, and his comments are recorded. The client is then questioned as to whether he feels any occupational areas of interest were omitted from the original seventy-six cards, and is also given the opportunity to elaborate on his earlier responses. Steps are then taken to be certain the client has specific directions to take upon leaving the counseling session. Dewey suggests the counselor refer the client to such resources at the *DOT, Occupational Outlook Handbook,* or college catalogs.

A Case Study Using the NSVCS

William, a twenty-one year old man, shows high scores on the SVIB Artist Scale. However, he grouped "artist" on the NSVCS in the "Would Not Choose" pile, saying that he was not at all certain he had the necessary drawing ability for such a profession. The counselor noted that Bill was pursuing a business management major, but that his grades were below average. In further discussing his future plans, Bill stated that his father, an eminent businessman, wanted him to become a partner in his firm when he graduated from college. He had frequently told Bill that he would not be able to succeed as an artist because artists were not "he-men" and they didn't make enough money to support themselves. Nevertheless, Bill had spent the past three summers working as an artist at a nearby vacation resort. He also said that despite working against stiff competition, he had received substantial remuneration for his work, and had spurned several offers from patrons to exhibit his work in order to return to school on a full-time basis in the fall. When the discrepancy between his statement and the earlier reason he had given for rejecting the profession of art was pointed out to him (his lack of drawing ability), Bill realized the conflict between making his own decisions and relying on his father to make them for him. This theme subsequently became the focus of several follow-up sessions.

Here, the NSVCS helped the client to explore a vocational alternative, as well as focusing on the criteria he was using in vocational decision-making. In addition, it served to open up another broad area of concern to the client which was discussed in further visits, namely, his relationship with his father.

In addition to the advantages of the card sort mentioned by Dewey, such as discouraging sex-role stereotypes, encouraging further vocational choice alternatives, and making it possible for the client to actively participate in the administration of the instrument, other possible strong points are: (a) it focuses on *how* the client makes his vocational decisions and the criteria he uses, rather than focusing only on *what* decision he makes; (b) either group or individual administration is possible; (c) the administration is relatively simple and brief; and (d) as with Q-sort techniques in general, the card sort permits the counselor to arrive at a more comprehensive picture of the client's choices than if he were only asked to rate the occupations numerically.

Some possible disadvantages of the card sort might be: one-to-one counseling contact appears to be necessary, which is time consuming for counselors with busy work schedules; and, as with Q-sort techniques, the instrument requires the client to make a forced choice when dividing the occupations into groups. Thus, the counselor should be careful to elicit information regarding the particular criteria the client uses to place the occupations within groups.

The Vocational Preference Inventory

Another interest inventory which is gaining acceptance is Holland's *Vocational Preference Inventory* (Consulting Psychologists Press). Holland designed this instrument primarily as a personality inventory rather than a vocational inventory. It is composed of 160 occupational titles and the client indicates his amount of interest by responding "yes" or "no" to each occupation. A profile is then compiled (Holland, 1965) consisting of eleven scales, such as Intellectual (a high score on this scale would be indicative of a person who thinks through problems more than acting them out); Social (those who score high have social interests and tend to be relatively more insightful in interpersonal relationships); and Artistic (those who tend to be imaginative, original and somewhat unconventional).

There appear to be several advantages to this instrument. First, it provides a very broad range of information concerning the client's life style, coping mechanisms, vocational interests and self-concept in a short period of time. Secondly, it has several timesaving advantages in that it is self-administering, scoring is quickly accomplished, and the time of administration is from fifteen to thirty minutes. Third, Holland (1965) states that the occupational content of the VPI reduces the need of the client to fake his answers, since the VPI is not usually perceived as a threatening test of personality. Last, this is an instrument which can be used to complement and provide a further check on data obtained by other instruments in a test battery to provide the counselor with a multifaceted view of his client. Holland suggests it may be very helpful as a screening inventory to gather information which will help the counselor determine what path to take regarding the client's career planning in future sessions.

One possible disadvantage of this instrument is that it lacks adequate empirical evidence to permit anything other than a subjective, clinical interpretation of the profile data (for a comprehensive discussion of the merits of the actuarial versus the clinical interpretation of tests, see Meehl, 1954, or Goldman, 1961).

Inherent in the above is the implication that interpretation of the information is best left to the counselor with a sound clinical background grounded in testing and personality theory. This is, as was previously mentioned, a personality inventory as well as an instrument to assess vocational interests, and the counselor should be aware of this.

ASSESSMENT OF VOCATIONAL MATURITY

Crites (1973) developed the Attitude Scale of the *Career Maturity Inventory* (formerly the *Vocational Development Inventory*) as a way of assessing a person's vocational maturity through determining his attitudes toward various occupations in terms of empirical behaviors. This instrument consists of fifty true-false statements regarding the attitudes the student takes toward work which may determine his later vocational choices when he finishes his schooling, such as "A person can do any kind of work as long as he tries hard," or "It is probably just as easy to be successful in one occupation as it is in another." The data is summarized and presented as a vocational maturity scale. Herr and Cramer (1972) suggest that although this instrument is largely experimental, it may certainly help the counselor in terms of planning if he knows his client's stage of career development. The rationale behind this assumption is that if the counselor assumes the client is proceeding in a series of steps toward maturity, then he can keep him up-to-date with changes and help him personalize the information. For instance, should the college student indicate that he has little or no idea what work will be like when he graduates, or that he is having difficulty preparing himself for a vocation, he needs to be given very basic information on vocational possibilities, in addition to working on improving his decision-making skills. It would probably also be helpful to help him explore the possibility of taking a summer job in order to familiarize himself with "the world of work." However, if another client who is a high school senior indicates he feels there is only one occupation that is "right" for him and thinks that by the time he graduates he should make that decision, his counselor might want to discuss whether he has been exploring other possibilities. He may have narrowed his alternative plans for the future to too great a degree should his present outlook change. This instrument helps the counselor validate his personal impressions of how his client's development is progressing, as well as checking the client's feelings about decisions he must make about his future career.

The Vocational Decision-Making Checklist

Harren's *Vocational Decision-Making Checklist* (1966) has been developed largely on an experimental basis. However, it may be of interest as a useful tool in determining the client's level of vocational maturity.

The Checklist is based on Tiedeman's Vocational Decision-Making Model (Tiedeman, 1961; Tiedeman & O'Hara, 1963). It purports to measure where the client is situated on the following continuum of vocational decision-making (Harren, 1972):

Exploration: This stage is marked by random, exploratory considerations. It is characterized by generalized vague concern with little or no apparent progress toward choice. Knowledge of self and the occupational world is a felt need, but the individual has developed no strategy or plan of action for satisfying this need. There is an absence, or near absence of definite negative choices (exclusions from the range of possibilities). This is accompanied by vague anxieties and doubts about the future.

Crystallization: This stage represents progress toward, but not attainment of choice. The individual recognizes alternative possible choices and at least some of the consequences of these alternatives. Conflicts are recognized; advantages and disadvantages are weighed; the bases for a decision are being developed at least implicitly. The process of narrowing down the range of possibilities through negative choices is operating. False steps and inappropriate earlier decisions are recognized and used as bases for further decisions.

Choice: This stage represents a definite commitment with some degree of certainty toward a particular goal. It is accompanied by expressions of satisfaction and relief for having made the commitment . . . This stage further represents a swing from the pessimism characteristic of the exploratory stage to a kind of naive optimism about the future. The individual usually expresses . . . eagerness and impatience to reach the goal. Focus upon the consequences of the decision and further planning are not yet in evidence.

Clarification: This stage represents a process of closure in which the individual is involved in clarification and elaboration of the consequences of his commitment, as well as in planning the details and next steps to be taken to follow through on the commitment . . . In addition, the individual is usually engaged in a process of elaboration and perfection of his self-image and his image of the future. Although planning the overt action to carry out the commitment is characteristic of this stage, the overt action itself may be delayed until the environmental conditions are appropriate for action.

There are fifty-six items on the checklist. The client is instructed to check any statement which would accurately describe himself, or one of his current needs, concerns, or problems. The time of administration is approximately 20 to 30 minutes. Scoring is simple, and is done by hand. There are two subscales; Choice of Major, and Choice of Occupation. These two problem areas are interpreted as being particularly relevant to vocational choice.

It is possible for the counselor to determine whether the client's decision-making is relatively mature, and whether he is more mature with regard to his choice of major field or future occupation. This instrument has the advantages of being quickly administered and easily scored. Harren has suggested it may be useful as a preliminary screening device in career counseling or as an introductory way of going over individual responses for future clarification of the client's goals. Normative data are being collected which may make the scores more meaningful and permit comparison between clients.

ASSESSMENT OF WORK VALUES
The Work Values Inventory

One of the more promising instruments is Super's *Work-Values Inventory* (Super, 1970). It is designed for grades seven through adult and takes only fifteen minutes to administer. It attempts to measure fifteen values which are associated with vocational success, such as intellectual stimulation, creativity and esthetics. These fifteen factors are then further subdivided into four more inclusive categories, termed by Super (1970) as material, goodness of life, self-expression, and behavior control. Although no predictive validity has yet been established, this approach may have practical implications for the counselor in that it attempts to measure a number of values related to work that have previously not been tapped.

SUMMARY

This chapter has discussed the use of assessment procedures in five different areas of career development; aptitude, achievement, interests, vocational maturity, and work values. Several criticisms of assessment procedures were presented, and selected assessment procedures were discussed with descriptions and suggestions for employing them in counseling. It has been shown that there are new assessment procedures that may be usefully employed, and that counselors are limited only by their innovativeness, imagination and flexibility within the framework of their training in attempting different ways to interpret and personalize the data obtained from these instruments.

BIBLIOGRAPHY

The American College Testing Program. *Handbook for the ACT Career Planning Program.* (1972 ed.) Iowa City, Iowa: Author, 1969.

Anastasi, A. *Psychological Testing.* (3rd ed.) New York: MacMillan, 1961.

Crites, J.O. *Career Maturity Inventory.* Monterey, California: McGraw-Hill, 1973.

Cronbach, L.J. *Essentials of Psychological Testing.* New York: Harper & Row, 1960.

Dewey, C.R. Exploring interests: A non-sexist method. *Personnel and Guidance Journal,* 1974, *52,* 311-315.

Dolliver, R.H. An adaptation of the Tyler Vocational Card Sort. *Personnel and Guidance Journal,* 1967, *45* (9), 916-920.

Goldman, L. *Using Tests in Counseling.* New York: Appleton-Century Crofts, 1961.

Harren, V.A. A study of the vocational decision-making process among college males. *Journal of Counseling Psychology,* 1966, *13,* 271-277.

Harren, V.A. *Preliminary Manual for the Vocational Decision-Making Checklist*. Carbondale, Illinois: Author, 1972.

Herr, E.L., and Cramer, S.H. *Vocational Guidance and Career Development in the Schools: Toward a Systems Approach*. Boston: Houghton-Mifflin, 1972.

Holland, J.L. *Manual for the Vocational Preference Inventory*. Palo Alto, California: Consulting Psychologists Press, 1965.

Holland, J.L. *The Psychology of Vocational Choice*. Waltham, Mass.: Blaisdell, 1966.

Holland, J.L. *Making Vocational Choices: A Theory of Careers*. Englewood Cliffs, N.J.: Prentice-Hall, 1973.

Meehl, P.E. *Clinical Versus Statistical Prediction: A Theoretical Analysis and Review of the Evidence*. Minneapolis: University of Minnesota Press, 1954.

Prediger, D.J. The role of assessment in career guidance. In Herr, E.L. (Ed.), *Vocational Guidance and Human Developemnt*. Boston: Houghton-Mifflin, 1974a.

Prediger, D.J. Innovations in test interpretation. A symposium presented at the national convention of the American Personnel and Guidance Association, New Orleans, April 1974.

Super, D.E. *Work Values Inventory*. Manual. Boston: Houghton-Mifflin Co., 1970.

Tiedeman, D.V. Decision and vocational development: A paradigm and its implications. *Personnel and Guidance Journal*, 1961, *40*, 15-21.

Tiedeman, D.V., and O'Hara, R.P. *Career Development: Choice and Adjustment*. New York: College Entrance Examination Board, 1963.

Chapter Five

SIMULATION TECHNIQUES IN CAREER COUNSELING

PATRICK SWEENEY

How MANY TIMES IN RECENT years while watching a moon shot on television have you gotten into an argument over whether what you were seeing was really the moon or a simulation. Only the periodic flash "SIMULATION" on the screen would identify definitely which it was. The space program made all of us familiar with simulations as "mock ups" or models of the real thing. Our working definition of simulation in this chapter is the taking on or assuming of appearances or attributes of an entity without the reality of that entity.

No doubt the space program has provided the most dramatic use of simulations, not only in reporting the Apollo missions to the taxpayers, but also in training the astronauts for the unique, "unearthly" experiences they were to encounter. We were made aware of simulations through the space program but they had, in fact, been around for a long time. Prehistoric man simulated the hunt by drawing on cave walls, primitive tribes simulate hunting and warfare in their ritualistic dances and ceremonies, and wild animals are able to simulate their physical environment to avoid capture by their predators. Man first used verbal or pictorial simulations before he progressed to scale models in planning and design. Many advertisements seen in the media attempt to simulate the good life and the successful people who result from switching to Brand X. If Madison Avenue and NASA can use simulations effectively, why not counselors?

The social sciences utilize simulation in studying interpersonal behaviors or interaction between an individual and his environment. By making use of simulation in a system designed for certain conditions, data can be gathered to expand an area of knowledge, specific tasks can be taught to others, or principles can be generalized to new situations, all under controlled, replicable conditions. Gangé (1962) and Dawson (1962) stress that the presence of systematic control is the critical difference between a simulation and an operational situation; the difference is between predictable and unpredictable variation. Phenomena that are rare, random, expensive, dangerous, or self-consuming are often observable only through simulations. Simulation is ideally suited to a systems framework because of the availability of immediate feedback that allows for a series of replications with variable modification. An admitted disadvantage of simulation is the degree of deviance between the simulation and the operational concept.

The key to the effectiveness of simulation as a learning model lies in reinforcement theory. Rather than waiting for accidental or random behavior to occur, a variety of stimuli are presented to elicit behavior which can then be reinforced. The learner, as simulation user or observer, establishes or recognizes a given $S_1 \longrightarrow R_1$ relationship, which can be generalized to $S_2 \longrightarrow R_1$ and eventually to $S_n \longrightarrow R_1$. In other words, the stimulus presented in the simulation must be similar to the real stimulus so that generalization will occur. Interference can occur resulting in a transfer response ranging from positive (as desired) through zero (no response) to negative (opposite of desired). After transfer of learning has taken place, practice and review will serve to stengthen the new $S \longrightarrow R$ bond.

So far we have established a working definition of simulation, described certain useful applications of the concept and described the psychological mechanisms that make simulation effective. The remainder of this chapter will attempt to develop a rationale for using simulation in career counseling and will suggest ways of doing this. Different types of simulations will be discussed including gaming, which is a special type. Examples of simulation in current use will be cited and certain research and evaluation will be presented. Finally, sources of information on simulation materials and techniques will be identified.

DESCRIPTION OF TECHNIQUES

Coleman (1971) noted that most learning takes place in the out-of-school world where the incentives to learn are quite different from those in the classroom. Experiential learning is an action-feedback-modified action sequence, while school learning is based on contrived, extrinsic rewards and punishments. Too often, and for too long, according to Sprague (1966), adolescents have been isolated from the adult world during their naturally inquisitive years when recognition of cause-effect relationships is most needed. Sprague believes teachers, as such, are not needed, but rather helpers and facilitators are needed. Serving as hosts, models, provocateurs, and resources, they should provide experiences where learning through natural inquiry is expected, rewarded and supported.

Simulation provides a student the opportunity to exercise skills, to apply insights and to gain immediate feedback. Consider the learning difference which occurs when one tells a child the stove is hot as compared to his discovering it by touch. This opportunity to observe cause-effect relationships firsthand allows one to alter his behavior and then observe the new consequence and gain extensive experience in a relatively short period of time. Young adults are often confronted with rarely occurring situations, such as a job interview, and the outcome may have far-reaching effects on their lives if their "trial and error" approach turns into "trial and disaster." If helping persons can assist students in anticipating, rehearsing, and preparing for such events, then students can devote their time and energy to structuring and planning alternative behaviors rather than recovering from consequences of those events.

Examples of simulation are many and varied. The military establishment used the WWII Link-trainer in flight training and has developed even more sophisticated mock-ups and simulators for warfare training. Management theorists and practitioners were quick to realize the benefits of simulation for training and for forecasting and decision making models. Sociologists have also simulated social systems to study human behavior. Educators too have utilized simulation in teacher education programs. These simulations, most notably reported by Twelker (1967), were to prepare more adequately student teachers for classroom behavior situations by adding an experiential dimension to the cognitive preparation they had traditionally received. Eisenberg (1971) cited a threefold use of simulation in counselor selection, counselor training, and research on counselor behavior, but these were directed toward the counselor rather than the client.

The evaluation of the effectiveness of a simulation is much like the evaluation of any other learning technique. Depending upon the behavioral objectives stated for the simulated experience, the evaluation is essentially a verification of the amount of learning that is transferred from the simulated to the real event. The final evaluation of the space program's simulation training was the actual landing of Eagle on the surface of the moon, but the effectiveness of a role playing simulation in counseling would more likely be satisfactory interpersonal transactions involving both client emotions and overt behavior. The latter is more difficult to assess; particularly the emotional counterparts of behavior which are difficult to operationally define.

SIMULATION IN CAREER COUNSELING

Given the tasks of assisting a person in investigating and choosing a career, one is typically faced with a situation where there is an abundance of demographic, economic, and statistical information available but little opportunity for the student to experience or personalize what he may learn. As the world becomes even more complicated *(Future Shock,* 1970) ironically providing man more leisure, there may be even less opportunity for youth to gain personal experience of the world. The youth of today can watch the world go by on television.

Simulation, including gaming, promises the opportunity to expose people to new experiences and to provide feedback. It also allows one to recognize cause-effect relationships often thought of as trial-and-error learning. Recognizing that deliberate behavior is the result of decision making (whether decisions are made well, poorly, or not made) counselors or career education specialists find that providing decision-making opportunities to be a worthwhile task. Of the several ways to accomplish this task, the most stimulating may be games.

Games as Simulations

Games are simulations, but not all simulations are games. Dawson (1962) saw the essence of games to be a contest of opposing forces with a stake to be gained or lost. In zero-sum games the total gains equaled the total losses so that one person's advantages were matched by another's disadvantages. In non-zero-sum games, however, it was possible for everyone to "win" by cooperating with each other and by competing against the game elements. Abt (1970) has stated that the formal essence of games is an activity among two or more independent decision-makers each seeking to achieve his objectives. He felt that game activity was most typical of real life activity and furthermore that games were a particularly useful way of looking at situations.

Simulation games clearly are exercises in making decisions and experiencing the consequences of those decisions in a safe environment. A safe simulation is not necessarily sterile or non-involved, for modeling and simulation can be effective in both cognitive and emotional learning. Crawford and Twelker (1970) discussed the affective outcomes of simulation learning and suggested that the long hours of concentration in continuous game play demonstrate an intense involvement with other players. The player interaction, whether with teammates or opponents, is characterized by joy, anger, elation, and even mild shock both during the game and at valuable post game discussions. Increased player awareness of self and others has also been noted by observers. Empathy is experienced with the problems faced by others; attitudes towards others and their problems are changed. Self-perception is best illustrated by the increased feelings of power and effectiveness reported by the players as many of them experience potency and control never known before. Scott (1966) says "information acquired while the individual is under stress and is emotionally involved is likely to be internalized more fully than information acquired casually."

Counselors have long encouraged the trial and error approach to career choice, e.g. sampling relevant courses, doing volunteer work, obtaining part-time jobs. The time, energy and money involved in this approach, however, are limiting factors. There is a need for games and other techniques that simulate actual experiences of a particular job. Abt (1970) believes that a student/player should be able to discover the following characteristics of a simulated occupation: nature of the job, rewards, entry requirements, advancement opportunities, and opportunities for self-realization. Replays of a game offer an opportunity to use a different strategy to obtain a different outcome, which is often impractical in real life. While it may not be desirable to eliminate all experience of trial and error for youth, neither should it be necessary for each generation to reinvent the wheel.

Modeling and Role Playing

Bandura (1969) has done extensive work in the field of social learning, a type of simulation where the student/client observes a genuine or contrived situation that may or may not be familiar to him. It has been demonstrated that both cognitive and affective learning takes place even without reinforcement. One could assume that learning had occurred when the observers adopted and executed the observed (modeled) behavior. The use of modeling to increase the rate of information seeking behavior was discussed in Chapter 3. Also it has been observed that clients viewing appropriate behavior prior to counseling have made better progress in counseling (Sauber, 1971).

Thoreson (1969) urged the use of social learning in his model of the "Applied Behavioral Scientist" where the counselor modeled the appropriate behavior for the client. In the past there had been too much reliance on one-to-one verbal interaction in counseling, he said, suggesting that no procedure was off limits as long as it was operationally evaluated. Earlier Krumboltz (1966) discussed imitative learning as one of the appropriate methods to promote adaptive behavior. He suggests the counselor model or arrange for models of appropriate behavior, e.g. listening to taped recording of a young person actively engaged in information seeking behavior.

Kelly (1955) describes Fixed-Role Therapy where a client acted "as if" he were the character in a sketch. The sketch, written by the counselor and based on interview, Q-sort or other test data, would be rehearsed or practiced during the session with the counselor and the student playing the roles. Kelly had come to the realization that psychoanalysis did not seem to be the answer to problems arising in a social, economic, or educational setting. The written role would be a positive one attempting to utilize the student's resources. Kelly's chapter on Fixed-Role Therapy is very readable, giving step-by-step procedures, a case history, and even an example of the technique used with an individual and with a group. It may be time for guidance counselors to renew (or gain) an acquaintance with Kelly.

Decision-Making

Matheny (1971) urged use of simulation in counseling to gain decision-making experience in a safe environment where results could be observed, alternatives selected, and mistakes corrected. Feedback, called knowledge of results by learning theorists, allows the participant to recognize control and cause-effect relationships in a simulation.

A career decision-making model with the unlikely acronym of MOLD was developed by Johnson and Myrick (1972). Using a six step format the student gathered personal data on himself, participated in discussion and exploration in a group meeting, explored alternative careers and made a tentative choice. After planning a year of activities on paper using locally relevant information the student then received feedback on probable consequences of his decisions. He then planned another year and continued the cycle. In a study of this model Johnson and Myrick found that the eighth grade students liked the model which had a positive effect on their acquisition of educational and occupational information. They are continuing their analysis of the model. This particular exercise appears to be similar to the *Life Career Game* except the profile is not fictitious, but of the student himself.

One way to experience decision-making consequences, the

Life Career Game (Boocock, 1966), can be played by any number of teams, each consisting of two to four players. Each team works with a profile or case history of a fictitious student. The game is organized into rounds which represent one year in the life of a person. During each round players plan their person's schedule for a typical week, allocating time among various activities: school, studying, work, family, and leisure time. Because most activities required certain investments of time, training, and money, one could not engage in all available activities. Thus the problem faced by the players was to choose the combination of activities which maximized their person's present satisfactions and enhanced his chance for a good life in the future.

In addition, for certain activities such as a job or higher education a person had to make a formal application; so students, in the process of the game, acquired the skills necessary for filling out application forms correctly. When players have made their decisions for a given year, scores are computed in four areas; education, occupation, family life, and leisure. Calculators used included a set of tables and spinners which indicated the probabilities of certain events happening in a person's life, given his personal characteristics, past experiences, and present efforts. A chance or luck factor was built into the game by the use of spinners and "unplanned event" cards. A game would run for a designated number of rounds and the team with the highest total score at the end of the game would be the winner. The game can be varied by using actual forms, catalogs, want ads, etc., from the local community.

Varenhorst (1968) examines the usefulness of the *Life Career Game* and emphasizes several points. The game can be used with students at a wide range of ability or achievement levels. The structure of the game is such that it can be varied to fit a number of differing situations or groups. Fitting the game into a guidance unit or system is easily done. This game may be the most easily useful simulation game for the uninitiated (in gaming) counselor to use and to enrich with relevant material suitable for a given locale.

One may gain knowledge about the subject of games by read-

ing about them in books and journals or by reading game instructions and examining game materials. Another way of gaining
knowledge would be to play one or more games and experience
the reactions that are reported by game participants. Learning
occurs in postgame discussions and analysis of cause-effect relationships and possible alternative strategies. From the emphasis
in this chapter on the value of experiential learning through
direct involvement, there is a strong suggestion that an effective
way for a guidance practitioner to learn about games is to design
one.

Many writers about games (Abt, 1970; Boocock and Schild,
1968; and Osmond, 1970) discuss the steps involved in game design. Prior to the design of the actual game, however, the desired
objectives must be stated in order to achieve the desired result.
Games have been known to affect different types of learning; a
decision about the kind of learning which is to occur is the initial
step in designing games. Initially certain technicalities about the
situation have to be determined such as limits on time, amount of
detail, geographical bounds, resources, etc. The next step is to
define the players and their roles because the players will have
certain objectives and resources, both physical and psychological.
Then, the "win" criteria must be set, a scoring or accounting
system devised, and a dynamic sequence of interactions which
yields alternative choices must be allowed for. Finally the game
must be field tested by actual play. Following the systems model
(see Part III) there is allowance for reentry into the cycle at any
point with continual retesting and feedback into the system. Perhaps one of the hats in the counselor's wardrobe should be labeled
"Gamesman" and another, "Simulation Agent."

SELECTED STUDIES AND RESOURCES

The techniques and principles of simulation are of little impact if not integrated into a systematic learning model. Long
range goals must be established in operational or behavioral terms
while considering both philosophical and ethical implications.
Initial behavior must be analyzed in order to plan strategies for
effective behavior change and to allow measurement of the differ-

ences between initial and terminal behaviors. Analysis and feedback of results are necessary to reenter the cycle in a true systems approach.

The Palo Alto (California) Unified School District adopted a decision making rationale (Clark, Gelatt, and Levine, 1965) for their secondary guidance program. Varenhorst (1969) used the *Life Career Game* in the program because of its relevance for decision making, which she believed to be the core of vocational planning. She went on to say that the emotional involvement, availability of relevant facts, value clarification, and practice necessary for decision making are provided by the *Life Career Game*. She then offered evidence that the social learning principles of modeling, reinforcement, successive approximation, discrimination learning, and skill development are used in the game play, but agreed that longitudinal research was needed to determine the effects of the game's influence.

Yabroff (1969), who was also at Palo Alto, studied ways in which counselors could train students to become better decision makers and the kinds of information which would be personally meaningful to students in making actual choices. He hoped to help students learn *how* to choose, not *what* to choose. In order to do this, he wanted to provide specific data based on experiences of recent graduates from the school. Expectancy tables were constructed on the past students based on academic abilities described in school records and on follow-up studies after graduation. Tables were constructed based on grades earned in the ninth through twelfth grades for several variables; high school grades, post-high school activities, first year employment activities, and colleges selected. Data in the tables generated much group discussion and individual reflection as students saw the possible consequences of certain actions. Using this kind of model proved very helpful to students who reported generalizing this type of decision making to situations outside of school choices. Many talked to their parents about their ideas; perhaps some for the first time. They also gained a realization that it was important to take personal responsibility for decisions that shaped their lives.

An "Effective Problem Solving" counseling model was offered

by Magoon (1969) as a self-directed learning program for students from the junior high level to the college level. Its purpose was for students to learn effective problem solving skills. After mastering the skills the student applied them to his own educational/vocational problems. The actual procedure involved an individualized, self-paced, programmed task of writing answers in a thirteen part booklet over a period of six to eight meetings. Topics covered in the booklet included effective problem solving, occupations, study time, ability and achievement, work experience, leisure time, interests, planning and taking action. Magoon felt that the advantages of the model were in its structure, flexibility of work pace, ordering tendency, written record, availability of alternatives, and emphasis on student responsibility. Disadvantages appeared to be reduced verbal interaction, the lack of allowance for emotional concerns, minimal definition of individual problems, and difficulty in adapting the model to varying situations. This simulation compacted decisions usually made at random times into a structured, methodical task available for discussion, review, and revision.

Questionable attempts at counseling disadvantaged youths by using traditional methods prompted Adkins (1970) to develop a more relevant program for black, inner city youth called "Life Skills Counseling." These youths held a common belief and shared a low expectation that their life could ever be any different and there was no one to challenge their belief. They had very little information resources and could not sustain attention on anything. Adkins noted the potential for peer influence and the desire for active learning to design a program suggesting three essential requirements. The program had to be life-problem centered, be built on present knowledge and skills of the participants while providing a means for improving problem solving skills and utilizing new knowledge, and utilize peer relationships by maximizing group activities. He identified fifty common life problems (proper diet, dealing with discrimination, identifying interests); categorized them into five major areas (developing oneself and relating to others, managing a career, managing home and family responsibilities, managing leisure time, and exercising community rights, opportunities, and responsibilities) ; and built four stages of development (stimulus, evocation, objective inquiry, and application) in each area. A large portion of the activity and resources used in the program involved active participation by the youths in simulated situations where they would actually apply their learning. Multimedia kits that contained various simulations and models, e.g. films, tapes, and printed materials, were used extensively. Like most simulations this program is very flexible. Adkins felt "Life Skills" programs may have certain advantages over didactic and counseling approaches but he recommended using it with a conventional program of services.

There are various sources of information, materials, and ideas about the use of simulation. The Johns Hopkins University Center for the Social Organization of Schools has since 1966 been an early leader in attempting to understand the relationships between games and learning in general. This work has been under the leadership of Coleman's Academic Games Program. The results of these efforts have been disseminated in many of their own reports as well as through ERIC.

Several commercial ventures have resulted in simulation based programs. The Singer Corporation's *Career Assessment Laboratory* is a simulation based commercial project which is undergoing field testing at this time. The program is a self evaluation and career exploration system designed to increase the effectiveness of the career counselor and career educator. The College Entrance Examination Board introduced in early 1972 a course of study called *Deciding* to teach decision-making. It met with such success that in addition to the initial materials designed for junior high students, plans were immediately begun to develop materials for older students and adults. This program, *Decisions and Outcomes,* is described in Chapter 9. The Education Achievement Corporation has recently published comprehensive systems entitled *The Valuing Approach to Career Education, Creating Your Future,* and *Motivation for Career Success.* Various materials, including games, are utilized to present the concepts and to integrate them into existing curricula. As of this writing new materials are being introduced almost daily into the market as large firms such as Singer, Bell & Howell, Xerox and others are becoming more active in educational marketing.

SUMMARY

In essence, simulation is quite simple; it is like make-believe or pretending but with the critical additional element of control. Even though simulation has always existed in one form or another, its value lies in the ability to control the simulated process. Exercising control allows us to examine the simulated activity, change the variables and repeat the process in systematic cycles. The value of simulation for the user lies in the "as-if" experience that approaches reality but without the permanency that accompanies a real situation. Practice and experience can be gained in a safe environment so that "trial and error" is not synonymous with "trial and disaster." Although education in general has made significant use of simulation, counseling has not. However, this appears to be changing as games and decision making models are increasingly being made available for career counseling and guidance programs.

Games were discussed as a special type of simulation very popular with learners because they involve the psychomotor, affective and cognitive realms of their behavior. Games emphasize decision making activity since choices are made which have observable consequences. Immediate feedback is obtained thereby providing the basis for the next choice, round or move. In this increasingly complex society where students are more insulated or detached from the out-of-school learning environment there is a need for students to become independent, autonomous learners rather than objects of abstract instruction. Students not reached through traditional programs may be reached through experientially based simulation activities.

BIBLIOGRAPHY

Abt, C.C. *Serious Games.* New York: Viking Press, 1970.

Adkins, W.R. Life Skills: Structured counseling for the disadvantaged. *Personnel and Guidance Journal,* 1970, *49,* 108-116.

Bandura, A. *Principles of Behavior Modification.* New York: Holt, Rinehart, and Winston, 1969.

Boocock, S.S. *Life Career Game.* New York: The Simulatics Corporation, 1966.

Boocock, S.S., and Schild, E.O. *Simulation Games in Learning.* Beverly Hills, California: Sage Publications, 1968.

Clark, R., Gelatt, H.B., and Levine, L. A decision-making paradigm for local guidance research. *Personnel and Guidance Journal,* 1965, *40,* 40-51.

Coleman, J.S. New incentives for schools. In Guthrie, J.W., and Wynne, E. (Eds.), *New Models for American Education.* Englewood Cliffs, N.J.: Prentice Hall, 1971.

Crawford, J., and Twelker, P.A. Affect through simulation: The gamesman technologist. In National Special Institute, *The Affective Domain.* Washington, D.C.: Communication Service Corporation, 1970.

Dawson, R.E. Simulation in the social sciences. In Guetzkow, H. (Ed.), *Simulation in Social Science Readings.* Englewood Cliffs, N.J.: Prentice-Hall, 1962.

Eisenberg, S. Implication of video simulation of counseling, *Educational Technology,* 1971, *11,* 50-52.

Gagné, R.M. Simulators. In Glaser, R. (Ed.), *Training Research and Education.* Pittsburg: University of Pittsburg Press, 1962.

Johnson, R.H., and Myrick, R.D. MOLD: A new approach to career decision-making. *Vocational Guidance Quarterly,* 1972, *21,* 48-51.

Kelly, G.A. *The Psychology of Personal Constructs.* New York: Norton, 1955.

Krumboltz, J.D. *Revolution in Counseling.* New York: Houghton-Mifflin, 1966.

Magoon, T.M. Developing skills for solving educational and vocational problems. In Krumboltz, J.D., and Thoreson, C.E. (Eds.), *Behavioral Counseling: Cases and Techniques.* New York: Holt, Rinehart, and Winston, 1969.

Matheny, K. Counselors as environmental engineers. *Personnel and Guidance Journal,* 1971, *49,* 439-444.

Osmond, M.W. The method of simulation games in family life education. *Experimental Publication System,* 1970, *9,* 346-356.

Sauber, R.S. Approach to precounseling and therapy training: An investigation of its potential influence on process and outcome. Unpublished doctoral dissertation, Florida State University, 1971.

Scott, A.M. *Simulation and National Development.* New York: Wiley, 1966.

Sprague, H.T. Changing education in America. Unpublished manuscript, Western Behavioral Sciences Institute, La Jolla, California, 1966.

Thoreson, C.E. The counselor as an applied behavioral scientist. *Personnel and Guidance Journal,* 1969, *47,* 841-848.

Twelker, P.A. Classroom simulation and teacher preparation. *The School Review,* 1967, *75,* 197-204.

Varenhorst, B.B. The life career game: Practice in decision-making. In Boocock, S.S. and Schild, E.O. (Eds.), *Simulation Games in Learning.* Beverly Hills, California: Sage Publications, 1968.

Varenhorst, B.B. Learning the consequences of life's decisions. In Krumboltz, J.D. and Thoreson, C.E. (Eds.), *Behavioral Counseling: Cases and Techniques.* New York: Holt, Rinehart, and Winston, 1969.

Yabroff, W. Learning decision-making. In Krumboltz, J.D. and Thoreson, C.E. (Eds.), *Behavioral Counseling: Cases and Techniques.* New York: Holt, Rinehart, and Winston, 1969.

ADDITIONAL REFERENCES AND RESOURCES

Adair, C.H., and Foster, J.T. *A Guide for Simulation Design.* Tallahassee, Florida: Instructional Simulation Design, Inc., 1971.

Adams, D.M. *Simulation Games: An Approach to Learning.* Worthington, Ohio: Charles A. Jones Publishing Co., 1973.

Charles, C. L., and Stadsklev, R. *Learning with Games.* Boulder, Colorado: The Social Science Consortium, Inc., 1973.

Education Achievement Corporation, P.O. Box 7310, Waco, Texas 76710.

Gamed Simulations Inc., P.O. Box 1747, FDR Station, New York, New York 10022.

Inbar, M., and Stoll, C.S.: *Simulation and Gaming in Social Science.* New York: The Free Press, 1972.

Kietsch, R.G. *An Introduction to Learning Games and Instructional Simulations.* Instructional Simulations and Co., 1969.

Simulation and Games, An International Journal of Theory, Design, and Research. Beverly Hills, California: Sage Publications.

Simulation/Gaming/News, P.O. Box 8899, Stanford University, Stanford, California 94305.

Tassey, P.J., and Unwin, D. *Simulation in Gaming in Education, Training and Business: A Bibliography.* The Education Centre, New University of Ulster, Coleraine, Northern Ireland, July, 1969.

The American Behavioral Scientist. Sage Publications, 275 South Beverly Drive, Beverly Hills, California 90212. (October and November, 1966 issues.)

Western Behavioral Sciences Institute, 1150 Silverado, La Jolla, California 92037.

Zuckerman, D.W., and Horn, R.E. *A Guide to Simulation Games for Education and Training.* New York: Western Publishing Co., 1970.

Chapter Six

A SHORT TERM CONTRACTUAL APPROACH TO CAREER COUNSELING

DAN MONTGOMERY

IN THE PAST DECADE THERE has been a great deal of attention given to the development and implementation of complex information delivery systems and simulated models for teaching career decision-making. Combining sophisticated computer technology with the insights of career development theorists, researchers have made an important contribution to the career development literature. Unfortunately, the focus on computerized systems for career counseling has, in the writer's opinion, led to an over emphasis on the information and cognitive needs of the client and to the neglect of the idiosyncratic emotional problems that may accompany a career choice. Individuals seeking career counseling are often plagued with a myriad of inter and intra-personal concerns which cannot necessarily be relieved by exposing the client to career information or by teaching him the ins-and-outs of rational decision-making.

As career counselors know, exposing an individual to decision-making skills or vocational information is different from showing the client how, given his doubts, anxiety and past history, he can make use of the information in his life—and it is the latter that has been neglected in the career development literature. With the exception of Krumboltz (1969), Hoffman (1973), and a few other writers, there has been very little attention given to devising treatment strategies for helping clients deal with the emotional problems inherent in the selection of a career. Questions such as: how can one help the unmotivated client, how can one help the client whose parents want him to do one thing and he wants to do another, or how can one help the individual who has no interests or too many interests, remain largely unanswered. Consequently, career counselors are placed in a dilemma: they are asked to help clients make meaningful career choices, but they have not been equipped to handle the variety of psychological problems that are involved in such a decision. Basically, the counselor has two alternatives: fit the individual into the existing model or refer him for psychotherapy or personal counseling.

The author proposes an alternative approach. Rather than relying on depersonalized methods of referring clients to a therapist or counselor when a personal problem is encountered, it is apparent that many of the techniques developed for short-term psychotherapy can be adapted and applied to career counseling. In this way, the career counselor could function as an expert on career information and decision-making, while at the same time deal more effectively with the psychological concerns that may accompany a career choice. Questions dealing with client confidence, maturation, and ability to relate to others would no longer be treated superficially or left to a therapist. Instead, the client's psychological problems would be seen as necessarily related to his career concern and be treated as such.

The purpose of this paper then, is (1) to show how a short-term treatment procedure based on the contractual approach to therapy can be applied to career counseling; (2) to demonstrate the potential of the technique in dealing with career related problems; (3) to stimulate other theorists to study and apply brief treatment procedures to career counseling; and (4) to encourage counselors to take a broader view of career counseling by focusing their attention on the social and psychological problems encountered by an individual facing a career decision.

One of the most promising of the techniques being used in brief treatment is the therapeutic contract. The notion of therapeutic contracts evolved from a variety of schools including behavior modification, Transactional Analysis, and Egan's encounter group (Egan, 1970). Broadly defined, a contract refers to a legal, ethical and mutual agreement between the counselor and client pertaining to some aspect of treatment, e.g. fees, number of sessions, and goals of treatment. This paper will discuss how contracts can be used in career counseling to clarify and define treatment objectives. The ideas presented in the paper are derived from the work of Claude Steiner, (1971b), Morris Haimowitz (1971), and Gerard Egan (1970) as well as the author's personal experience.

ADVANTAGES OF A
CONTRACTUAL APPROACH TO CAREER COUNSELING

When compared to noncontractual approaches, the contractual model has several distinct advantages. First, it is efficient. By clarifying what the client wants and by translating his wants into behavioral objectives, the counselor and client know what needs to be accomplished and they are less likely to waste time working toward an ill-defined goal. Moreover, a mutually agreed upon and behaviorally defined objective ensures that the client and counselor will not be working at cross purposes. A client who enters treatment to deal with one problem will be treated for that problem and not for another. Furthermore, the contractual approach provides a built in means of assessing outcome. Since the goals of treatment are stated ahead of time, progress can be judged in terms of whether or not the client reaches the stated goal. In other words, both the counselor and the client are in a position to assess the efficacy of treatment and to take the appropriate steps, including referral to another counselor, to remedy a therapeutic impasse.

In addition, the contract provides some safeguards against game playing. Because the client's and counselor's roles are clearly defined and the obligations of both parties are stated in relation to the goals, game playing is minimized. For example, games such as "Yes, but," where the client responds to each of the therapist's intervetnions with a subtle, but nonetheless evasive reply, can be avoided. Thus, if a counselor suggests that the client study some career related literature and the client counters the suggestion with an excuse, the therapist can fall back on the contract and the obligation of both parties in fulfilling the agreement. With a contract, the counselor can confront client resistance in a straightforward, nonmanipulative way. He does not have to make a rebellious client cooperative unless that is part of the contract. If the client chooses to undermine the counselor's efforts, then that is his decision. As hurt, disappointed or frustrated as the counselor may be, he knows that he has fulfilled his part of the bargain. Similarly, if the client feels the counselor is failing to comply with his obligations, he too can openly take steps to remedy the situation, thereby minimizing frustration and expediting his development.

CHARACTERISTICS OF A
WORKABLE THERAPEUTIC CONTRACT

Although it is difficult to specify all of the characteristics of a sound or workable therapeutic contract Morris Haimowitz (1973) and Claude Steiner (1971a) have developed some helpful criteria. As already mentioned, the contract should be *mutual,* i.e. both parties must agree to it; *moral, ethical* and *legal;* and defined in terms of *observable behaviors.* Although the criteria of mutuality and legality need no further explanation, the importance of behaviorally defined goals requires discussion.

Counselors and therapists in general are prone to accept nonbehavioral treatment goals as a legitimate basis for treatment. However, this may be unwise. A goal which is not defined in behavioral terms is likely to be vague, ambiguous, and difficult to achieve. Objectives such as "make the right career decision," "narrow my interests" or "understand how to make a better decision" are all legitimate requests, but they are vague and ambiguous. How will one know if one has made "the right career decision," "narrowed one's interests" or whether one can make "better" decisions? Relying on the client's opinion is inadequate. Clients are human and prone to errors. They may make a very poor career decision, but conclude it is the "right one" because they feel they have no other choice. Clients may reduce their interests from 10 to 4, but feel they have not made substantial progress. Or they may erroneously conclude that learning how to make a decision in a laboratory setting, *ipso facto,* prepares them for decision making in the real world. Obviously, one can make similar observations regarding the counselor's perception of his client's progress: the counselor's criteria for improvement may be too stringent or too lax; he may project his own standards of "good" and "bad" on the client's behavior; and he is likely to confuse his need for success with a successful outcome.

Given the ambiguity of non-behavioral objectives, an adequate contract requires the client and counselor to define treatment goals in terms of observable behaviors, the counselor and the client will know when and if the contract has been fulfilled, whether some additional or alternative form of help is necessary, and at the same time avoid the misunderstanding resulting from vague and unspecified objectives.

In addition to the characteristics of mutuality, legality, and behavioral goal definition, a valid contract should be one which the client (4) *wants to carry out,* (5) *is capable of carrying out,* and (6) *one which is consistent with his values* (Haimowitz, 1971). If any one of the three characteristics is in doubt, then the chances of the contract being achieved are reduced. For example, a client may feel that he should be a lawyer because his parents want him to. Furthermore, he may know that he is capable of legal work, but he may have no real interest in law or in being a lawyer. Under these circumstances his chances of successfully practicing law are greatly reduced. It is seldom the *should* or the *ought* that determines behavior, but rather the client's habits and needs. Stated simply: "wants are more potent energizers than shoulds" (Montgomery and Montgomery, 1974).

This is also true in the case of ability and values. If the client lacks the ability or is considering a career that is not in accord with his values, then the outcome may be jeopardized. An absurd, but nonetheless telling example appeared in an advice column where a young man wrote in asking if he should become a minister. Citing evidence favoring the decision, the man noted the excellent fringe benefits including a longer than average vacation, social status, and the use of a house and car. The one drawback from his standpoint—and this he wasn't sure was a drawback—was that he was an atheist. Wisely the editor of the column pointed out the problems of such a choice, but it is interesting to speculate just how often individuals pose similar but less extreme choices and receive enthusiastically affirmative replies. If one does not take the time to arrive at a contract that the client wants, can do, and is consonant with his values, the counselor risks doing the client a disservice.

NEGOTIATING A CONTRACT

Negotiating a contract is an educational and therapeutic experience. It involves helping a client move from a poorly defined goal to a clearly defined behavioral objective.

Depending on the client and the skill of the counselor, a sound contract may be accomplished in a single session or may require a considerable expenditure of time and energy. To assist the counselor interested in using the contractual approach, some tentative guidelines are identified below.

Step No. 1

Given the fact that many clients seek counseling because they are unable to rely on their own judgement, the first step in contract negotiation is for the counselor to firmly, but gently, *question the client's objectives*. When a client states that he wants to change some aspect of his life, the counselor can ask two questions: (1) ask the client to define *what* he wants to change in behavioral terms, and then (2) ask the client to tell *why* he wants to change the stated behavior. If, for example, the client says he wants to become more involved in his work, the counselor would ask him to define what he means by involved. To help the client in translating his goals into observable behavior, the counselor might ask: "What exactly do you mean by involvement?" "How would you behave or act differently if you were involved?" "If I were watching you, how would I know that you were involved?" If the client replies by stating that he would be more "interested," "happy," etc., the counselor needs to prod the client to tell him what he means by "happy." Some clients will have more difficulty with this step than others, but with continued perserverance the client will eventually arrive at a behavioral definition.

When the client has arrived at a behavioral objective, it is important for the counselor to assess the client's motives for wanting to change the target behavior. To do this the counselor needs to ask "why?" In this instance the question why is asked to find out the purpose behind the client's stated goals. By asking why, the counselor is saying "What's the purpose of your wanting to choose a major or wanting to become more assertive on your job etc." The client's response to the question is important in determining the reason the client sought treatment. If his response suggests that he entered treatment in order to please his boss, wife, family or others; or if he says he wants to change some particular behavior because he knows he should, then caution is in order. As stated earlier, people seldom change because they should change or ought to change. This would be too simple. In order for a contract to work, there needs to be some clear incentive for the client; otherwise, the contract will resemble a New Year's Resolution and be just about as effective. From the perspective of Transactional Analysis, a "should" or "ought" represents some ideal or prescribed behavior pattern which the individual or society is asking him to live up to. When he fails to do this, he disparages himself or his behavior becomes a problem for those around him. Usually, he will try and adjust his behavior, but if this does not work he will seek the "expert" advice of the counselor. And, as Allen (1971) has pointed out, this may be a set-up. As in other areas of life, an individual will seek an expert for any of several reasons: he may truly want help, he may be looking for someone to confirm the futility of the situation, or in some cases, he may be looking for someone to take the blame. In other words, the client who defines his problem in terms of "shoulds" or "oughts" may be asking the counselor to try to accomplish what everyone else has failed to do; and if the truth were known, the client may not even want to do.

To demonstrate how the counselor can use the "why" question to assess client motivation, the author has included an excerpt from an intake interview:

Client: I need to take an interest test.
Counselor: Why?

Client: (surprised) To find out what I am interested in of course!

Counselor: Yes, but why do you want to find out what you are interested in?

Client: Because my wife said I should.

Counselor: Yes, but why do you want to find out?

Client: (pause) I guess I really don't. I mean I really don't care right now. I like what I'm doing.

Counselor: In other words, it's not you who wants the test, but your wife.

Client: Right.

In this exchange the counselor skillfully uses the why question to help the client see exactly what he was doing, and how he would probably get very little out of taking an interest inventory. When the client admitted his motivation for entering counseling, he was in a better position to decide for himself exactly what he wanted. In this instance, he wanted to discuss the pressure from his wife to obtain a better job. If the counselor had not questioned the client's motives, it is unlikely that the client would have benefited from counseling. He would have taken the test to pacify his wife and ignored the results. However, by asking "why" and by focusing on what the client wanted, the counselor was able to let the client know that he was unwilling to help the client's wife; but that he was willing to help him.

Step No. 2

The second step in contract negotiation might be labeled the *challenge* or *confrontation phase* (Steiner, 1971a). Having arrived at a behaviorally defined contract which takes into account the client's values, capabilities and desires, the counselor can begin to help the client move toward his objective. The means which the counselor and client will use to carry out the contract will depend on the nature of the problem and the parties involved. Nevertheless, there are some general considerations which are likely to enhance the chances of successful outcome.

The responsibility for change must be given to the client. If the client suspects or even hopes that the counselor possesses some magical prescription for his woes, which he won't unveil until after the N*th* session, then the prognosis is poor. The best way of dispelling the client's ill-found hopes is to repeatedly challenge his efforts to avoid or transfer responsibility. If the client says he doesn't know what he likes or doesn't like, then the counselor needs to ask what he plans to do about it. Or if the client says he needs to make a decision, the counselor needs to ask what's stopping him. Common questions that can be used to facilitate the confrontation phase are: What is it you want to change? What additional information do you need to make a decision? What's the next step? How are you stopping yourself from reaching your objective? And what are you avoiding? Each of these questions is designed to help the client move from discussion to action while at the same time leaving the responsibility for action with the client.

CARRYING-OUT THE CONTRACT

The success of a therapeutic contract will depend largely on the contract negotiation process. If the counselor has applied the guidelines set forth in the previous section, then the chances of successful outcome are greatly enhanced. However, implementing a contract inevitably creates problems and some additional points need to be made.

First, it is important that the contract be broken down into small and specific steps. Given an overall set of objectives, specific sub-goals should be delineated and the steps necessary to reach the subgoals should be specified. Each step the client takes should help him advance toward his objective. In short, the counselor should design a program which allows the client to work toward his goal through a series of successive approximations.

Second, the counselor needs to be firm, but supportive. Backsliding and game playing are inevitable, and a competent counselor should realize this and develop effective strategies for dealing with it. Getting angry or irritated doesn't usually work. A client's inability to engage in a particular behavior must be recognized as part of his problem and treated as such (Haley, 1961). To dismiss it as manipulative or lazy will not facilitate treatment. When such behavior occurs, it is important to find out why. Obviously there are a variety of ways of doing this, and the particular method one chooses will depend largely on the counselor's beliefs regarding the efficacy of certain approaches. The approach favored by the author and adopted from the work of Haley (1961), is illustrated in the transcript at the end of this chapter. In addition to using humor and warmth to communicate concern, the counselor attempts to gain control of the problem behavior by agreeing with the client, taking his view to its logical extreme, and at times using Ellis' rational emotive approach to examine how the client indoctrinates himself with irrational ideas regarding his life and career. For further information on these approaches, see Haley (1961) and Ellis (1973).

Finally, if the contractual approach is to be used successfully, the counselor must continually reexamine and alter the original contract to correspond to new information. In the process of thinking through and carrying-out a contract, the client and the therapist will receive continual feedback. For a contract to be effective the counselor must reassess his goals in light of the information and make the necessary changes. For example, if a client repeatedly fails to carry out homework assignments such as reading through some vocational literature, then the therapist needs to examine the contract in terms of this feedback. It may be that the client is incapable of carrying out the contract; feels he should carry-out the contract, but doesn't want to; or he may be engaging in some form of repetitive self-defeating behavior which needs to be dealt with before career counseling can continue. Whatever the case, it is essential that the counselor and client see the contract as a tentative set of objectives which can be modified when and if additional data is generated.

A PARTIAL TRANSCRIPT

To help the reader use and understand the ideas presented in this chapter, a transcript from a typical career counseling interview is provided below. The transcript highlights several of the critical steps in contract negotiation and illustrates difficulties a counselor may face when helping a client translate his goals into concrete behavioral steps.

Joe, age 21, sought career counseling because he was doing poorly academically, had little or no interest in his work, and was being pressured by the Dean of his college to declare a major. As you will see from the transcript, his attitude toward the counseling interview is much like his attitude toward life and can be adequately summed-up by the simple phrase: "do something for me."

Joe: I need some help choosing a major.

Counselor: You are undecided?

J: Yes, I was told that the counselors here would be able to give me an idea what I should be doing.

C: What do you want to be doing?

J: I need to chose a major—just like I said.

C: Why?

J: Because, the Dean said so, and my parents are on my back.

C: Yes, but *why* do *you* *want* to choose a major? How would your life be different if you had a major?

J: I don't think this is going to be very helpful. I thought you could give me some tests or something and then tell me what to do.

C: Tests don't do that.

J: (Silence)

C: I have heard you say several important things. First, that you *should* choose a major and second that the College and your parents would be upset if you didn't; but what I haven't heard is a clear statement from *you* about what *you* want to be doing, and that leaves me feeling uneasy.

J: What do you mean?

C: I'm not sure, but it sounds like I'm being asked to help your parents or your Dean out rather than you.

J: Hmph, never thought of it that way. (recognition smile)

C: What's the smile about?

J: Oh, I don't know—well, actually I had this idea that—sort of strange—of what it would be like to be sending my parents or the Dean over to see you.

C: That turns you on?

J: Yea.

C: They need it?

J: And how. They are, I don't know if uptight is the word, but it's pretty close. Really good at telling everybody how to do everything including run their life.

C: (Interrupts) Try "my life."

J: Yea, especially my life.

C: How do they do that?

(At this point J. proceeds to launch into a long and somewhat angry recitation of the crimes and grievances afflicted on him by his parents and other authority figures. The counselor allows him to ventilate for a while, but staying within the framework of the short term problem centered, contractual approach to treatment, he intervenes as soon as he feels the client can move beyond his feelings to deal with the problem on a rational level).

C: It's good to hear you get some of that off your chest, but time is running out and if we keep talking about what's happened to you in the past twenty years, I may have some understanding of what you have been through, but you won't be any further ahead. So, what do you want to do about your current situation?

J: I don't know.

C: My guess is that you do know.

J: Not really, all I know is that I don't care for the classes I have taken and I doubt if I ever will. If it were possible, I would drop out, but I don't know how that is going to help me choose a major or get ahead in life.

C: You don't. Well, to me that's confusing. I hear you saying that you want me to help you do something which you don't want to do, and I can't imagine why you want to do that?

J: It's the only practical thing to do. I have to choose a major that will get me a job—like business or science.

C: Why? Why is it the only practical thing to do? Why do you have to choose business or science? Who's forcing you? I didn't see your parents or the Dean forcibly bring you to the Counseling Center. I don't see anyone waiting outside the building to punish you if you don't make the right choice.

J: Now I'm confused.

C: Yea, you get confused when I ask you to think for yourself, to say what you want to, to decide for yourself what *your* goals, not your parents goals, are.

J: Yea, (slightly dejected) it's frightening too.

C: I don't understand.

J: Well, I mean deciding for myself is frightening. I guess I have never really done that much before.

C: Now we're getting somewhere. Let's talk about your fright.

The remainder of the hour was spent exploring Joe's irrational fears about what would happen if he didn't select a career in business or science. Although Joe was unable to make a decision regarding a major by the end of the hour he realized that not everyone felt like his parents, and that alternative careers and majors not only existed, but were regarded as respectable by society.

Session II

C: What do you want to work on today?

J: Let's take up where we left off.

C: O.K.

J: I thought a lot about what we talked about, but I'm still hung-up on what I'm going to do.

C: What do you want to do about it?

J: I don't know—I guess I want to do what I want to do, and not what someone else wants me to do.

C: That would be a mistake (jokingly). After all, think of all the awful things that might happen: like you might enjoy your work, be happy and maybe even respect yourself. Pretty scary stuff all right. God forbid that you do what you want to do.

J: Yea. (laughing).

C: If I were you I would do what all these people are telling you to do—after all isn't popularity more important than happiness?

J: Are you serious?

C: I'm always serious.

J: Bull.

C: Watchout, I may not like you if you start standing up for yourself—show some respect.

J: Hey, look, let's cut this out. I want to tell you what I figured out. I've always wanted to be an artist—I'm really pretty good, but my parents laughed at me; but I think I am willing to risk it anyway.

C: That surprises me. I think you are actually going to do what you want. Let's talk about what you will need to do if you are going to become an artist.

The above interview provides a typical example of how the process of contract negotiation can help an individual clarify and act on what he wants. The key steps in the process were as follows:

1. Refusal to accept the client's goal as valid without first checking his motivation.

2. Repeated use of the question 'Why?' to force the client to separate his wants or objectives from the wants or objectives of significant others in his life.

3. Insistence that the client does know what he wants, or if he doesn't, that he is capable of finding out.

4. Continual confrontation of client avoidance responses by placing the responsibility on him, by using questions such as "What do you want to work on?" "How do you want to change?" and "What do you want to do differently?"

5. The communication of acceptance and respect through warmth, humor, and respect for the individual's capacity to think for himself.

6. The uncovering of the irrational ideas and beliefs that prevented the client from engaging in constructive problem solving behavior.

SUMMARY

In the preceding pages the attempt has been made to show how the therapeutic contract, a brief treatment procedure developed for psychotherapy, can be used to facilitate and improve current career counseling practices. In addition to discussing the advantages of the contractual model, the chapter has attempted to set forth specific guidelines for counselors interested in using the approach with career related problems. Topics such as client motivation and problem definition are discussed and a transcript from a counseling interview was included to further illustrate the negotiation process.

BIBLIOGRAPHY

Allen, T.W. Adlerian interview strategies for behavior change. *The Counseling Psychologist*, 1971, *3*, 40-49.

Berne, E. *Games People Play*. New York: Grove Press, 1964.

Egan, C. *Encounter*. Belmont, California: Brooks/Cole, 1970.

Ellis, A. *Humanistic Psychotherapy: The Rational Emotive Approach*. New York: Jullian, 1973.

Haimowitz, M.L. Short term contracts. *Transactional Analysis Journal*, 1973, *3*, 24.

Haley, J. *Strategies of Psychotherapy*. New York: Grune & Stratton, 1963.

Hoffman, S.D. A comparison of two "Future Group" approaches to self-exploration/career development with college students. Unpublished doctoral dissertation, The Florida State University, 1973.

Krumboltz, J.D., and Thoresen, C.E. *Behavioral Counseling*. New York: Holt, Rinehart, and Winston, 1969.

Levitsky, A., and Perls, F.S. The rules and games of gestalt therapy. In Fagan, J., and Shepherd, I.L. (Eds.), *Gestalt Therapy Now*. New York: Harper & Row, 1970.

Montgomery, A., and Montgomery, D. Contractual psychotherapy: Guidelines and strategies for change. *Psychotherapy: Theory, Research, and Practice*, in press.

Steiner, C. Contractual problem solving groups. *Radical Therapist*, 1971, *2*, 13. a

Steiner, C. *Games Alcoholics Play*. New York: Grove Press, 1971. b

---

Chapter Seven

GROUPS IN CAREER COUNSELING

S. DAVID HOFFMAN AND
DONALD J. COCHRAN

INCREASING ATTENTION IS BEING paid to career development *action.* In academic circles there is a need to bridge the gap between theory and practice; and in the field there is a need for performance and demonstrable impact on the deciding-selves of students and clients. For years we have been able to talk about: implementation of self-concepts, value clarification, needs assessment, congruence of personality and environments, and self-awareness in vocational psychology and career development. Somehow though, a distinction between counseling and career development perpetuates itself. Career counseling has continued to be considered as dealing with only part of the person. And this view is reinforced partly by economic conditions and client expectations.

Many students come to us in a decision crisis, asking for the test that tells them what to do. It is interesting that students continue to approach counselors with this request. We obviously do not have such a test, and most college freshmen and sophomores have had experience with interest inventories of one kind or another. Apparently many come with this request after hearing of a roommate's or friend's experience with the counseling center's test. Yet, students come, perhaps in desperation, looking for that objective answer.

One of our beliefs about this is that lower division students are in what Tiedeman and O'Hara (1963) call the implementation stage of educational/career decision-making, and are thus adjusting to the new situation with new sources of identity formation and affirmation. They arrive on campus not really prepared to begin approaching the decisions which the university says must be made as early as possible.

Admissions, academic advising, registration, departmental messages in catalogue descriptions all call upon the student to decide as though answers and goals were out there simply to be chosen. The student looks around in this array of external presses seeking answers, looking to some authority for the right decision, and soon discovers the difficulty in such a search. He's looking in the wrong place.

Another of our beliefs, we owe to the thesis of William Perry (1968), that students begin their college lives with a basic dualistic belief system. Perry suggests that students frequently enter college thinking of the world as either: good-bad, right-wrong, and resting authority in the absolute and in external sources. Perry distinguished nine stages in the development of commitment by college students proceeding from this dualistic view to a relativistic view of the world. The revelation occurs gradually, that answers to life are not simple; and that there may not be any external authority to divide the world so neatly or to provide any answers.

Realizing the relativistic nature of the world and of intellectual and personal development creates the setting for the development of internality. The self comes to be seen as the central critical evaluator of experience, and adherence to traditional and external authority becomes less acceptable. During this period of growth, discovery and self-development, which educational experience is intended to be, tentative commitments are made, and the individual experiences the implications of commitment through processes of trial and error, of assertion of self and the implications of choosing and acting in a world of relativity (Perry, 1968; Kroll, et al., 1970).

We are looking at lower division college students as adolescents in the beginning phases of the kind of growth and development described by Perry; and in the new environment of the campus with its expectations, cues and pressures to decide and succeed. These students come to us asking for information about themselves and the environment. They want help in finding the answers to the "Who am I?" questions, but they seek the answers in external sources.

There are also many students who come to us looking for an experience rather than an answer. These students are stuck, not in a decision-making crisis or specific problem situation, but in a struggle with broader, less clearly defined issues of development or identity. It is the developmental process, rather than content which is of central concern to these students who seem to be able to function somewhere between awareness of their own needs, values and wants and the realities of their environments. They are seeking direction from their own self-awareness, and ways to increase that awareness. They seem to be aware of a kind of flow between inner and outer realities to which they must respond and are generally more experiential participants . . . doers. Attention to developmental levels and dynamics of students is implicit in our work with career development groups.

RATIONALE FOR GROUPS

There is presently a proliferation of group approaches to counseling at all educational levels. And while there are those with a healthy skepticism, it appears that group counseling is an essential part of counseling services. Carl Rogers (1970) judges the group experience to be the most potent and rapidly spreading social invention of the century, and many believe that the group experience has already made individual counseling obsolete. The point is that group approaches are here as viable, potent strategies for helping.

Any rationale for using groups in career development is essentially the same as for using group approaches in counseling generally. There are the economy or utility arguments, the benefits of social modeling, the sharing of common difficulties, reality testing in a social situation, a microcosm of the larger society, etc. Further, many counselors and students alike *want* to do groups. The average student seen in counseling is in developmental difficulty with adolescent identity struggles often manifested in decision-making or career development terms. We believe the goal in working with these students is self-understanding or, as Volsky and Hewer (1960) have stated it, self-understanding in relation to the educational-occupational world.

Group career counseling provides the setting and opportunity to learn effective ways of being mature, self-supportive adults in the world. The groups described in this chapter encourage participants to examine themselves in a setting with others. They provide opportunities for participants to compare their styles and problems with those of other students. They help to develop confidence in one's abilities and skills of relating through processes of trial and error and reality testing. They provide opportunities for deeper self-understanding and skill in seeking alternatives to solve problems and make decisions. Further, the groups help the counselor to gain better understanding of participants (clients) by observation in a broader, more active social setting (Volsky & Hewer, 1960; Mahler, 1969). The group experiences described in this chapter are, by and large, experiential learning situations, theoretically and practically sound, and they are fun.

As guidance and counseling has grown as an identifiable profession/discipline alongside its relatives, education and psychology, the development of a professional role has presented a series of conflicts and reversals. The group approaches presented here reflect this development. Some are akin to what used to be called group guidance and have roots in occupational information classes and group test interpretation. Others are direct outgrowths of the human potential and so-called group movements, and place greater emphasis on group process and psychological growth. Still others bear witness to both of these, and are combinations of content and process emphasis. It may be productive for some to think of these examples as existing on a continuum from focusing on didactic, content orientation to focusing on an experiential, process orientation. The groups presented in this chapter are organized on this kind of continuum, beginning with the Career Development Group which is the most didactic and content oriented and ending with the Future Group as the most experiential and process oriented. The others fall, in order of presentation, between these ends. We sometimes find this kind of dichotomizing to be problematic and somewhat arbitrary; and present in table 7-I what seems to be an alternative way of differentiating groups.

TABLE 7-I
DIFFERENTIATING GROUPS

	Career Development Group	Vocational Exp'n. Group	Case Conference Group	Life Planning Workshop	Future Group
SETTING	Secondary, College, Adult	Employment Service, Secondary, College, Adult	Secondary, College, Adult	Secondary, College, Adult	Secondary, College, Adult
TIME	4 sessions/2 hours	Varied, 3 sessions/ 2 hours, 6 hour workshop	6-8 sessions/2 hrs.	6-8 hour workshop	3-4 hour workshop or 6 sessions/ 2 hours
SIZE	8	8	6-8	Varies, Sub-groups of 6	Varies
LEADERSHIP	Co-led, teacher, counselor, para-professional, active structuring	Teacher, counselor, co-led — facilitating, reinforcing, reflecting	Counselor, shared among students, re-inforcing-reflecting	Counselors co-led in sub-groups, re-inforcing-reflect-ing	Counselor, cata-lyst, stimulator
PROCEDURES	Didactic and discussion	Didactic, discussion, feedback Planning	Discussion, parti-cipants function as catalyst help-ers; feedback	Discussion, struc-tured exercises Projecting into future	Structured exer-cises, guided fan-tasy, discussion

FOCUS	Content, present and future — Objective and subjective assessment data	Content — past, present and future, job environments	Content/process — past, present, future Individual data packets	Process — present, future self as instrument	Process — past, present and future, deciding self
MEMBERSHIP	Self — other selected low level functioning in educational/career decision-making	Self — other selected by need for assistance in career development	Self — selected by need for assistance in education/career development	Self-selected, experiential, career development and personal growth	Self-selected, experiential, career development & personal growth
GOALS	Impart general and specific information	Impart information re: personal, social and man-job links	Increased sense of own interests, abilities & needs; support, organized approach to problem solving	Specific but flexible plan of action — increased internality	Values, goal clarification increased internality

Our aim is to give the reader an overall view of the five groups under discussion which differentiates and yet gives some sense of integration. We want to simplify—recognizing the danger of over-simplification.

CAREER DEVELOPMENT GROUP (CDG)

Rationale

At the Counseling Center, Illinois State University, an exploration group has been developed and implemented. The CDG is aimed at lower division students who are undecided about choice of major and career plans. This is a content oriented group dealing with some of the information that these students need and want.

The CDG provides the context for students to look systematically at existing information related to career/educational planning. Both subjective and objective means of self-assessment are used with emphasis on integrating material into the members' self-systems. Discussion of past experiences and perception of present decision-making pressures and problems provide the subjective self-assessment. Use of test results from the *Strong Vocational Interest Blank* and the *Self-Directed Search* provide objective assessment. The group introduces identification of decision-making strategies, identification of values as they relate to educational career plans, and the formation of short and long range goals.

The CDG is intended to address broad informational needs with an emphasis on expanding alternatives.

Procedures

Participants in the Career Development Group take the *Strong Vocational Interest Blank* (SVIB) and Holland's *Self-Directed Search* (SDS) prior to the first group meeting. The group meets for four, one hour sessions.

The leader needs to be sure that the SVIB is administered to all participants with sufficient time for the profiles to be returned for use in the second session.

The group experience begins by the leader structuring an introduction of the members to each other. This is done by asking the group to form pairs and to interview each other briefly. Each member introduces his partner to the group using the information gained from the short dyad experience. The leader can structure this experience further by initially asking the members to introduce each other in terms of their past experiences and interests, and future plans. This exercise is intended to open the subjective side of the self-assessment process and to help members get a feeling for their own and others' interest and experiences.

The objective assessment also begins in the first session. Members are asked to look at their measured interest patterns via the SDS.

An exploration of as many environmental/behavior styles as possible is encouraged in this session without stressing specific occupations within any one category (Cochran, Vinitsky, and Warren, 1974). A broadening of possible alternative behavior styles is the underlying goal of this process.

The second session is devoted to: (1) a discussion of informational sources, and (2) the continuation of objective self-assessment. The session begins by discussing all the possible sources of information related to career choice that are available on campus. Sources include career center libraries containing all kinds of written information on career and educational alternatives, placement service and academic advising, various academic department personnel, etc. A tour of the career center and introduction to the materials and paraprofessionals who work there is included in this session.

The SVIB is discussed in the second session with emphasis on the general meaning of the profiles and more importantly, the specific meaning of profiles to individual members. At this point an effort is made to merge the subjective information (e.g., past experiences, current picture of self, and future expectations) with objective information from the behavior inventories (SDS, SVIB). The important goal of the leader in this process is to help group members to articulate the personal meaning they attach to this information.

Examples of statements that the leader might make at this point are:

"When your past experience was related in the introductions Bob, I remember that in the past you were involved in a lot of leadership activities. Yet your SDS results don't support that preference of activities. I wonder how you're going to put that conflicting sounding information together for yourself?" "Janet, from what we've heard about you in the group, it sounds like supportive, helping relationships have always been important to you. Your SVIB results seem to go in that direction also. Your measured interests on the SVIB compare closely to people in social service areas of work."

The third session looks at another important dimension of self-assessment, the clarification of values. A game format (Mc-Holland & Trueblood, 1972; Simon, Howe, Kirschenbaum, 1972) is used to stimulate interaction. Members are asked to budget an amount of imaginary cash to each of a series of value statements such as, having recognition as a powerful person, having an opportunity to help eliminate social ills, etc. They are then asked to bid on the various value statements and write down the amount they bid for each value. Finally members are asked to look at 1. the difference between their budgeted amount and their bid amount, and 2. the hierarchy of their values. This game helps members understand their cognitive orientation to values (budgeting) and their emotional reaction (bidding) to competing for the same values.

Here the leader might point out some of his observations during the exercise and encourage the group members to do so. "Mark, I don't know how much you budgeted for the statement about having lots of prestige, but you sure got involved in the bidding on that statement."

The session is summarized by the leader who draws implications of values as mediating forces in self-assessment and decision-making.

The fourth and final session consists of two more activities. The first is on identification and discussion of decision-making styles; the second, a goal setting exercise. The decision-making styles described by Miller and Gelatt (1971) supply content for a group exploration of personal decision-making. These strategies include: "the long shot" strategy, "mini-max" strategy, "safe bet" strategy, and "highest expected values" strategy. Members are encouraged to elaborate upon, add to, evaluate, and identify elements of their own decision-making style using the examples from Miller and Gelatt as a starting point. No attempt is made to change individuals' strategies; the objective is simply to identify.

The leader reinforces and stimulates exploration of these styles of behavior. "Yes, I think you're right. The safe bet strategy does involve a high valuing of security and not much risk taking." "The stereotype of the long shot strategy has its place in folklore. This type of individual was a pioneer, an adventurer, sometimes an entrepreneur."

In the final activity, goal setting, members are asked to identify short and long term goals that relate to their career/educational planning. The SPIRO model (Pfeiffer & Jones, 1972) is used as a guide to effective goal setting. Identifying criteria of effective goal setting (*S*pecificity, *P*erformance, *I*nvolvement, *R*ealism, and *O*bservability) is the process of the structure, while individual goals are the content. The leader encourages members to share their goals with the group, and to give feedback to others regarding their goals.

Throughout the Career Development Group the leader plays a highly active role by structuring, giving information, introducing discussion topics, and encouraging members to participate. The group might be described as a medium-heavy discussion group centering on the leader most of the time.

Critique

Evaluation of the groups to this point has been primarily of a descriptive nature. At the conclusion of the group, members have been asked to rate the experience on two dimensions. Statements which represent objectives for the group are reacted to as they are important as objectives, and as they have been met for individual participants. Reactions have been mixed. Most participants appreciate being introduced to available sources of information both about themselves and the world of work. Also, the CDG puts use of tests into perspective as a valuable tool in the process of self-assessment without magic properties or instant answers.

The most prevalent problem with the Career Development Group has been holding the members over the entire four sessions, or attrition. Since the group is highly content and leader oriented the group conditions of cohesion, and openness develop very slowly. Also, participants of the Career Development Group have typically come to the Counseling Center looking for the tests, and may leave the group as soon as they have the results of the SDS and SVIB.

Spending more time on developing interpersonal communication patterns in the group and hence lengthening the experience is one method being implemented at this time to lower the dropout rate.

VOCATIONAL EXPLORATION GROUP (VEG)*

Rationale

The Vocational Exploration Group emphasizes man in the world of work, and man-job links. It is a group approach using group dynamics and phenomena such as self-disclosure, peer acceptance and sharing to enhance the process of learning about jobs in a new way, i.e. what can the job give the person? The process is concerned with thoughts about jobs, and member acceptance of others' thoughts about jobs.

The rationale for the VEG (Daane, 1972) is the relationship between man and his work, and the goal of the VEG is the clarification for individuals of the man-job relationship. The originators of VEG present four basic dynamics which occur in the VEG: members gain in self-confidence, sharing of job knowledge and resources, gain in understanding of man-job relationships, and job personalization (Daane, 1972).

VEG has five phases. Phase I is an inclusion phase which encourages exploration in the group setting, and presents a two-fold

*The authors wish to thank Drs. Calvin J. Daane and William L. Elster of Studies for Urban Man, Inc., Tempe, Arizona for their correspondence and sharing of VEG materials for this chapter.

matrix through which participants view the world of work. The matrix consists of 1. the job function, and 2. job preparation. Phase II is the sharing of previously gained job information, and study of a prepared job information book. Phase III examines job demands and job satisfactions. Phase IV is expansion, relating one job to several others which are similar, and a feedback chart which is used for members to give each other feedback regarding the jobs they see for each other. Phase V is a planning phase in which members look at the "next step" (Daane, 1972).

Procedures

The VEG begins in much the same way that the CDG begins, that is by the members introducing each other with information gained from short interviews. This inclusive phase of the experience proceeds with a group exercise. As a way for the group members to get to know each other better they tell a story about themselves. The theme is relating a fantasy about how each might spend a million tax free dollars if this were just given. In the final part of the inclusion phase, group members brainstorm and share their ideas about jobs via a job matrix chart. On one axis job function (data, people and things) is shown, and on the other level of preparation (on the job training, HS graduation, college, professional certification, etc.) is shown. Members are asked to fill in the cells with jobs they have either done or have heard about. In this exercise there are no wrong answers. The leader supports and acknowledges *all* of the members' responses and works toward an inclusion and acceptance of *all* of the members and their ideas.

Members continue to share information and disclose more about themselves in the next phase of the experience. Members are asked to name their top and bottom job choice—the job they would most like to have and least like to have. Here the leader reinforces by repeating what members say and "pairs" similar responses. For example, the leader might say, "Sounds like both Joe and Phil are interested in jobs in the science field." These leader responses are meant to help members feel more comfortable in self-disclosure (repeating and reinforcing) and to help members identify with each other (pairing).

The next exercise relies heavily on the dynamics of the group. Members give feedback to each other based on their initial impressions of each other and the information that has been shared in previous exercises. Each member is asked to sit in the "cool seat" while the other group members assign a top and bottom job to him. After the leader models by accepting feedback from members, each member has an opportunity to occupy the cool seat and get the impressions of the other members regarding what jobs they think he would like or dislike. After this exercise the members respond to each others' feedback. Examples of what group members might say to each other are: "Gee, I didn't think I was smart enough to be a teacher." (HS student) "What makes you think I'd be a good accountant?" (College freshman) "I'm glad you put stable cleaner on the bottom instead of top!" (Group leader).

At this point written exercises are used to summarize some of the information gathered. Members are asked to write three alternatives they are considering for themselves and to identify the data, people, and things dimensions of their alternatives as well as the level of preparation necessary. To familiarize members with these dimensions more fully, ambiguous photographs depicting people doing various work tasks are shown. Members are encouraged to project their views into the photos and to name job titles that apply to the photos. These titles are listed on large sheets (e.g., newsprint) according to their place on the data, people, things, and preparation matrix. As an additional stimulus to generate and share information about jobs, job information booklets are used to familiarize the members with different job titles. In these information sharing exercises there are no wrong responses. The leader acknowledges all of the contributions of group members. If one picture stimulates more than one job title, all of the titles are used for the matrix. For example, members might identify the same photo as a social worker, lawyer, salesperson, managerial supervisor, etc. Likewise members might say that an insurance salesman fits in with "data" jobs *and* "people" jobs. The leader treats both of these as acceptable responses. The main objective of these exercises is to help members generate and share information about jobs and accept each other in the process.

The next phase of the group experience is designed to explore job demand and job satisfiers. The first exercise of this phase is introduced in the frame of reference that jobs do more than just supply money, they supply satisfactions of many varieties. A group of job satisfiers are presented (prestige, team work, service, craft work, etc.) discussed, and defined by the group. Each member is asked to identify his top and bottom job satisfier and to share this with the group. Next, members look at interests and skills that they bring to the job setting and need to fill jobs. The leader and group discuss and define interests and skills (ability with members, design, relationships, selling, etc.) and assign a top and bottom skill to themselves. The final job demand focused upon is training. In this exercise members focus on four possible job situations:

1. Jobs they would like to have that they currently have enough skill and training to enter.
2. Jobs they would like to have but *don't* have enough skill and training to enter.
3. Jobs they would not like that they currently have enough skill and training to enter.
4. Jobs they would not like, and that they do not have the skill and training to enter.

During this series of exercises the leader can pair responses to increase the identification of group members with each other. Examples of these kinds of responses are: "Fred, you and Brenda have both expressed some strong feelings about prestige as a job satisfier." "Jobs that demand a strong interest and skill in directing don't have much appeal to you or Al; do they Marty?" As a summary exercise to this section a written exercise is introduced. Members list three alternatives again, either ones they listed before (see above) or new ones. This time they are asked to consider the dimensions of satisfiers and demands (interest and skill) along with training requirements and functions (data, people, and things). As members consider each of these alternatives they use a check list to identify elements of the above four dimensions in their choices.

The next exercise is directed toward more expansion of the member's alternatives. Members are asked to review the training alternatives (jobs they either like or dislike and for which they may or may not have appropriate training) and to add as many alternatives to these areas as possible. Likewise they are asked to consider their needs (satisfiers) and job demands they can meet in order to generate more alternatives for themselves. Job booklets may be used again at this point. Since the objective of the workshop is to help members learn how to make good choices rather than to make one final choice at the end of the group experience, this expansion exercise is included. Its objective is to give the members additional alternatives on which to practice their choice making skills.

The final phase of the group experience is the planning phase. Again a written exercise is used to summarize the thoughts and feelings of the members. Members record their current job goals and list their next step in moving toward the goals. A what, how, and when format is used to stimulate interaction. Each member shares his goals and plans with the group. For example, "I plan to get more information about apprenticeships (what) by writing to the State Labor Commission (how) as soon as I can find out where they are located (when)." "I need to talk more to my teacher about being a shop teacher (what). He's been very high on the possibility of my getting a scholarship to college (how). I think he'll be around after school later today (when)." At this point in the experience it is important that the leader facilitates as much support as possible by the group for various group members and their plans. This is the point at which the group process can be most helpful. Simple examples of how this might be done are: "Ann, you have mentioned some good ideas about what you want to do but you seem a little confused about what your next step might be. Does anyone have some ideas that might be useful for Ann?"

As the group terminates, the goals and plans give the leader an idea of whether further counseling and/or information would be appropriate for various members. At this point the leader can either ask to talk to some members individually or give information to all of the group on continued counseling/information options.

Critique

The VEG is an effective group model for those who need to make an immediate career decision, e.g. manpower training and employment service clients. It has also been effectively used in educational settings with participants whose needs were less immediate and/or broader. In personal correspondence Elster (1973) has pointed out that the VEG required adequate programming in career guidance to back it, and that the VEG could stimulate development of guidance programs.

VEG seems to be most appropriate for participants who require a great deal of structure in their approach to learning a decision-making process. The group is content oriented with an emphasis on internal and external dimension (i.e. job satisfiers—job matrix).

CASE CONFERENCE GROUP

Rationale

The case conference approach has been patterned after that reported by Hewer (1959), Hoyt (1955), and Volsky & Hewer (1960). The goals of the group are: to define the members' problems in educational/career decision-making, to understand the self and other members in the career development process, to explore various alternatives available, and to seek courses of action.

Sprague and Strong (1970) report three general goals for the case conference group: 1. the sessions attempt to improve the helping skills of participants; 2. each participant develops a picture of himself, better sense of interests, abilities and needs regarding goals and career; and 3. each participant has opportunity for interaction with peers which generates mutual support, organization in thinking, and strategies for problem solving.

Each participant takes the SVIB and the SDS before the first session and writes a short autobiographical statement including work history, interests, aspirations, and present difficulty in the educational/career decision-making process. This material is put together in a package for each group member.

Procedures

The first session is set up to be an introduction by the leader of the materials in the package and a technique to introduce members to each other. The leader facilitates inter-personal communication, modeling listening, attentive, and feedback behaviors. He explains the SVIB profile and the SDS to members, and discusses the goals and purposes of the group. The procedures are discussed and members are encouraged to participate in the helping process with each other by considering individual members' presence in the group, and the material that each will present and to work toward finding solutions and compromises that would enable each to clarify and move toward achievement of personal goals.

The leader discusses career development as a process, and the importance of "Who am I?" questions as well as occupational and educational information.

Members introduce themselves to the group, and are encouraged to discuss their present educational/career concerns which brought them to the meeting.

Subsequent sessions deal with individual members as they present themselves to the group in a case conference. Members try to help by becoming, in effect, career counselors. The leader participates as facilitator of communication, test interpreter and process director. If necessary, the leader can point out inconsistencies or insufficiencies in information and offer suggestions.

Critique

As with many of the group approaches, there is little data on which to base evaluation of the case conference group. Sprague and Strong (1970) found that students enjoyed the experience even though some were left in various stages of indecision. A decision is not an expected outcome of any of these groups; however, half of the small sample used by Sprague and Strong did make a vocational choice at the conclusion of the group experience. The case conference group, according to data reported by Hewer and Volsky (1960), had a very low attrition rate. This approach seems worthy of further trial and examination.

LIFE-PLANNING WORKSHOP (LPW)

Rationale

As the title implies, the Life-Planning Workshop is aimed at experience and skill development broader than job selection and the use of occupational information. It represents movement toward a more affective growth experience. LPW was developed at the Colorado State University in 1969 (Hinkle & Thomas, 1971; Birney, et al., 1970-71).

The LPW is described (Greer, 1972) as a powerful, impactful, structured growth group designed to involve participants in the process of influencing their own future. The workshop is a one-day, six or seven hour mini-marathon experience, focusing on self-assessment in the present and projection of self into the future. The objective of the workshop is increased self-awareness and realization of the need for specific and flexible plans for the future.

Procedures

Workshops involve approximately eighteen to twenty participants who meet in small groups with facilitators. Members act as consultants, probers and facilitators for each other, as the workshop moves through a series of structured exercises. The exercises described below are the primary activities of the workshop. These descriptions are drawn largely from Hinkle and Thomas (1971, pp. 3-5) and Greer (1972).

LIFE-LINE: Participants draw a life-line on paper and divide it into two parts to emphasize the workshop's focus on the future. The members discuss how much living remains rather than focus on past failure or accomplishment.

IDENTIFICATION AND STRIPPING OF ROLES: Participants identify significant roles in their lives, and beginning with the least im-

portant, strip themselves of each role. Discussion of feelings resulting from the loss of the role takes place after each role is stripped.
Participants have time to fantasize about themselves without roles,
followed by group discussion. Most of the remainder of the workshop is conducted while participants are free of the influence of
roles.*

TYPICAL DAY AND SPECIAL DAY OF THE FUTURE: Participants,
free of roles, are asked to imagine the future and to be whatever
they want to be. Then, participants write a brief description of a
typical day and a special day. Members help each other look for
inconsistencies and realism of goals.

LIFE INVENTORY: Questions are posed for participant reaction
(i.e., things I do badly and would like to stop doing, things I do
well . . .). The exercise focuses on areas of potential change or
areas of strength, and may be thought of as a preliminary goal
setting exercise.

NEWS RELEASE: Here, participants reflect on their lives from
some point in the future, and write a news release which emphasizes role, accomplishment, pleasures, etc. Focus is on how a person is or is not moving in directions he wants. As in other
exercises, discussion follows.

REASSUME ROLES: In this exercise, participants reassume their
discarded roles, or substitute other roles they now wish to assume
in place of the original ones. Focus is on change and involvement
in decision-making about the present and future.

GOAL SETTING: Participants are asked to write specific behaviors which can be performed immediately and in the near
future to direct themselves toward goals. Focus and importance of
this exercise is on the individual's own involvement in change
and planning toward his desired goals.

The leader encourages members to participate as fully as they
can in the exercises, and facilitates interaction between members
which helps draw meaning and implications of the experience.

---

*Hinkle & Thomas (1971) report no problems with this exercise, but emphasize
a note of caution, suggesting screening of individuals with tenuous reality contact
who may actually withdraw from reality following imaginative withdrawal.

Critique

While the LPW does not contain any specific kinds of information about jobs, curricula, or the world of work, it does provide an opportunity for information about the self of the participants which can be used to measure external kinds of information. The content of discussion following the fantasies and exercises often centers on the educational/career issues with which students are faced.

Who is the LPW most appropriate for, or who seems to get the most out of this kind of program? Students at a crisis point in planning, or students with very specific information needs are probably not going to get what they need from the LPW. This approach seems helpful for those who are aware of some difficulty with decision-making generally, or who are unclear about the extent of their own impact and power in choosing. Students struggling with the "Who am I?" questions inherent in career development, and who value self-awareness and direct experience seem to get most involved and enjoy the Life-Planning Workshop. Research on the LPW is available in Birney, et al. (1970), Cochran (1972), and Mencke and Cochran (1974).

FUTURE GROUP

Rationale

Future Group is a growth group, similar in some respects to the Life-Planning Workshop. It was developed by Don Sanz at the Florida State University and is currently being refined and studied. In a sense, it is experimental career development group approach.

The underlying assumptions of the Future Group are that students are largely unaware of the patterns of career decision-making in their pasts, the processes and bases of decisions they are making in the present, and the questions they want to ask about their future careers. As one becomes more aware of the process by which antecedents of past and present choices are centered in his environment or situation, he will be able to make more satisfying and appropriate decisions about the future (Sanz, 1973; Hoffman, 1973).

The goal of the Future Group experience is to provide a set-ting of experiential self-awareness of the processes and antecedents of present choices, and to make some guesses about the future.

Procedures

The Future Group is a highly structured group workshop which can be completed in three to four hours. This time length gives the Future Group some advantage of being portable and easily introduced in classes, outreach, and school programs. Struc-tures used are taken from the work of Sam Keen (1970) and Herbert Otto (1970). It has been used with small groups of six to ten, and with large groups of up to ninety.

The workshop begins with a short introduction of the ration-ale, the Future Group experience, and career development and decision-making. The leader explains that the deciding-self exists within some fantasy dimensions: 1. remembering the past in ways that may have some debilitating impact on present deciding; 2. fantasies of the future; 3. the reality dimension—the way the past helps determine who we are; and 4. the present situation and reality, abilities, and real interests.

The first exercise is designed to focus members on the past, and to involve the group in activity which gets people together. It begins with milling. Participants walk around the room look-ing for a partner with which to spend some time. When each per-son is with another, the dyads are instructed to introduce them-selves and to explain why each picked the other.

Next, all draw on paper the floor plan of the house in which they lived as a child. The dyads then take their partners on a tour of this house showing all the special places, and describing the house. The exercise is fun, usually characterized by loud talking and laughter. It brings the past, including family relationships and memories into awareness, and seems to be a pleasant way for participants to get to know each other. When the leader senses that the group has finished with the tours, each person is in-structed to take turns telling a story which is to consist of two parts: 1. how messed-up and un-together he or she is, and who helped to make him/her that way; and 2. how together, healthy, and okay he or she is, and who helped to make him/her that way. This discussion in dyads moves the group to more intense levels of sharing, and focuses more directly on the relationships of the past. The relationship of this exercise to career development is seen to be a focus of environmental and historical impact on who one is. Further, and less explicit at this point, is the issue of self-responsibility, choosing one's way, and being centered in the present. Talking about how one is and who helped make him that way can focus awareness on one's ability to choose.

At this point in the Future Group, members are brought into subgroups of four. The instructions are for partners to introduce each other to the new dyad, with attention to the "now" rather than simply retelling the partner's story or revealing information from the house portion of the exercise.

After the introductions, a short break may be taken. These activities take about one and a half hours.

The group returns to the sub-groups of four. Guided fantasy imagery is used next to project the self into the future. Participants are told they will be guided in fantasy, and they are encouraged to participate as fully as possible. Emphasis is placed on the importance, sometimes lost or forgotten, of using the imagination in creative and useful ways. The group members are asked to make themselves as comfortable as possible, lying down or sitting comfortably with eyes closed. The Paradise Fantasy is then read or structured from memory (Otto, 1970). Here, the instructions are to picture a personal paradise, asking oneself what it would look like, where it would be, who would be in it and what would be the essential ingredients. The fantasy lasts about five minutes. At its conclusion, members are asked to share the experience in the small groups. Following this sharing, the group is told to meditate on what this means. While each member is spending some quiet time alone, meditating on the fantasy, the leader asks three questions: 1. what does it mean; 2. does it, or should it lead to action; and 3. are changes in life style indicated?

After allowing sufficient time for each member to consider the fantasy and the questions, the group reconvenes as a total group. The leader encourages anyone who desires to share the experience with the group. Here the leader focuses awareness on values, life-style, and occupation as these are implied in the fantasy experience. No interpretations are made, but members are encouraged to try to determine meanings for themselves. When all who desire have shared and discussed their experience, the leader introduces the question: How can we create a paradise in the here and now? The question is presented for two reasons. First, the paradise fantasy sometimes generates anger or resentment as members become aware of discrepencies between their wants and their present activities; or how far they are from what they consider their paradises. Creating a paradise in the here and now facilitates channeling the energy into some consideration of action. Second, the question is presented to encourage participants to consider their ability to plan creatively.

The leader can then present a summary, using the material from the group, and initiate a discussion of decision-making and career development.

Critique

The Future Group workshop has advantages of relative ease in scheduling, economical use of time, low attrition rate and ability to be incorporated into existing, on-going programs. The Future Group is usually enjoyable and is a low risk growth group relative to intensive marathons, encounter, sensitivity and T-groups. Further, a program such as the Future Group which encourages imagination, playing with fantasy and developing self-support, enhances the learning experience of the individual in a para-academic career planning program. Hoffman's research (1973) indicates that the Future Group increases internality and time-competence, and to a limited extent, career maturity.

SUMMARY

All of the group approaches included here are short-term helping strategies for so-called healthy or normal individuals. Some are clearly anchored in imparting information about the self and the world of work while others are less clearly related to occupational environments. Groups such as Life-Planning Workshop and Future Group involve some experience in self-exploration and intra-personal growth with implied impact on educational/career development and decision-making.

The development of group therapeutic forces such as cohesion, belonging and trust, inter-personal and intra-personal experimentation, openness and involvement, are necessary elements in these activities. Ample experience and skill on the part of the group leader in observing and facilitating group process cannot be overemphasized as a requirement for any of these approaches. Original sources for structured exercises should be read and precautions appropriately noted.

Counselors who are now doing group counseling in various settings could introduce any of these models to attempt to enhance the career development of their client populations. The process and content can be introduced to on-going group counseling programs.

In this chapter some of the newer, innovative uses of groups which attempt to facilitate a person's career development have been presented. There is some incompleteness and perhaps more questions have been raised than answered. Nonetheless, these group approaches will help practitioners use some alternative avenues to further understand their clients and meet their career development needs.

BIBLIOGRAPHY

Birney, J., Hinkle, J. and Thomas, L. *Life Planning Workshops.* Student Affairs Publication, Ft. Collins: Colorado State University, 1970-71.

Campbell, E., Walz, G., Miller, J., and Kriger, S. *Career Guidance: A Handbook of Methods.* Columbus, Ohio: Charles Merrill, 1973.

Cochran, D. The effects of a developmental outreach program on vocational choice processes. Unpublished doctoral dissertation, University of Arizona, 1972.

Cochran, D., Vinitsky, M., Hoffman, S., and Warren, P. Conceptual model of theory and practice of career development services. Unpublished paper, Student Counseling Center, Illinois State University, 1974.

Cochran, D., Vinitsky, M., and Warren, P. Career counseling: Beyond test and tell. *Personnel and Guidance Journal,* 1974, *52,* 659-664.

Daane, C. *Vocational Exploration Group: Theory and Research.* Tempe, Az: Studies for Urban Man, Inc., 1972.

Elster, W. Personal correspondence to authors, December 4, 1973.

Ginzberg, E. *Career Guidance: Who Needs It, Who Provides It, Who Can Improve It?* New York: McGraw-Hill, 1971.

Greer, N. Life planning workshop: Description of exercises. Mimeo, Ft. Collins, Colo.: Colorado State University, 1972.

Hewer, V. Group counseling, individual counseling, and a college course in vocations. *Personnel and Guidance Journal*, 1959, *37*, 368-370.

Hinkle, J., and Thomas, L. Life planning workshops: A future oriented program. Mimeo, Ft. Collins: Colorado State University, 1971.

Hoffman, S. A comparison of two "Future Group" approaches to self-exploration/career development with college students. Unpublished doctoral dissertation, The Florida State University, 1973.

Hoffman, S., and Rollin, S. Implications of Future Shock for vocational guidance. *Vocational Guidance Quarterly*, 1972, *21*, 92-96.

Hoyt, D. An evaluation of group and individual programs in vocational guidance. *Journal of Applied Psychology*, 1955, *39*, 26-30.

Keen, S. *To a Dancing God*. New York: Harper & Row, 1970 .

Kroll, A., Dinklage, L., Lee, J., Moreley, E., and Wilson, E. *Career Development: Growth and Crisis*. New York: Wiley, 1971.

Mahler, C. *Group Counseling in the Schools*. Boston: Houghton-Mifflin, 1969.

McHolland, J., and Trueblood, R. Values Auction. In McHolland, J., *Human Potential Seminars: Leaders Manual*. Evanston, IL: Kendall College Press, 1972.

Mencke, R., and Cochran, D. The impact of a counseling outreach workshop on vocational development. *Journal of Counseling Psychology*, 1974, *21*, 185-90.

Miller, G., and Gelatt, H. *Deciding*. New York: College Board of Review No. 82, 1971.

Morrill, W., and Forrest, D. Dimensions of counseling for career development. *Personnel and Guidance Journal*, 1970, *49*, 299-305.

Otto, H. *Group Methods to Actualize Human Potential: A Handbook*. Beverly Hills: Holistic Press, 1970.

Pfeiffer, J., and Jones, J. *The 1972 Annual Handbook for Group Facilitators*. Iowa City: University Associates, 1972.

Perry, W. *Forms of Intellectual and Ethical Development in the College Years*. New York: Holt, Rinehart, and Winston, 1968.

Reardon, R. The counselor and career information services. *Journal of College Student Personnel*, 1973, *14*, 495-499.

Rogers, C. *On Encounter Groups*. New York: Harper & Row, 1970.

Sanz, D. Future Group. Unpublished paper, University Counseling Center, The Florida State University, 1973.

Simon, S., Howe, L., and Kirschenbaum, H. *Values Clarification: A Handbook of Practical Strategies for Teachers and Students*. New York: Hart Publishing Co., 1972.

Sprague, D., and Strong, D. Vocational choice group counseling. *Journal of College Student Personnel,* January, 1970.

Tiedeman, D., and O'Hara, R. *Career Development: Choice and Adjustment.* New York: College Entrance Examination Board, 1963.

Volsky, T., and Hewer, V. A program of group counseling. *Journal of Counseling Psychology,* 1960, 7, 71-73.

Part III

PROGRAM STRATEGIES

For several years now, many leaders in the counseling field have been arguing that counselors and counseling psychologists should disengage themselves from the total commitment to direct services, one-to-one and small group approaches. For example, they have been describing "the Cube" (Morrill, Oetting, and Hurst, 1974), systems approaches (Hosford and Ryan, 1970; Korn, 1969), outreach (Morrill and Banning, 1973), subcultural needs of women and minorities (Lewis, 1972; Palomeras, 1971; Smith, 1970), and other ideas as alternatives to traditional practice. The concurrent theme has been concern about the survival of the profession. "I don't have much hope that a counselor, however good he or she may be, who can only deliver direct service to one client at a time will make enough impact on our society to continue to support that activity" (Parker, 1974, p. 439).

Perhaps this very brief background serves to set the stage for the introduction to the chapters in Part III. The remainder of this introductory section (1) identifies some of the common themes in the following eight chapters, (2) describes the development and use of the model in Appendix A, and (3) briefly reviews salient points of the eight chapters in Part III.

COMMON THEMES

There are four common themes in the chapters. First, each chapter offers or reviews practical programming ideas which a counselor could implement or modify. Of course, the program descriptions or counseling techniques presented are not inclusive, only illustrative. Second, the systems approach is a common theme. The authors refer to such topics as environmental assessments, writing goal and objective statements, using a wide variety of intervention techniques, pilot testing and feedback, product evaluation, and accountability. A third common theme is the use of instructional design principles. Students

127

and others with career development needs can learn to solve problems, become assertive, get information, make and implement choices if they are systematically exposed to planned learning experiences. And fourth, each chapter suggests the need for counselors who can change organizations, be advocates for clients, endure and even thrive in spite of personal sacrifice, and who are primarily judged by a commitment to help people effectively.

A MODEL

The presentation of the conceptual model for academic advising and career development services in Appendix A also deserves special mention. After carefully reviewing the literature, Ms. Ashcraft created a comprehensive career development model, complete with goals and objectives statements. She then reviewed the existing programs and services in the academic advising, counseling, and career planning area at her institution and categorized each one of them in relation to the model. Although it is still incomplete, the model is included in this book as an illustration of one way in which a school or college might try to "get it together" regarding career development services. Anyone desiring to review existing or proposed programs could quickly categorize them in terms of the model. In fact, Ashcraft has illustrated this process in Appendix A.

OVERVIEW

The eight chapters in Part III can be separated into three groups according to format and themes.

The chapters by Bonar, "Developing an Educational/Career Guidance Program," Gimmestad, "Curricular Approaches and Self-Help for Career Development," and Peterson, "Accountability in Program Evaluation: A Case Study," each stress the interrelation of educational and vocational guidance programs. They also emphasize the ongoing need for evaluation and the systems approach as a guide to program development and accountability. Bonar and Gimmestad clearly advocate establishing career guidance programs as instructional activities, and offer concrete, specific steps for a counselor to follow in this regard. In addition, Peterson offers some examples of how career counselors can demonstrate accountability within the overall educational mission of the institution.

The next two chapters by Minor and Oliver describe specific activities a counselor might do to increase the resources available for facilitating career development. In "Developing a Career Resource

Center," Minor offers suggestions on establishing, locating, staffing, stacking, operating and evaluating a multipurpose career information/resource center within a school. Oliver's chapter, "Using Community Resources," reviews past problems and possible benefits of increased use of nonschool personnel and resources in facilitating individual career planning. A job placement service, a resource directory and career conferences are among the strategies described.

Chapters Twelve, Thirteen, and Fourteen each examine the special career development needs of three sub-cultural groups, women, homosexuals, and ethnic minorities. In these chapters, each author carefully reviews releveant historical, theoretical, or research literature and summarizes what it reveals about the subpopulation needs and characteristics. Following this review, Burkhart, Brown, and Stone describe the implications for the counselor in terms of counseling practice, consultation, and program development. Finally, each author identifies and describes strategies which might improve the delivery of career development services for the three subgroups.

The establishment and maintenance of programmatic interventions to facilitate career development must not be done at the expense of all direct services. However, in spite of deficiencies in prior training and low priorities, counselors must begin to move into programming. The eight chapters in Part III are designed to help the career counselor develop initiatives in this area.

BIBLIOGRAPHY

Hosford, R.E. and Ryan, T.E. Systems design in the development of counseling and guidance programs. *Personnel and Guidance Journal,* 1970, *49*, 221-230.

Korn, H.A. Higher education programs and student development. *Review of Educational Research*, 1969, *30*, 155-172.

Lewis, J. (Ed.), Women and counselors. (Special issue) *Personnel and Guidance Journal*, 1972, *51*, 84-156.

Morrill, W.H. and Banning, J.H. *Counseling Outreach: A Survey of Practices*. Boulder, Colorado: Western Interstate Commission for Higher Education, 1973.

Morrill, W.H., Oetting, E.R., and Hurst, J.C. Dimensions of counselor functioning. *Personnel and Guidance Journal*, 1974, *52*, 355-359.

Palomares, V.H. (Ed.). Culture as a reason for being. (Special issue) *Personnel and Guidance Journal*, 1971, *50*, 83-147.

Parker, C.A. Epilogue: . . . the more they remain the same. *Personnel and Guidance Journal*, 1974, *52*, 439.

Smith, P.M. (Ed.). What guidance for Blacks? (Special issue) *Personnel and Guidance Journal*, 1970, *48*, 707-789.

Chapter Eight

DEVELOPING AN EDUCATIONAL/CAREER GUIDANCE PROGAM

JOHN R. BONAR

Student: "Mr. Rambow, do you have a minute to help me with a problem? I've changed my mind and now think I'll go on to college. Dad wants me to go to State and take up Nuclear Physics. What do you think?"

Counselor: "Joe, I'm really glad you're thinking about continuing your education. Look, could you come in tomorrow and I'll tell you what to do to get into State. Right now I'm sort of rushed to get these attendance figures in to the principal."

xxxxxxxxxx

Student: "I just don't know what to do Mr. Peabody! I just can't seem to decide on a major and Mom and Dad are getting pretty mad about spending a lot of money on college for me when I can't make up my mind what I want to do. Can you help me?"

Advisor: "I've noticed that more and more of the students in college these days are undecided about a major. Sarah, I'm afraid I'll have to tell you what I tell the other undecideds. If you are interested in my field I can help you plan a program. But, if you are not, it would probably be best for you to request another advisor more closely associated with your interests. Sarah, you're just going to have to quit fooling around and sit down and decide on a major—and then get going on it!"

xxxxxxxxxx

Student: "Mrs. Jones, I feel like I have a strong interest in helping people as a possible career and I have a half-credit elective

130

to fill next semester. Can you help me select a subject that might be useful to this interest?"

Counselor: "Well, Suzie, I don't have any test scores available for you, so that makes it a bit difficult to recommend anything, but if you're going on to college you had better just stick to our College Track Program and earn the best grades you can."

Contrived situations? Yes, but also a reflection of the reality of couselors' offices in many schools and colleges. The purpose in presenting these situations is to point out that counselors at the secondary and college level frequently perceive their role as one of providing assistance to students who are having problems related either to education *or* career. Less frequently is the counselor ready, willing and able to work with students simultaneously in both the educational and career development areas.

This chapter will develop these ideas:

1. The educational and the career development of students are not inherently separate domains and should not be separate areas of endeavor for counselors. Together educational and career development constitute the warp and weft of the fabric of individual development. Therefore, the educational and career development needs of students can and should be met through an integrated educational/career guidance program.

2. Counseling for educational and career development can be viewed in terms of instructional design. Both educational and career guidance involve providing instruction to facilitate decision-making about educational and career choices.

3. The systems approach models used so effectively in the design of instruction are also an appropriate set of strategies to use in conceptualizing an integrated educational/career guidance program.

EDUCATIONAL AND CAREER DEVELOPMENT IN A COMMON CONTEXT

Continued attempts to rehash the distinctions between educational and career guidance are probably not fruitful. Development of an educational program and identification of an occupational choice are not distinct and separate end-points. Educational planning cannot be divorced from career planning, nor should the opposite be true. They should be viewed as two aspects of a single helping process which facilitates self-definition and personal growth in the student.

In practice, however, it appears that many secondary level guidance counselors are largely consumed by shuffling paper, assigning students (tracking), giving information about colleges, and providing students with occupational materials. What seems to be missing is meaningful educational guidance which integrates the student's formal education with the career development process. At the collegiate level, the emphasis is largely on educational guidance as it relates to coursework selection with little attempt to relate courses and majors to the career development process. Theory and practice in educational and career guidance can be brought into closer alignment by redesigning the program format, the way in which these services are delivered to students.

EDUCATIONAL AND
CAREER GUIDANCE AS INSTRUCTION

The educational/career guidance program should be viewed in terms of providing instruction, in the same sense that instruction is provided in English, science, or any academic discipline. There are skills to be developed, concepts to be mastered, and generalizations to be arrived at. There is both content and process to be learned. Chapter 2 of this book identifies many of the basic concepts in the career development process. The educational/career guidance program relates educational planning and career planning in a framework of decision-making strategies. This process can be learned if proper instructional opportunities are provided.

In recent years a new technology known as instructional design has emerged. As the field has developed, systems analysis approaches have been used extensively to facilitate the development of instructional materials. More recently the method has been used to guide the design of entire educational programs. An article by Hosford and Ryan (1970) illustrates a systems approach model for program design in the area of guidance and counseling. This procedure is further analyzed and described in Part III of this book.

Since the educational/career guidance program is largely instruction, it should be possible to design that instruction using the best available methodologies in instructional design. The remainder of this chapter is devoted to utilizing a systems approach model to conceptualize an educational/career guidance program. A total and completely detailed systems analysis for the program would probably constitute a small book, so it will be necessary at many points in the analysis only to allude to topics and procedures in a total design which should be considered in much greater detail.

USING A SYSTEMS APPROACH MODEL TO DESIGN AN EDUCATIONAL/CAREER GUIDANCE PROGRAM

In all systems design approaches there are three essential elements: 1. the statement of desired outcomes, 2. the treatment, or instructional procedures, and 3. a method of evaluation. The systems approach model used in this chapter includes these elements and is illustrated in Figure 8-1.

Clarifying the Problems

The first step in the design process calls for an intensive review and thorough understanding of the problems the program is to address. The counselor as program designer and others close to the endeavor are likely to have developed some notions about the nature of the problems. For example, when talking with colleagues about existing educational or career guidance programs one often hears such comments as "We need more opportunities for college bound students to explore the academic implications of saying, 'I want to be a doctor,' or 'I'm going to be a nuclear engineer;' " and "Career information should be available for our students, but I don't even have the time to keep on top of sources of information— let alone acquire it and make it available to students." These statements identify operational problems existing within the educational and career guidance program. What they lack as sufficient problem statements is succeptibility to generalization to program-wide pervasive underlying goals and objectives.

In applying the first step of the model, it is desirable to reconceptualize these specific complaints into larger, overarching categories. It is helpful to ask into what broad categories one may place

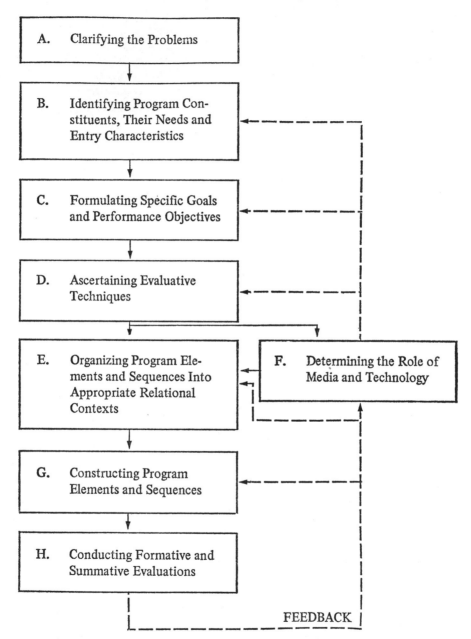

Figure 8-1. A Systems Approach Model for Use in Designing an Educational/ Career Guidance Program.

specific criticisms of the existing program and how these categories relate to underlying program goals. When the program designer begins to think along these lines, categories generally begin to emerge that relate identifiable goals to existing criticisms of programs. For example, certain criticisms may relate to either educational or career guidance. Other possible categories are: 1. program constituencies—the students, professionals, paraprofessionals, lay persons and so on, who will interact with the program; 2. needs assessments of program constituents; 3. informational and instructional components of the program; and 4. program administrative, physical, political and financial considerations.

In the formative stages of program development the necessity for both individual and committee input cannot be overemphasized. All constituents should be involved and should be asked their opinions of the problems and potential solutions. This diversity of input would undoubtedly produce a number of potential program alternatives and statements of the needs of various program participants and possible tasks to be included in the program in order to resolve the identified problems. Models and constructs could also be formulated at this point and introduced for consideration. Committee input, constituent input, individual suggestions and modeling techniques all serve to sharpen the issues to be addressed.

After listening carefully to all sources of representative input, the program designer is ready to formulate tentative statements of the problems. Three examples are offered to illustrate such statements:

1. The problem to be addressed is to develop an integrated educational/career guidance program which recognizes individual differences and needs, yet at the same time recognizes that the educational and career development of students can best be facilitated in the common context of a program in which they are merged.

2. The problem is to provide comprehensive educational and career guidance services to students in the most efficient and functional administrative and instructional formats.

3. The problem is to design, develop, implement and evaluate a comprehensive, integrated educational/career guidance program

appropriate to adolescents, organized for delivery in individual and group settings designed to meet special needs and utilizing the most efficient and functional administrative, instructional and technological formats available.

The sample problem statements vary considerably in specificity; the third one includes the largest number of variables identified as relevant to the design. Identifying relevant variables in a problem statement is highly desirable, as this begins the process of delineating clearly the parameters of the developing program. Perhaps in a particular operational setting one comprehensive and carefully developed problem statement would suffice. Then again, perhaps half a dozen would be required. The perceived complexity of the problem is obviously the overarching factor which governs the variety and number of problem statements to be developed. The important point is to capture the essence of the problems to be addressed in the clearest, largest contexts possible.

As they are applied in an operational setting, the first several steps in the systems approach model are not discrete, but comprise a structured series of activities which guide one's thinking from the general to the specific. The program designer's thinking may, at times, vacillate among problem statements, specific program objectives, program alternatives and tasks, and entry characteristics of the clientele. This fuzziness and overlapping is natural and is symptomatic of the general difficulty involved in developing problems clearly enough to allow for systematic treatment.

Identifying Program Constituents, Their Needs and Entry Characteristics

While the problems are being brought into sharper focus, input should be solicited to further identify the students and others who will interact with the program. It is necessary to understand their needs and the kinds of skills and compentencies they would be expected to bring to the program. As thought is given to the needs of constituents and their entry characteristics, specific questions begin to develop. For example, in regard to program constituents, it is necessary to ask who will be involved. Students, certainly, but they do not generally cluster in homogeneous groups. Instead, typically they are heterogeneous in abilities, aspirations, life-styles, and so on. The emerging educational/career guidance program will need to identify any special groups that are to receive attention. Other questions regarding student constituents of the program need to be considered.

1. How will the needs of the "undecided" student be met?
2. Are college-bound and non-college-bound students to be identified and provided different kinds of assistance?
3. Will educationally disadvantaged students be provided with special programs and services?
4. Do grade level distinctions appear pertinent to the development of programs to meet the special needs of special groups?
5. Should special service programs be developed for minorities and women?

Professional personnel constitute another group of program constituents. The counselors, advisors and other professional personnel associated with the program must be considered. Will special requirements be placed on them in terms of training, interests, participation patterns and so on? Program administrators are also professional personnel who must be considered. Will the program require new behavior and performance on their part?

A third potential group of constituents consists of lay persons as they impinge on the program. Here again, a number of questions arise.

1. Are parents; professional, religious and civic groups; the business community; outside educational establishments and so forth necessary to the successful operation of portions of the program? If so, how are they to participate?

2. What will lay groups bring to the program in the way of attitudes, skills and abilities? What will they be expected to carry away from the program in the way of attitudes, learnings and appreciations?

Answering these questions requires careful perusal of existing data and means gathering additional data from representative samples of the intended program constituents. For example, if one assumes that students who are undecided about their future educational plans are to be helped by the program, then certain specific questions must be formulated in order to obtain reliable data about the entry characteristics of that group. The data obtained should provide answers to such questions as:

1. How many undecided students are there in the total student population?
2. How long have these students been undecided?
3. Are there different kinds of undecidedness? If so, what are they?
4. Is undecidedness as to future educational plans more prevalent in males, females, blacks, whites, or any other discernible group?
5. Do undecided students have aptitudes, motivations, compentencies, interests, or comparable characteristics by which they differ from other students? If so, how and to what extent are they different?
6. Does student undecidedness result primarily from a lack of information upon which to make decisions or from a lack of decision making skills?
7. To what extent is student inability to identify future educational plans related to indecisiveness about a career?

It is important that the program designer obtain as much reliable information as possible about the entry characteristics of the constituents of the developing program. The need to do this almost concurrently with the previous step in the design seems obvious.

Formulating Specific Goals and Objectives

The activities undertaken in the previous two steps of the systems approach design would give rise to much discussion, soul searching, questioning, and data gathering. From this should develop rather clear conceptualizations of the larger goals and objectives for the program. That process of conceptualization culminates in the identification of all overarching program goals and more highly detailed objectives. This process is to many practitioners the most onerous task in a systems approach design. (Designing evaluative materials usually runs a close second.) However, it is crucial to designing the program efficiently, effectively and in a way that insures the optimum opportunity for program constituents to achieve the stated objectives.

Classification schemes which make it easier to conceptualize objectives and to relate them to an underlying model help introduce order and reason to this process. Multi-level classification schemes are very frequently used. Some program designers have systematized goals and objectives in terms of basic concepts; others have established domains for overarching goals and then proceeded to detail specific objectives within those domains. Obviously there are many ways to classify and codify identified program goals and objectives. The important point, however, is that they form a comprehensive, inclusive set of desired outcomes for all program constituents.

In the past few years much has been written about the processes of goal clarification and objective writing. Two books by Mager (1962, 1972) are extremely useful in sorting out and analyzing goals and in developing performance (or behavioral) objectives. In addition to the books by Mager, reviews of attempts by others to apply systems design techniques in the area of educational and career guidance can be very helpful in identifying strategies for developing goals and objectives (Hays, 1972; Hamilton and Jones, 1971; Conyne and Cochran, 1973; Hosford and Ryan, 1970; Shearn, 1973; Cunha et al., 1972).

Ascertaining Evaluative Techniques

Programs and services in educational and career guidance usually lack systematic evaluation. Services have frequently been developed and offered on the basis of gut level feelings of student need. Evaluation of a program's effectiveness has also been overly subject to personal "feelings."

Stating program goals and objectives in performance terms affords the program designer an opportunity to relate evaluation to predetermined objectives. This minimizes the necessity for "biologically induced" evaluations. By tying performance objectives and evaluative procedures together, the designer is required to show the relationship between the two and to demonstrate empirically the effectiveness of the program in helping the intended constituents to achieve the desired program outcomes.

Both the *process* and the *product* of the program should be evaluated, and thought should be given to the evaluative techniques to be employed. Process evaluation focuses on providing information regarding the adequacy and efficiency of the various processes (delivery systems) used to deliver instruction and information to program constituents. Product evaluation focuses on behavioral changes in the program constituents as a result of their interaction with the informational and instructional aspects of the program.

Further detailing of the role of evaluation in program design will not be undertaken here; reviews of its theory and application appear in other chapters of this book. (See Chapter 5 by MacAleese and Chapter 15 by Peterson.)

PUTTING IT ALL TOGETHER

After detailed objectives have been developed and related to evaluative procedures, it is possible to begin designing new or improved ways in which services will be provided, in other words, ways in which the instruction will be developed and delivered to program constituents. Steps E, F and G in the systems approach model shown in Figure 8-I all deal with aspects of putting the program together.

Organizing Program Elements and Sequences
Into Appropriate Relational Contexts
and
Determining the Role of Media and Technology

The objectives for the educational/career guidance program do considerably more than simply identify desired outcomes for the program. They provide insight into the nature of the instructional and informational components of the program and into the related systems required to deliver the content of the program. Steps E and F of the systems approach model involve the concurrent activities of identifying and relating the concerns of instructional and delivery systems.

Because the instructional content of the program must relate directly to identified program objectives, it is necessary to make assumptions about those objectives in order to discuss instructional and delivery system considerations. Seven such assumptions are stated and discussed in succeeding pages.

1. The program will address both the educational and career guidance needs of students. It will be both instructional and informational and will utilize a variety of formats.

A somewhat artificial distinction has been created in this writing between instruction and information. This has been done because it is helpful in visualizing the delivery systems for various program components. If the student needs help in understanding and clarifying values, in developing decision making skills, or in understanding the career development process, these needs may be viewed as primarily instructional in nature. On the other hand, if the student needs help in identifying the skills requiring in various careers or coursework requirements of various educational programs, those needs may be viewed as primarily informational in nature. (Chapter 10 is an excellent illustration of a program that is largely informational.)

A considerable portion of the educational/career guidance program will consist of instruction and information dissemination. With this fact in mind, a number of questions occur:

1. Should segments of the program involve dispensing information with little instruction taking place? Should other segments be primarily instructional? In other words, what should be the relationship between information dissemination and instruction for specific program tasks?
2. Are required informational and instructional materials to be produced locally or can they be obtained commercially? Can there be some combination of the two? Under what circumstances is it advisable to opt for either commercially or locally produced materials?
3. Will different types of instructional and informational materials be required for different age groups?

4. Will both group and individual information dissemination and instruction approaches be used? If so, when and how?
5. Should the developed materials be essentially independent of the counselor? What are the most appropriate uses of self-help materials?
6. Are the informational and instructional materials to be used in passive or active settings? In other words, will the instruction and dissemination of information be outreach or "reach-in" oriented?

The educational/career guidance program must serve both the informational and instructional needs of program constituents. Basic informational resources must be readily available, as this information is the basis upon which sound educational and career decisions are to be made. It is necessary to make available information on various careers, on educational program requirements, the relationship between educational programs and careers, various community resources that the student may use to clarify his perceptions of various educational programs and careers, and so forth. Instructional packages must also be available to assist students in such tasks as value clarification, improving their decision-making skills, exploring the career implications of educational choices, understanding the career development process, and so on.

As the presentation of instruction and information is planned, multi-media applications should be considered at every point. Modern man has become so accustomed to the bombardment of entertainment and educational materials in all the visual media that he has become a very passive learner. The educational/career guidance program must be able to compete for attention in this learning environment. There is another reason, too. In these times of shrinking resources, it becomes increasingly necessary to look for ways to provide information and instruction to larger numbers of people at smaller dollar costs. It is precisely in this area that pre-packaged multi-media programs have made great progress. The diversity of media applications in instruction and guidance are identified by Perrone and Thrush (1969), Scates (1969), and Chick (1970).

The one-to-one helping relationship must be supplemented by

extending instruction and information to larger groups. (This is aptly illustrated in Chapter 5.) The use of self-help instructional materials such as tape-slide presentations, video recordings and cathode-ray tube computer terminal programs should be explored. As instructional and informational components are developed, the program designer should be concerned with the manner in which they are to be "packaged," in order to have maximum impact at minimum overall cost. A handbook by Espich and Williams (1967) is helpful in identifying relevant packaging considerations.

2. The program will be competency based to the extent possible.

Competency based instruction provides a way to evaluate whether program objectives are being met. In the face of vigorous demands for accountability, it becomes increasingly necessary to design instructional and informational programs in a way which makes it vividly clear that objectives are being met. Since funding is increasingly dependent on proving program effectiveness, emerging programs should pay more than lip service to systematic efforts to introduce accountability through competency based program design. For a much more comprehensive treatment of this subject, the reader is referred to Chapter 15.

3. The program will address the needs of special groups through the design and delivery of specialized instructional and informational materials.

A comprehensive educational/career guidance program should address the special needs of identified target sub-populations. Specialized materials and delivery systems may be required for the college-bound student, the overdecided student (low ability but high interest and commitment to an extended educational program), the undecided student (interest in an extended educational program but with little or no direction), women, minority groups, the educationally disadvantaged, etc. (For reviews of programs for women, homosexuals and minorities, see the chapters in this book by Burkhart, Brown and Stone.)

The program designer must carefully consider ways to package and deliver special services to special groups. The counselor's activities can be enlarged upon if portions of these service programs can be designed so that they are largely self-contained, voluntary self-help instructional packages. It is also desirable to design many of these services in an outreach format, making the programs readily available where the intended users may usually be found. This may help to counteract the high level of passivity and poor voluntary utilization usually associated with programs designed to meet specialized needs.

4. The program will have an outreach orientation and make use of carefully developed referrals.

Outreach programs to address the needs of identified sub-populations are desirable. But those portions of the program designed to utilize community resources could also profit from an outreach orientation. Furthermore, since much educational and career counseling at the collegiate level can take place in residence halls, any programming efforts in this area should also be heavily outreach oriented. A publication by Hoelting (1973) provides a diversity of leads regarding possible residence hall programs. There is another excellent publication detailing outreach programs by Morrill and Banning (1973).

In addition to being outreach oriented, many facets of the program will need to make heavy use of referrals. For example, if paraprofessionals are used to assist in the program, they may frequently need to refer students to other professionals for specialized assistance. However, this does not preclude the professionals working in the program also making extensive use of referrrals. A student who needs information about careers might be referred to a careers information service. A student experiencing education and career concerns which are interwoven with serious emotional problems might be referred to a professional counselor. Minority students, women, homosexuals and undecided majors might be referred to special programs designed to meet their needs for educational and career guidance. Students who want to experience various careers through limited involvement at low personal risk could be referred to appropriate community resources which have been identified as willing to help.

The list of referral possibilities is long, indeed. In fact, the entire program may be viewed as a network of referral resources in which units in the program may make referrals to many other units. The informal, casual referrals often associated with existing programs are not what is envisioned here. If the referral network is to be effective, it is essential to consider the referral process carefully. The referral delivery system must be carefully developed and formalized to insure consistency and accuracy in making referrals. The system must also insure that referral contacts are made and then evaluated in terms of their success in addressing student needs.

5. The program will make use of individual and group instructional settings, voluntary and required participation patterns, and professional and paraprofessional staffing.

Both group and individual instructional (counseling) techniques should be used in the educational/career guidance program. Chapter 7 provides an excellent review of the use of groups in career guidance. The program designed by Brown (1972) contains an excellent blending of individual and group instructional techniques using paraprofessionals at the college level.

Although a considerable portion of the educational/career guidance program will involve voluntary participation, there may be instances in which manditory participation is both desirable and feasible. Self-motivation certainly cannot be discarded as the primary mechanism for getting students involved with the program. If a student doesn't perceive a need to make a career choice, then instruction in career decision-making will probably seem very unappealing. But mandatory participation in certain facets of the program may also merit consideration. For example, early in a student's educational program it might be advantageous to have him complete an instrument or battery of tests to obtain base-line data regarding his interests, goals, aspirations, possible career directions and so on. Perhaps it would also be desirable in certain situations to require mandatory attendance at a careers course, career seminar or career day, or at group sessions relating educational programs to careers. Other possibilities present themselves, but suffice it to say that mandatory participation should not be completely ruled out as a possible program delivery mechanism.

As program designers look for new ways to get additional mileage from existing resources, the value of peer instructional techniques is increasingly recognized. In this regard, the use of paraprofessionals as program staff members has been receiving increased attention. Paraprofessionals can often lead outreach programs designed to meet the needs of special groups. They can be used to monitor or proctor self-help information resources and may also provide direct instruction in both individual and group settings. With very careful selection, training, supervision and evaluation, paraprofessionals can do much to extend the sphere of influence of a single professional associated with the program. With this kind of assistance available, the professional becomes a resource person, a referral agent for the more difficult individual clients, a designer of instructional and informational materials for individual and group use, and a trainer/evaluator of the paraprofessionals. The program designed by Brown (1972) at Southwest Texas State College stands out as a most comprehensive collegiate use of students serving as counselors to other students. The programs designed by this author at The Florida State University have also successfully blended individual and group techniques using both professionals and paraprofessionals. The use of paraprofessionals in guidance and counseling at the secondary level is also gaining impetus (Carroll, 1973). This movement at the secondary level is particularly necessary if the public desire for increased personalization and relevance in the guidance program is to be satisfied in the face of continuing high student-to-counselor ratios.

6. *Although the program will probably be tied to a fixed, limited resource base for operation and program development, every effort will be made to secure protected funding to perpetuate basic services.*

It seems valid to assume that in most educational settings, programs are generally saddled with a fixed and limited resource base. In many ongoing programs much of the potential for new programming thrusts lies in extracting additional mileage from existing resources. The program designer cognizant of this hard reality constantly looks for ways to obtain a little extra from every dollar spent. Some would argue that this is an inappropriate activity for the program designer. Theoretically, that may well be true, but if he is committed to the redesign of an existing program or the development of a new one, practical reality dictates that he show concern for funding during the program development phase. This concern shows up most clearly in the delivery systems picked for all the facets of the program being developed. A number of promising mechanisms have already been mentioned, among them multi-media self-help materials, group instructional techniques to reach increased numbers of people, and the use of paraprofessionals to extend the professionals' spheres of influence.

The program designer should also wrestle with the problem of insuring continued, protected funding after the developmental phase is complete. The task is somehow to incorporate program operational costs with other recurring essential expenses. If the program is funded in a highly visable, identifiable and singular way, it is more subject to cutbacks than if it is less visable and combined with other long-standing recurring funding commitments. Once the program is carefully incorporated with essential services, attempts to make cuts in the program tend to be viewed as attempts to cut essential services. It is also important to note in passing that in arranging for protected, continuous funding, the program designer is also insulating the program from the shock of political whim.

7. The program will be appropriately situated from an administrative point of view and will be, to the extent possible, oriented toward student needs rather than toward administrative needs.

Are the administration and services of the educational/career guidance program to be centralized or decentralized? Is some combination of the two feasible and desirable? What agency or agencies will be administratively responsible for the program? How is this to be determined and what are the political and programatic implications of these decisions? These are but a few of the questions that should be considered when identifying the administrative structure for the program. Here again, the program designer should assume a prominent role in decision-making.

The educational/career guidance program can work well in any administrative unit of the educational system: the academic, student personnel, or central administration. Whether it does in fact work well, depends largely on the strength of commitment and overall leadership of the chief administrative officer in the unit through which the program is offered. Other administrative variables crucial to the success of the program are the visibility and viability of the relationships between the program and other units and constituencies in the total educational setting, and the establishment of a secure, equitable resource plan for generating program finances, facilities and personnel.

When considering how the program can best be administered, two approaches need to be examined. One is in common practice; the other is largely just talked about. The most prevalent administrative style is one in which program constituents are presented with a "standard fare." The program is available for the taking as long as the constituents fit the administrative pattern which is predetermined as appropriate for the program. In this administrative needs model, the constituents are being told, "Here are the institution's administrative needs; meet them if you wish to participate in the program."

The other view of program administration, though frequently favorably spoken of, is seldom viably applied in practice. Based on a student needs model, it tends to be much more flexible and student oriented. Administration is viewed as a facilitator of program objectives and thereby is tied to the needs of program constituents. In essence, in a program of this administrative style, constituents are told, "The administrative needs of the program are flexible and developmental, and depend on how your perceived need for the program may best be satisfied."

In designing the delivery systems for various aspects of the program, the designer should carefully consider both of these administrative models. It is recommended that the student needs model be considered seriously for implementation to the extent that the prevailing administrative style will permit, for it is this model which complements a focus on the development of the individual through programs designed to meet individual needs.

Constructing Program Elements and Sequences
and
Conducting Formative and Summative Evaluations

When steps E and F of the systems approach model are completed, the educational/career guidance program should be clearly identified, although in skeleton form. It is then possible to begin the task of developing each program element and sequence in a completed version suitable for an initial field trial. Evaluative material should also be completed in trial version. The various program elements and sequences being developed need to be tested with small samples of the intended constituents in order to obtain feedback for possible revision before the extensive field trial of the program takes place. This formative evaluation is highly useful in identifying problems with the materials as they are being developed. As part of the full field trial, the last step in the systems approach model calls for a summative evaluation in which representative samples of all program constituents provide feedback. It is this feedback that serves as the basis for subsequent program revision.

In considering the full development of each element of the program, it is important to understand that the first pass through a systems approach model results in a broad conceptual view of the program constituents and their needs, of program objectives and of strategies for meeting identified objectives. Additional passes through the design steps of the model are required to completely detail each of the major program components identified as being desirable. It is through this repetition of passes that the final program takes shape.

It is easy to visualize the model's usefulness in developing instructional and informational materials to be used by students, but there are less visible tasks in the instructional area to which the model may also be usefully applied. Consider, for example, the matter of using paraprofessionals in the program in some instructional capacity. A systems approach model may be used to develop the instruction the paraprofessionals will be working with; less obviously, their own preparation for their assignments may be amenable to a systems approach design. There are instructional and informational aspects to any preservice training requirement for paraprofessionals, and they are just as amenable to a systems approach design as are materials to assist students with values clarification or educational course selection. The program designer is advised to look continually for additional applications of the systems approach model as he or she moves from the first pass through the model to segments requiring more detailed development.

SUMMARY

This chapter has argued for considering educational and career guidance as two aspects of a single helping process. As such, student needs in these areas are best met through an integrated educational/career guidance program. In this unified approach, much of the resulting program can be viewed as a matter of providing instruction to facilitate decision-making regarding educational and career choices. The instructional aspects of the program are just as subject to development by current methodologies in instructional design as is instruction in English or science. Systems approach models have been used with considerable success in many instructional design settings, and they may appropriately be used to design instruction for the educational/career guidance program. The methods used to deliver the instruction in the program can also be more aptly designed using a systems approach model. This design process was illustrated in the chapter using a systems approach model as a way to discuss the instruction and delivery systems associated with an educational/career guidance program.

BIBLIOGRAPHY

Brown, W.F. *Student-to-Student Counseling: An Approach to Motivating Academic Achievement.* Hogg Foundation Research Series. Austin, Texas: University of Texas Press, 1972.

Carroll, M.R. The regeneration of guidance. *The School Counselor,* 1973, *20,* 355-360.

Chick, J.M. *Innovations in the Use of Career Information.* Guidance Monograph Series, Series IV. Career Information and Development. Boston: Houghton-Mifflin, 1970.

Conyne, R.K., and Cochran, D.J. Academia and career development: Toward integration. *Personnel and Guidance Journal,* 1973, *52,* 217-223.

Cunha, J., et al. (Eds.). *Career Development: A California Model for Career Guidance Curriculum K-Adult.* Monograph No. 5. Fullerton, California: California Personnel and Guidance Association, 1972.

Espich, J.E., and Williams, B. *Developing Programmed Instructional Materials.* Palo Alto, California: Fearon Publishers, 1967.

Hamilton, J.A., and Jones, G.B.: Individualizing educational and vocational guidance: Designing a prototype program. *Vocational Guidance Quarterly,* 1971, *20,* 293-298.

Hays, D.G. Responsible freedom for the school counselor. *The School Counselor,* 1972, *20,* 93-102.

Hoelting, F.B. *How To Do It In Residence Halls: 1001 Ways To Program.* Macomb, Illinois: Western Illinois University, 1973.

Hosford, R.E., and Ryan, T.A. Systems design in the development of counseling and guidance programs. *Personnel and Guidance Journal,* 1970, *49,* 221-230.

Mager, R.F. *Goal Analysis.* Belmont, California: Fearon Publishers, 1972.

Mager, R.F. *Preparing Instructional Objectives.* Belmont, California: Fearon Publishers, 1962.

Morrill, W.H., and Banning, J.H. *Counseling Outreach: A Survey of Practices.* Boulder, Colorado: Western Interstate Commission for Higher Education, 1973.

Perrone, P.A., and Thrush, R.S. Vocational information processing systems: A survey. *Vocational Guidance Quarterly,* 1969, *17* 255-266.

Scates, A.Y. (Ed.). *Computer-Based Vocational Guidance Systems: Summary of Papers-Fourth Symposium for Systems Under Development for Vocational Guidance.* Washington, D.C.: U.S. Office of Education, 1969.

Shearn, R.B. Guidelines for Constructing an Optimal Academic Advising Program in Non-Traditional Higher Education Adaptable to the University Without Walls Institutions. Unpublished doctoral dissertation, The Florida State University, 1973.

Chapter Nine

CURRICULAR APPROACHES AND SELF-HELP TECHNIQUES FOR CAREER DEVELOPMENT

MICHAEL J. GIMMESTAD

A S COUNSELORS AND EDUCATORS are confronted with increasing demands for effective career guidance they are faced with two major challenges: first, to make career guidance efforts relevant and interesting to their clientele, and second, to increase the delivery of systematic career guidance services while operating under *cost-efficient* constraints. Two responses to these challenges are discussed in this chapter: curricular approaches to career development, and self-help techniques in career guidance. Curricular approaches are defined as systematic efforts to meet career development objectives for groups of students through courses or units of courses offered as a part of the regular school or college curriculum (including both credit and non-credit offerings). Self-help techniques are defined as those processes and materials which are self-directing and self-paced, and which can be used by an individual either completely on his own or in conjunction with curricular approaches or counseling.

Included in this chapter are a discussion of the special needs of adolescents and young adults as related to curricular approaches and self-help techniques; common goals ascribed to by representative curricular approaches and self-help techniques; summaries of selected strategies which are representative of these approaches; and a closing summary which includes the author's recommendations for implementing curricular approaches and/or self-help techniques in a unique setting with unique clientele.

NEEDS ASSESSMENT

Curricular approaches and self-help techniques can be especially responsive to a variety of student needs. In addition they can provide a means for institutions to respond within the constraints of limited financial resources. Ways in which curricular and self-help techniques have demonstrated particular responsiveness to these needs follow.

Need For Systematic, Developmental Approach

Various facets of career development and career guidance have been extensively described in texts on vocational development theories, occupational/educational information, and vocational guidance (see Chapter 2). Chronological developmental constructs such as Erikson's (1950) eight stages of man and hierarchical developmental schemes such as Maslow's (1962) steps toward self-actualization are familiar to counselors. Guidance services such as individual appraisal, information services, counseling, placement, and follow-up are described in almost every standard text on guidance.

The facilitation of career development necessitates integration of knowledge of human development (including vocational development) with the offering of guidance services which are consonant with principles of individual differences, motivation, and learning as well as interest and ability. This clearly calls for a view of career development that is broad in scope. It is this breadth and unity that makes the new curricular approaches different. Careers courses are not new. Holcomb (1966) reported the existence of college-level courses focusing on career guidance as early as 1917, and the high school unit on careers has a long history, generally in the context of either 9th or 12th grade English or social studies (Mezzano, 1969). What, then, is new and exciting? It is the integration of self-assessment, values clarification, mastery of new information systems, and the teaching of decision-makng skills. It is the design of materials and procedures that respect the wide range of individual differences of students, both in stages of maturation and in interests and abilities. It is in the use of a full range of teaching technology, multi-media presentation of information, modules, electronic media, and other means of maximizing the motivation and the learning of *each individual*. Traditional curricular approaches which focus primarily on extensive testing, the study of a small number of selected occupations, or preparation for placement cannot adequately respond to the needs of all students. What is demanded is an approach which pulls the pieces together in accord with principles of human development and sound instructional methodology.

Need to Legitimize Career Development as Academic Experience

Efforts to facilitate career development in schools and colleges have typically occurred in *ancillary* services, rather than in the mainstream of the academic curriculum. The major exception to this is in vocational education courses, which are considered by many educators to be *nonacademic*. Borow (1960) traced the growth of career guidance activities offered within formal college curricula, and found significant increases from the early 1930's until the post-Sputnik era, when pure academics controlled the curriculum. Recent years have witnessed another turnabout; the public has become disenchanted with education for education's sake, and is demanding a new respect for career development activities as a legitimate credit-earning aspect of the curriculum. As Reardon (1973) points out, "In general the impetus appears to be for the college to provide preparation for making a living as well as living." In colleges and universities, the last bastion of academics in a pragmatic world, the receptivity has changed. Devlin (1973) has identified over seventy colleges and universities in the U. S. currently offering academic credit for courses which focus on the teaching of career decision-making skills.

The career education movement is also a reflection of public sentiment regarding a need for increased attention within the formal school curriculum to career development concerns. The movement to infuse career information and decision-making into all aspects of the curriculum, from kindergarten up, has already left its mark in the legitimizing of career development activities. Curricular approaches offer units which can receive academic credit; self-help techniques can be implemented at many stages in career education models.

Need to Respond to Individual Differences

The counselor working with high school or postsecondary students should be well aware of the fantastic range of individual differences of his clients. Many of these relate directly to career development: differences in decision-making skills, ability to evaluate information, skills in goal-setting and priority setting, reading level, ability to understand self and others, and many other differences. There is a need to provide systematic facilitation of career development which has a flexibility and responsiveness to individual differences. Curricular approaches can include this flexibility, and self-help techniques *must* do so.

Need to Maximize Impact of Professional Personnel

Systematic facilitation of career development implies comprehensive services to all students. No educational institution is likely to underwrite a "guidance for all" approach which is based exclusively on direct services of professional counselors, either through individual or group counseling. Schools and colleges are struggling to maintain their current numbers of counselors, let alone meet the need for additional counselors which system-wide direct services would dictate. Counselors have demonstrated considerable multiplier effects in offering services indirectly, through training and consultation with teachers (Parker, 1974) and through program development activities, development of curricular methods and materials and self-help techniques (Reardon, 1973). The counselor's specialized expertise in human development and career guidance, when merged with skills in consultation and curriculum development can result in significant system interventions (Blocher, Dustin, and Dugan, 1970).

COMMON PROGRAM GOALS

Among the curricular approaches and self-help techniques reviewed by the author there are a number of common program goals. Obviously they all have the same general objective: to facilitate the career development of students. Common goals are: 1. to facilitate awareness of self, which encompasses a broad spectrum of specific approaches, e.g. testing of interests and aptitudes and values clarification techniques; 2. to facilitate awareness of the world of work, including the identification, evaluation, and use of occupational and educational information; 3. to develop goal-setting and decision-making skills, which typically involves the processing and integration of information from 1. and 2. above; and 4. the development of a personal career action plan based on sound personalized decision-making.

TYPICAL KINDS OF INTERVENTION STRATEGIES

This section contains a brief discussion of curricular approaches and of self-help techniques used in facilitating career development of adolescents and young adults. Each type of strategy is illustrated by summaries of representative approaches.

Curricular Approaches

The curricular approaches include courses, both credit and non-credit, which are offered in schools and colleges, as well as those materials and procedures which comprise an intact *package* for use as a unit within a course. These are to be distinguished from the increasing volume of career guidance materials which are designed for intermittent use or to be interwoven with courses in the regular curriculum.

Curricular approaches are not new. Holcomb (1966) identified a high school course devoted entirely to the study of vocations offered in 1908, and a college course offered in 1917. What is offered in current curricular approaches may best be contrasted with the old by comparing titles: "career development" and "career decision-making" as opposed to "the study of vocations" and the "choice of an occupation." The focus is on career as a dynamic, developing concept, and on teaching decision-making skills which can be used throughout many career decision points, rather than emphasizing the selection of one occupational choice as an outcome of the course. Summaries of selected approaches follow.

Deciding and Decisions and Outcomes

These two curricular materials are published by the College Entrance Examination Board (Gelatt, et al., 1972; 1973). Similar in design, they both focus on the development of decision-making skills on 1. examination and recognition of personal values, 2. knowledge and use of adequate, relevant information, and 3. knowledge and use of an effective strategy for converting this information into action. *Deciding,* designed for junior high school students, consists of three units entitled Values, Information, and Strategy. *Decisions and Outcomes,* for senior high school and college students and adults, has four units: The Starting Point, The Deciding Self, Before Deciding, and Applying Skills. Both are presented in a consumable workbook format. Leader's guides accompany both, outlining the "Theory underlying the decision-making process and providing detailed instructions on how to conduct effective group sessions." Both *Deciding* and *Decisions and Outcomes* can be used effectively as the framework for a course in decision-making, as major components in counseling and guidance programs, or as units in subject areas such as English, history, human relations, drug education, and health education. Both can be completed in as few as fifteen class sessions or extended to as many as forty-five. Although focusing on personal values clarification and the development of personalized decision-making skills, both rely very extensively on peer interaction and group discussions.

Life/Career Development System

This is a set of nine modules developed by Garry Walz and associates (Walz, undated) for use with students in grades 9 to 12 and college. Each requires six to nine hours to complete, and can be used in large classes or individually. The system is designed for a trained facilitator to present the modules and coordinate the learning experiences of the participants. The modules are not available separately, but are purchased as part of a kit, including pre/post measures, facilitator's manuals, participant journals, telephone consultation with the publisher, and training of facilitators. The nine modules are: 1. Exploring Self, 2. Determining Values, 3. Setting Goals, 4. Expanding Options, 5. Overcoming Barriers, 6. Using Information, 7. Working Effectively, 8. Thinking Futuristically, and 9. Selecting Mates.

Careers Courses

A variety of descriptions of courses were reviewed, with considerable overlap. Calvert, Carter, and Murphy (1964) identified four different types of careers courses: 1. the course on personal-vocational selection or career planning, with emphasis on self-appraisal; 2. introduction to the world of work, involving analyses of occupations and use of occupational information; 3. job-seeking techniques, focusing on actual job placement; and 4. adjustment to careers, examining problems one might expect to encounter in making the transition from school or college to the world of work. Most of the courses reviewed are hybrids of these four types, and appear to be based heavily on the Borow (1960) prototype. Highlights of selected courses, representing a variety of institutions at several levels, follow.

FLORIDA STATE UNIVERSITY: A three quarter-hour course entitled Career Planning and Occupational Choice is offered as an elective to any upper division students by the College of Business. The course is designed to "provide an investigation of careers, the world of work, and the career planning process" (Lee and Anthony, in press). Students engage in several self-evaluation exercises and take the SVIB in early class sessions. Students are introduced to broad occupational categories and assisted in locating sources of occupational information and career planning literature. The student then develops a career plan and formulates a career strategy to achieve his goals. Related course activities focus on job-seeking skills including interviewing, resume writing, and negotiation, as well as an introduction to the services and resources of the Career Planning and Placement Center and the Counseling Center.

The course is designed to initiate self-motivated individual study through use of structured exercises, videotapes, guest lectures, and readings. Course format is primarily didactic, but individual counseling and consultation between students and instructors is provided. The distinguishing characteristic of this course is the interplay between the academic unit (Management Department, College of Business) and two student service units, the placement center and the counseling center.

UNIVERSITY OF UTAH: The staff of the Counseling and Psychological Services at the University of Utah have developed a series of career counseling packages. Built on a common theoretical rationale (Fuhriman, 1972), these packages have taken the form of one-shot career exploration workshop for entering freshmen (Packard, 1972), extended marathons on career development (Warsaw, 1972), career development workshops for disadvantaged students (Carney, 1972), and a career development seminar (Stoddard, 1972). The Career Development Seminar is a 10-week course open to all students, for which general education credits are received. Each section of the seminar is limited to ten students, and is led by a member of the Counseling and Psychological Services staff and a graduate student in counseling psychology. During weeks 1 to 4, the seminar includes group discussions of personal experiences, characteristics, and values. Included is information relating to each student's scholastic aptitude (ACT scores), achievement (grades), and vocational interests (SVIB and Kuder OIS). During this time span each student also has individual conferences with one of the instructors, in which results of the *Maudsley Personality Inventory* and the *Personal Orientation Inventory* are discussed. Occasional referrals for further counseling result from these conferences. Weeks 4 and 5 find the groups integrating information from the tests (SVIB, OIS, MPI, and POI) with individual life plans. Objectives for these sessions include the students' assessment of individual progress in career development *and* readiness for further movement. Weeks 5 to 9 focus on goal-setting and implementation, with each student setting specific goals and designing an action plan for reaching those goals. He negotiates a behavioral contract with the instructors, with input from the seminar group. Remaining weeks in this segment involving sharing of experiences and progress with peers. The tenth and final session consists of individual reports of efforts to complete contracts, evaluation of individual progress in decision-making, and defining of future goals.

Distinguishing characteristics of this course are (1) its theoretical basis (Fuhriman, 1972), (2) its individualized behavioral contracting system, and (3) its use of a peer group as both a support system and reinforcer for progress on individual action plans.

PHOENIX COLLEGE: The Counseling Department at Phoenix

College has offered a course in Educational and Vocational Planning since 1966. This course was designed to "focus on educational choices and to make career decisions based on test results, occupational information, and discussions of the changing world of work" (Kass, Nobel, and Tobiason, 1973). Evaluation of this community college course, however, indicated that too much was being attempted in one term, and that students were experiencing difficulties in making decisions without first exploring their values, interests, and strengths.

As the department responded to the need for first exploring personal values and developing decision-making skills, the course evolved into two separate one-credit courses, entitled Personal Resources Assessment and Personal Resources Development. The objectives have shifted from defining a specific educational or vocational objective for each student to helping each individual to assess his personal strengths and to make choices consistent with his strengths, interests, and values.

Classes, limited to eighteen students, meet twice weekly for fifty minutes over an eight week period, or one night weekly for two and one-half hours. The focus of almost all class activities is the development of self-awareness. This occurs through role-playing and a variety of structured exercises. The SVIB is given and interpreted, followed by a vocational image-sharing exercise. The only other specifically career-oriented session is one in which job interviews are role-played.

The distinguishing characteristic of the Phoenix courses is the evolution from purely vocational in nature to more of a personal growth orientation as a foundation for career decision-making, while maintaining academic credit for the experience.

LANGLEY HIGH SCHOOL, MCLEAN, VIRGINIA: the old careers course is not dead! At this large suburban high school it has been revived as a nine-week elective unit in English for juniors and seniors. Two counselors, both former English teachers, teach the course (Johnson and Martin, 1973). The format is fairly traditional: testing, counseling, research on specific occupations, and simulations of the job-seeking process. The reported successes of this course might be related to three characteristics which distinguish it from the usual high school careers course: first, it is elective, and more students request the course than can be admitted; second, the course activities are designed, to a large part, around the expressed career interests of the students (i.e. guest lecturers and industrial or business field trips which the students have requested) ; and third, the learning of career decision-making skills is stressed, rather than actually arriving at a tentative career choice.

CALIFORNIA STATE UNIVERSITY, SAN DIEGO: A credit course entitled Self-Concept and Careers is offered by the School of Education. With joint sponsorship of the placement and counseling services. Somewhat similar to the Phoenix College course, the focus is on students attempting to deal with six questions: "1. Where am I?, 2. Who am I?, 3. What are my resources?, 4. Where am I going?, 5. What is keeping me from getting there?, and 6. What plan of action should be undertaken in order to include information and reality testing" (Webb, 1973). A distinguishing characteristic of this course has been the offering of a special section for women only, with emphasis on consciousness-raising (see Chapter 12). The self-concept approach was considered incomplete for women, since ". . . for women, vocational choice may not be merely an assessment of values, interests, aptitudes, and self-image. . . . Many women are handicapped primarily by the psycho-socialization process to which they have been subjected, and many need some expansion of consciousness before they can change their position in the work world" (Ramsey, 1973). Thus the special section focuses less on self-concept exploration and more on sociological perspectives relating to women and the changing world of work.

Self-Help Techniques

Self-help techniques do not have the long history which characterizes curricular approaches. These involve materials and processes which are self-directed and self-paced, and can be used by an individual on his own or in conjunction with curricular approaches or counseling. A variety of modes of presentation can be utilized: paper and pencil materials, multi-media modules, programmed instruction materials, and use of computers.

A review of selected self-help techniques shows considerable variations in their complexity and degree of sophistication of technology employed. Most are designed for use with college students, but it is expected that the Career Education movement will result in the creation of many such packages for high school students. A review of selected self-help techniques follows.

Curricular-Career Information Service

The Curricular-Career Information Service at Florida State University is a multi-media, self-managed career guidance program designed for lower division students (Reardon, et al., 1973). CCIS is located in a small three-room suite off the lobby of a residence hall centrally located on campus. The primary objectives of CCIS are to provide accurate information on a variety of careers and the academic curricula related to them, as well as to provide self-help techniques for students to learn sound decision-making skills and to use them in integrating CCIS information.

Located in an outreach setting, CCIS is used in a variety of ways: walk-ins, attracted by CCIS literature or friends' recommendation; students referred by advisors; students referred by the Couseling Center or Placement Center; and students referred by residence hall staff. Five individualized modules guide students through a variety of self-selected activities, including career decision-making skill-building, learning to locate and evaluate desired information, reading selected articles and essays on career development for college students, completion of Holland's *Self-Directed Search,* viewing simulated video tape interviews between students and faculty regarding academic programs in the University, and referral information about sources of specialized assistance.

CCIS was initiated with limited financial support from the Division of Student Affairs, partial release time for a director (staff member of the University Counseling Center), contributed space from the residence halls, and a pledge of cooperation from the Head Counselor and Resident Assistants of the dormitory in which it was located. A full-time Career Guidance Specialist and two half-time graduate assistants staff the service, serving both as resources to the students and working to maintain the currency of both the occupational and the academic information maintained in the files and on approximately 120 audio and 12 video cassette tapes.

Self-Directed Search

The Self-Directed Search is the major component of the *Self-Directed Career Program* developed by John Holland and his associates at the Center for Social Organization of Schools, Johns Hopkins University (Holland, et al., 1972). The SDC consists of five sets of materials: 1. an instruction sheet; 2. the *Self-Directed Search* (SDS) booklet; 3. the *Occupations Finder,* which accompanies the SDS; 4. a checklist to help the student assess the accuracy and validity of his SDS experience; and 5. the *Occupational Outlook Handbook,* providing comprehensive descriptions of jobs and careers.

The program may be used in conjunction with counseling or strictly as a self-help technique which may be made available wherever students may be found. The instructions and materials are very clear, and assistance ought not to be required except when a student may seek help from a counselor in exploring implications of information he has discovered about himself or about a particular career. It is appropriate for use with high school students, college students, and adults.

The SDS bears brief description. The 15-page booklet is used by the student to record his occupational daydreams; his assessment of likes and dislikes for specific activities grouped according to Holland's theoretical framework (realistic, investigative, artistic, social, enterprising, and conventional) ; his assessment of competencies on activities grouped similarly; and his expressed like or dislike of specific occupations, also grouped in Holland's six categories. This is followed by a self-rating of ability, as compared with others of the same age, in the following areas: mechanical ability, scientific ability, artistic ability, teaching ability, sales ability, clerical ability, manual skills, math ability, musical ability, friendliness, managerial skills, and office skills. All of the information collected is synthesized and weighted in a way that produces a score for each student on each of the six Holland categories. The student works with a three-letter "summary code" consisting of the first letters of his top three scoring categories. He is directed to the *Occupations Finder,* where he "finds" all occupations which have summary codes identical with his. If he finds none, or very few, he is encouraged to look for occupations with similar codes.

Having engaged in a self-directed search for occupations which are consistent with his expressed interests, likes, and abilities, he is then directed to the *Occupational Outlook Handbook* to learn more about those occupations.

Career-Education Planning Services Self-Instructional Materials

The Career-Education Planning Services of the University of California, San Diego has developed a set of self-instructional materials to assist the student in making the transition from UCSD to graduate or professional school or to the world of work. These are hard-copy materials which help the student to acquire new skills and knowledge related to career decision-making, identifying and applying to graduate or professional school, and the process of seeking and obtaining employment. They also provide assistance in identifying resources available, including the Counseling and Psychological Services, for further career guidance. The specific self-help materials are:

1. The CEPS Questionnaire. This instrument informs the student of the services provided by CEPS, and helps him identify which may be of help to him.
2. A Flow Chart. This is a graphic representation of the steps in the processes of career planning and job seeking, with recommended action to be engaged in at each step.
3. The Career-Education Planning Library. This paper describes the reference materials available, and how to use them.
4. The Guide to Career Planning. The paper is designed to help the student who is uncertain as to career direction. It introduces the concept of career development as an ongoing process, and provides beginning self-assessment experiences.
5. The Job Market, Employer Research, and Job Hunting. This paper is designed to assist the student who has some idea where he is headed but is unaware of specific job opportunities, current job market conditions, and future trends.
6. Job-Seeking Techniques. Specific assistance is provided in this paper in the development of skills in writing a resume, letter of application, and interviewing skills.
7. Information for UCSD Students Who Are Considering a

Career in Medicine, Dentistry, and Other Health Professions. This long title betrays a special interest in promoting a program which has received special attention at UCSD, the Premedical Advisory Program.

The model used by the CEPS has several distinct characteristics. It is intended to assist students who are headed primarily toward professional or graduate schools or beginning level professional and executive positions. Heavy emphasis is placed on student motivation to read extensive amounts of written materials.

Effective Problem Solving

The Counseling Center at the University of Maryland, under the leadership of Thomas Magoon, has developed a set of self-help materials entitled, "The Process of Effective Program Solving Applied to Your Vocational and Educational Planning." This self-directed learning program (Magoon, 1969) is designed to assist college students to learn the steps in effective problem solving and then to apply that process to their own vocational and educational planning. The program is primarily in written form, consisting of an introduction and instructions, eleven sequential units, and an evaluation. The materials are designed to teach a problem solving process through the gathering, analyzing, synthesizing, and application of information about the student, his university, and the world of work.

The eleven units are as follows:

1. Effective Problem Solving. A description of a six-step problem solving paradigm.
2. Occupations for Investigation. A work sheet on which the student lists occupations for further investigation.
3. Taking Stock of Your Study Time and Efficiency. A self-assessment step, with possible referral to the Reading and Study Skills Laboratory.
4. Taking Stock of Your Ability and Achievement. Self-assessment of skills, both potential and current.
5. Taking Stock of Your Work Experience. Investigation of personal satisfactions and dissatisfactions observed in previous work experiences.

6. Taking Stock of Your Leisure Experiences. Self-assessment of non-work preferences.
7. Taking Stock of Your Interests. Compares expressed vocational interests with measured interests (based on SVIB).
8. Taking Stock of the Opinions of Others. Assessment of the opinions of others with regard to one's career decision, with emphasis on personalizing the meaning of these opinions.
9. Occupational Facts. This unit consists of gathering a variety of facts on at least six different occupations, and relating them to educational opportunities available at the University of Maryland.
10. Summary and Evaluation. Synthesis of information gathered in all previous steps.
11. Choice of Plans and Taking Action on Them. Goal-setting, and the development of alternative action plans.

As with the materials from the University of California, San Diego, the Effective Problem Solving materials are primarily written materials, and the motivation and sophistication of the student could be a big factor in the utility of the materials. The EPS system, while teaching a process, does encourage the student to set several alternative goals, and to develop action plans which are appropriate for those goals. It is likely that many, if not most, students might need assistance from a counselor in making the next step beyond the last unit in the EPS materials: they may well need help in assessing the probabilities of their succeeding in each of their goals. The counselor's intervention may be required to insure that students do not use the EPS as a crutch to support a premature career decision. The intent of the EPS must be kept in mind by the student—the learning of a process, rather than arrival at a final decision.

RECOMMENDATIONS FOR THE PRACTITIONER

Given a variety of possible curricular approaches and self-help techniques, how does a counselor decide what is most appropriate for his clientele in his institution? Are there any common bases for selection? Certainly there are, but the practitioner encounters factors which make each situation unique. The demographic characteristics of his school's student enrollment, the nature of the school or college curriculum, employment trends in the community, state and nation, administrative, faculty and parent interest and support are but a few of the factors which, in combination, must be considered in selecting or designing curricular approaches and self-help techniques.

Hosford and Ryan (1970) have presented a framework which might assist the counselor in examining his local situation. Their systems approach provides a model for developing a counseling and guidance program (in this case a subsystem of the overall program) which is based on the needs of the clientele, maximizes utilization of resources while adjusting to the constraints of reality, and is self-correcting. A modification of this system approach which has been used by students of Gimmestad and Reardon at Florida State University follows.

Needs Assessment

This step includes a thorough analysis of environmental and situational variables. For the counselor involved in developing materials and procedures to be used in facilitating career development there are several key factors which should be examined. First, a thorough knowledge of the student clientele to be served is of crucial importance. Factors such as socioeconomic status, academic capabilities, aspirations and interests must be looked at to determine several things: 1. the variability of individual differences to be dealt with in materials development, 2. the levels (maturity, reading level, etc.) to which materials must be addressed, 3. the interest factors which may be capitalized on to make materials most interesting, attractive, and fun. Second, a thorough knowledge of the school and community can be helpful. This becomes apparent in several ways: the school environment offers both opportunities and constraints. To the extent that materials resources can be made available, freedom has been increased in developing creative and effective materials. Limitations placed on a counselor because of a tight school budget will cause one to have to look for other resources (business and service organizations, for example) in the community which might help underwrite the costs of new approaches to facilitating career development. Knowledge about community labor trends, the extent to which students tend to leave (or not leave) the community after schooling to seek employment elsewhere, and information regarding training opportunities are all relevant data which should be in hand prior to attempting to build a program to facilitate career development. These are also the kinds of data which should be periodically updated in order to maintain the currency of materials developed.

Another aspect of needs assessment is the identification of problems which might properly be addressed by the development of curricular or self-help materials and techniques. Some of the typical problems which come up are: narrowness of the range of occupations for which students are preparing, lack of knowledge of decision-making skills, inability of students to identify and use career information, high number of changes of major and/or students who are undecided in colleges, high dropout rate from certain tracks in the school program, and many others. The more thorough the job done by the counselor in defining the problem(s) to be addressed, the more likely the resultant product will be on target.

Goal Setting

One of the leading causes of failure of well-intentioned programs is the lack of clearly stated objectives. Counselors, in particular, have been noted for their reluctance to speak of purposes of counseling in terms more specific than improved self-concept, self-actualization, and facilitating communications. It is essential in laying the foundation of a new approach to clearly define the desired outcomes. Obviously, a good job of problem definition will enable one to state desired outcome which reflect remediation of the problems. It is suggested that counselors should approach goal-setting in developing materials and procedures at two levels: general goals and more specific behavioral objectives.

General goals are statements which indicate general direction and purpose, and clearly flow from problem statements. Each general goal should be followed by one or more specific behavioral objectives. A behavioral objective is a statement which indicates desired outcomes in terms of specific observable and measureable behaviors of individuals. Several examples of problem statements, general goals, and behavioral objectives and their relationships are illustrated in Figure 12-1.

PROBLEM STATEMENT: Many college students are completing their sophomore year without having decided on a major.

GENERAL GOALS: College students should learn to make effective decisions regarding their educational/vocational goals.
College students should be aware of the educational opportunities available to them.

BEHAVIORAL OBJECTIVES: (1) The number of college students completing their sophomore year at this university without having decided on a major will have decreased by at least 25% by the end of this school year.

(2) After completion of this module, each student will identify, in priority order, his first three choices of majors.

(3) After completion of this careers course, each student will explain, to the satisfaction of two classmates, a step-by-step process for making career decisions.

PROBLEM STATEMENT: Large numbers of high school students are reporting to their counselors that they don't know what they want for a career except "something professional."

GENERAL GOALS: High school students should be able to identify general career areas in which they have interests.
High school students should be able to identify career areas in which they have the potential to succeed.

BEHAVIORAL OBJECTIVES: (1) The student will identify his top three interest areas as reported on the SVIB.

(2) The student will, to the counselor's satisfaction, relate his aptitude and achievement indicators to the requirements for three jobs.

Figure 9-1.

Note that a well-written behavioral objective involves more than meeting the technical criteria; it must also contain content that speaks to the general goals such that it answers the question "How do I want my client to behave differently, and how will I know when he's doing it satisfactorily?" The counselor who finds it difficult to convert general goals for counseling and guidance into behavioral objectives may benefit from the outstanding series of monographs published by the California Personnel and Guidance Association (Krumboltz, 1966; O'Hare and Lasser, 1971; Sullivan and O'Hare, 1971; Cunha, et al., 1972) dealing with goals and objectives, evaluation, and accountability.

Design Program and Materials

It is important to realize that up to this point no decision has been reached that would commit the counselor to the use of curricular approaches or self-help techniques. The counselor has surveyed the situation, defined problems, and generated goal statements and objectives which are desired outcomes. It is at this stage, and no earlier, that exploration of strategies which could be employed to reach those desired outcomes should begin.

Information obtained in the Needs Assessment must be integrated in this step. Knowledge of student characteristics, available and potentially available resources (including human resources) as well as a knowledge of strategies previously utilized in addressing the same problems must be considered. What are the pros and cons of structured group activities for all students as opposed to highly flexible individualized approaches? Can the students be expected to function independently with extensive use of written materials, or would structured use of non-print media be more likely to succeed? Do the problems focus more on a need for information or knowledge of self?

It may be obvious that any approach chosen will not necessarily be appropriate for all students. Options for multiple approaches should be considered. A frequent limitation about which counselors lament is financial restraint. Can multiple approaches be designed such that more expensive ones may be offset by extremely cost-efficient ones? Might high initial expense (such as purchase of videotape equipment) be offset in the long run by increases in the quantity and quality of services provided?

These are the kinds of questions which must be considered in designing an intervention strategy. Some are clearly educational in nature; what kind of strategy is best with regard to learning. Others are more political in nature, dealing with questions of resource allocation, administration, staff endorsement, and cooperation.

A variety of strategies might be selected at this point, many of which are discussed in other chapters of this book. For the purpose of this chapter we will examine strategies for the development of curricular and self-help approaches.

Curricular Approaches

Curricular approaches generally are more comprehensive in scope, and may include the use of self-help techniques. Principles of curriculum design should be applied as they would for any other academic course. Clear statements of objectives, coupled with the provision of learning experiences and assessment of student progress are included. One particular concern is the extent to which a curricular approach can be or should be individualized. Some advantages of curricular approaches are the peer group involvement used, as in *Deciding*, to assist the student in exploring his personal values. To the extent that individualized approaches are used, less use is made of peer interaction. Most curricular approaches reviewed utilize group discussion extensively, although often it is as a forum for dispensing information which has been gathered through individual students' research. It is important for the designer of a curricular approach to identify those objectives which might be attained through common activitites, and which are least affected by individual diffcrences. For those which are highly affected by individual differences, or which are not to be required of all students, individualized options should be designed. Rarely will a pre-packaged set of materials fit for a curricular approach. The designer must identify any such materials which might be included, design other experiences, and fit them together in a desirable sequence. He must line up the resources required, whether it be test materials (SVIB, Allport *Study of Values,* etc.) , guest speakers, simulation materials *(Life Careers Game, Job Experience Kit,* etc.) , self-help techniques *(Self-Directed Search),* or counselors to train peers to lead small group discussions.

Self-Help Techniques

Strategies for the design of self-help techniques are unlimited, but the designer must keep in mind one question: "Can the student profit from these materials even if he is given no other instructions and no other follow-up?" Key elements which should be considered for inclusion in self-help techniques are those suggested by Houston, et al. (1972) : 1. a prospectus, including an overview which spells out the objectives, any prerequisites, and instructions to the user; 2. a preassessment, which will assist the individual in deciding whether to go on, and diagnostic self-tests, which are helpful in multi-unit materials to enable the individual to move directly to those units which have not been mastered and thereby avoid any which would be redundant; 3. enabling elements, the individualized instructional units; and 4. a postassessment, which enables the individual to assess the extent to which he has met the objectives, and to assist him in identifying where and how to seek further assistance.

Self-help techniques need not employ gimmicks to be successful. A wide range of approaches have been reviewed, with Holland's *Self-Directed Search* illustrating a paper-and-pencil approach and Reardon's Curricular-Career Information Service illustrating a modular, multi-media approach. There are several factors which should be considered, however. For relatively low cost one can transcribe vast amounts of information onto cassette tape, with obvious benefits to the student with reading difficulties. Entire self-help units can be developed and used without presenting the student with a single written word. Why allow the student who suffers because of a reading problem to also suffer in learning career decision-making skills? That constitutes educational double jeopardy! Another factor to be considered in determining what mode(s) of presentation to use is that of motivation. This is a media-oriented era. What can be learned from Madison Avenue to make learning fun? With a little creativity, perhaps some volunteer student help, a few rolls of films, and a cassette tape, one can build a slide-tape presentation on using a career information file, or examining the requirements for job opportunities related to a given field of study. Computers and television provide even greater possibilities, although more costly. The point is that taking advantage of motivational factors that turn young people on does not have to be costly nor difficult to design. Some of the best resources for building motivation into materials are all around and eager to help: the students themselves.

Simulate or Pilot Study

This step is a debugging process, designed to help identify problems either in content or in procedures early enough to revise before attempting to implement materials and procedures on a large scale.

The first suggestion is simulation. This may involve, particularly for curricular approaches, assuming several roles (instructor, student) and walking through the prescribed procedures and materials (see Chapter 5).

The second suggestion is to subject the materials and procedures to a pilot study. For curricular approaches this might involve just one section of one course, or even just a part of a course. For self-help materials this could involve limited use with selected clients for whom the materials seem appropriate.

A variety of questions should be considered as you simulate or pilot test: are the objectives appropriate for this (these) client(s)? are procedures/materials properly sequenced? are there gaps or redundancies? can procedures or materials be simplified? where do students experience difficulties? of what nature? where should more options be designed? do additional resources need to be gathered?

Answers to the above questions should be analyzed and appropriate action taken to improve the materials and procedures before full-scale implementation.

Implement Program

Assuming the feedback received in the pilot study is of the "revise-and-proceed" nature rather than "you-blew-it-forget-it," the next step *appears* to be rather simple: implement on a large scale. Implementation, however, is far from simple, and is actually not a discrete step in this systems approach, but rather one which started in the needs assessment (step one).

Successful implementation of a new project is highly dependent on the nature and extent of the support given it by significant others, such as administration, faculty, students, parents and other staff in Student Affairs or Pupil Personnel Services. Blocher, Dustin, and Dugan (1970) stress the early involvement of others in building a support system. Go back to step one and look at ways in which the counselor can gather support. The needs assessment involved gathering a variety of kinds of information. Involvement of key people in obtaining and interpreting information, as well as in problem definition and goal setting will help considerably in gathering support. Commitment at the implementation stage can be heightened by getting others engaged in early planning.

What is the counselor's role in implementation? Thus far we have discussed curricular approaches and self-help techniques as though they were the brainchild and private domain of the counselor. Certainly the self-help techniques are appropriate for use in conjunction with counseling, but they are not limited to that use. Such materials can be incorporated in curricular approaches, and can be made available in a variety of locations: libraries, student learning centers, and residence halls, to name a few. But what of the curricular approaches? What is the counselor's role in the actual operation of them? Is he to go back willingly into the classroom as teacher of today's version of "Occupations"? Will he (or can he) get academic legitimacy (credits) for his invasion of the curriculum? Each counselor's local situation will differ with regard to these questions. What has been most successful in those approaches reviewed has been the use of team approaches, in which counselors work closely with interested faculty.

Evaluate Program

Accountability has been the counselor's bugaboo for years. At this step, however, one should not have too much difficulty with the accountability question. Again look back, this time to step two, goal-setting. If in fact the behavioral objectives were well written, they identified observable, measurable behaviors as desired outcomes. At that point criteria were established for evaluating the effectiveness of the strategies, whether curricular approaches or self-help techniques. Depending on the nature and time reference of the objectives, one may even build the evaluation into the curricular approach or self-help materials. Long-range objectives may require follow-up. Either way, the evaluation should be based directly on the stated objectives (see Chapter 15).

Modify Program

The evaluation should yield feedback which helps to identify the strengths and weaknesses of materials and procedures. A variety of modifications may result, ranging from changes in objectives to extensive revision of procedures. Where successful one can demonstrate the capability to facilitate career development; where less than fully successful problems can be pinpointed and the program modified to be more responsive to the clients' needs. At the point of evaluation and modification one has come full circle, and has begun a new cycle of needs assessment, goal-setting, and program development.

SUMMARY

Self-help techniques and curricular approaches offer systematic approaches to facilitating the career development of large numbers of people, while recognizing and providing for a great range of individual differences. Familiarity with representative strategies currently in use, when used within a systems approach, can enable the counselor to select and/or design those approaches which best address the career development needs of his specific clientele.

BIBLIOGRAPHY

Blocher, D.H., Dustin, E.R., and Dugan, W.E. *Guidance Systems.* New York: Ronald Press, 1971.

Borow, H. College courses in vocational planning. *Vocational Guidance Quarterly,* 1960, *9,* 75-80.

Calvert, R., Carter, E.M., and Murphy, I. College courses in occupational adjustment. *Personnel and Guidance Journal,* 1964, *42,* 680-682.

Carney, C.G. A career development workshop for economically disadvantaged students. Research and Development Report No. 43. Salt Lake City: University of Utah Counseling and Psychological Services, 1972.

Cunha, J., Laramore, D., Lowrey, B., Mitchell, A., Smith, T., and Woolley, D. (Eds.). *Career Development: A California Model for Career Guidance Curriculum K-Adult.* Fullerton, California: California Personnel and Guidance Association, 1972.

Devlin, T. Career development courses as part of the academic program. Paper read at the American College Personnel Association Convention, Cleveland, Ohio, April 1973.

Erikson, E.H. *Childhood and Society.* New York: W.W. Norton, 1950.

Fuhriman, A. A theoretical rationale for elements of developmental career counseling. Research and Development Report No. 43. Salt Lake City: University of Utah Counseling and Psychological Services, 1972.

Gelatt, H.B., Varenhorst, B., and Carey, R. *Deciding.* New York: College Entrance Examination Board, 1972.

Gelatt, H.B., et al. *Deciding: A Leader's Guide.* New York: College Entrance Examination Board, 1972.

Gelatt, H.B., Varenhorst, B., Carey, R., and Miller, G.P. *Decisions and Outcomes.* New York: College Entrance Examination Board, 1973.

Gelatt, H.B., et al. *Decisions and Outcomes: A Leader's Guide.* New York: College Entrance Examination Board, 1973.

Holcomb, J.R. College courses in careers: An historical and evaluative treatment. Unpublished paper. Pittsburgh: Duquesne University, 1966.

Holland, J. *The Self-Directed Search: A Guide to Educational and Vocational Planning.* Palo Alto: Consulting Psychologists Press, 1970.

Holland, J. *The Occupations Finder.* Palo Alto: Consulting Psychologists Press, 1972.

Holland, J., Hollifield, J.H., Nafziger, D.H., and Helms, S.T. A guide to the self-directed career program: A practical and inexpensive vocational guidance system. Report No. 126. Baltimore: The Center for Social Organizations, John Hopkins University, 1972.

Hosford, R.E., and Ryan, T.A. Systems design in the development of counseling and guidance programs. *Personnel and Guidance Journal,* 1970, *49,* 221-230.

Houston, R., Hollis, L.Y., Jones, H.L., Edwards, D.A., Pace, A.A., and White, S.J. *Developing Instructional Modules: A Modular System for Writing Modules.* Houston, Texas: College of Education, University of Houston, 1972.

Johnson, L.A., and Martin, R. A careers course. *Personnel and Guidance Journal,* 1973, *51,* 733-734.

Kass, E.L., Noble, V., and Tobiason, R. Van Cott. Human resource groups: Career counseling in the community college. Unpublished paper. Phoenix, Arizona: Phoenix College Counseling Department, 1973.

Krumboltz, J.D. *Stating the Goals of Counseling.* Fullerton, California: California Personnel and Guidance Association, 1966.

Lee, J.W., and Anthony, W.P. An innovative university career planning course. *Journal of College Placement,* in press.

Magoon, T., Krumboltz, J.D., and Thoresen, C.E. (Eds.). *Behavioral Counseling: Cases and Techniques.* New York: Holt, Rinehart, and Winston, 1969.

Maslow, A. *Toward a Psychology of Being.* New York: Van Nostrand Reinhold, 1962.

Mazzano, J. A survey of the teaching of occupations. *Vocational Guidance Quarterly,* 1969, *17,* 275-277.

O'Hare, R.W., and Lasser, B. *Evaluating Pupil Personnel Programs.* Fullerton, California: California Personnel and Guidance Association, 1971.

Packard, T. A career exploration workshop for entering freshmen. Research and Development Report No. 43. Salt Lake City: University of Utah Counseling and Psychological Services, 1972.

Parker, C.A. The new scope of counseling. *Personnel and Guidance Journal,* 1974, *52,* 348-350.

Ramsey, S.E. Career exploration for women. *Journal of College Placement,* 1973, *33,* 36-40.

Reardon, R.C. The counselor and career information services. *Journal of College Student Personnel,* 1973, *14,* 495-500.

Reardon, R.C., Dowkowski, D., Burkhart, M.Q., Minor, C.W., and Smith, J.D. The curricular-career information service (CCIS): Development and evaluation of the pilot project, 1972-1973. Mimeo report. Tallahassee: Office of Undergraduate Advising and Counseling, The Florida State University, 1973.

Stoddard, K.B. A career development general education seminar. Research and Development Report No. 43. Salt Lake City: University of Utah Counseling and Psychological Services, 1972.

Sullivan, H.J., and O'Hare, R.W. (Eds.). *Accountability in Pupil Personnel Services: A Process Guide for the Development of Objectives.* Fullerton, California: California Personnel and Guidance Association, 1971.

Walz, G.R. *Life/Career Development System.* Ann Arbor: Human Development Services, Inc., undated.

Warshaw, P. A career development "marathon" workshop. Research and Development Report No. 43. Salt Lake City: University of Utah Counseling and Psychological Services, 1972.

Webb, E.M. Placement moves to the classroom. *Journal of College Placement,* 1973, *33,* 30-35.

Chapter Ten

DEVELOPING A CAREER RESOURCE
CENTER

CAROLE W. MINOR

THE DEVELOPMENT OF AN ADEQUATE career resource center has long been considered necessary to a complete career development and placement program. Students need information about careers and educational opportunities open to them. LeMay and Warnath (1967), for example, found that almost 90% of the students they surveyed wanted a centrally located source of occupational information.

Each time he works with a client with a career concern, the practicing counselor verifies this need for conveniently located, easy-to-use information. The use of information in counseling is discussed by Reardon (see Chapter 3).

This chapter is written for the counselor who is both convinced of the need for information in career counseling and committed to the development of an efficient, complete career information center. It outlines a model for the development of a career resource center and makes specific recommendations regarding materials, equipment, staffing and organization. Topics addressed are (1) the goals of the information center, (2) considerations in the development of a center, (3) establishing the center, and (4) operation and staffing.

GOALS

The first, and perhaps most important, step in building a career resource center is to determine the goals to be met. Principal considerations at this point are the needs of the population to be served and the needs of the sponsoring institution.

Important questions include: What is the age level of the target population? What is their reading level? What is their level of vocational development? Will the library be used primarily for individual exploration (junior high), or will it be used for more specific information and decision making (senior high and college)? Will it be a placement library also? Will it serve only individuals seeking career information on a voluntary or referral basis, or is there also a need for materials which can be used by teachers in the classroom or by counselors in groups or classes? What kinds of staff will be available? Will counseling be available in or near the resource center, or will students have to be referred for counseling? Will the students be motivated already or will the center have to stimulate their interest in exploring careers?

Goals for most career resource centers should include:

1. Providing up-to-date information about careers on a level appropriate for the target population.
2. Providing up-to-date information about further education or training appropriate to the educational level of the target population.
3. Providing accurate information about local job availability and occupational outlooks.

Additional goals specific to various settings might be:

1. Providing exploration or information materials which can be used by teachers in the classroom or in planning units in career development.
2. Providing materials which counselors can use in group vocational counseling.
3. Providing resources which a student may use to gain experience in the world of work, e.g., job experience kits, lists of volunteer work experiences, or community referral resources.
4. Providing special stimulation materials to motivate students in career exploration.
5. Providing specialized materials for minorities, women, the handicapped, or other special subpopulations.

Other goals specific to individual settings could, of course, be added to the list.

CONSIDERATIONS IN THE DEVELOPMENT OF A CENTER

The most difficult part of developing a career resource center is likely to be obtaining the necessary resources: money, space, equipment, and personnel. A careful application of the systems approach can be of great help in this task. Using the model put forth by Hosford and Ryan (1970), the counselor may survey existing programs and resources and the career development needs of the students. He can use this information to develop a program to meet the needs in the environmental context. The career resource center must be viewed in the context of the complete career development program since neither will be effective without the other.

Using the systems approach to program development provides the counselor with a well-thought-out plan necessary in obtaining approval to proceed with the establishment of a career resource center. The counselor must have an effective case to present when requesting resources from principals, superintendents, univeristy officials, PTAs, alumni associations, or outside funding agencies. Gaining support from administrators is a key factor. The support of faculty members and other counselors may be helpful, and the counselor should be prepared to utilize academic politics or public relations skills if necessary. One example of the use of the systems approach in developing a career development program is discussed by Reardon, Domkowski, Burkhart, Minor and Smith (1973).

Each of the following factors should be considered in the development of a career resource center.

Location

The location of a career resource center will have a major effect on its usefulness. If possible, the resource center should be located in an area which is easily accessible to students as well as counselors. It should be available for browsing and independent use rather than available only to supervised groups. Locating the center in a high traffic area can greatly increase its use. The group of college students surveyed by LeMay and Warnath (1967) indicated overwhelmingly that they would prefer the location of a central library of occupational information in the union. Realistically, however, the simple existence of space is usually the most important factor in choosing a location.

The size of the space available will, in general, determine the number of students who may use the facility at any one time and the equipment which may be accommodated. It is suggested that sufficient space be provided for comfortable seating and/or work space for ten students.

Personnel, Materials, and Equipment

A career resource center needs to be monitored by at least one person whenever it is open. Personnel availability on the site is thus an important consideration. Will one or more counselors be available on the site to assist students, or will the monitoring duties have to be given to a well-trained paraprofessional or student assistant? Whoever is monitoring the career resource center needs to be completely familiar with the materials and information available as well as the operation of all equipment. He needs to be able to relate to students and to be sensitive to their needs.

In addition to personnel to monitor the resource center, part-time clerical assistance is necessary to obtain and maintain the current information. Careful consideration should be given to the necessity of providing adequate personnel to provide a quality service.

Decisions need to be made, with the goals as a guide, about what types of information are necessary, e.g. browsing materials, information about careers, educational information, employment outlooks, salary ranges, placement information, or career development materials. Next, decisions must be made about the vehicles for presenting this information. This may be accomplished through briefs, pamphlets, monographs, vocational biographies, filmstrips, microfilm, films, audiotapes, videotapes, slidetape presentations, or interactive computer programs. Special consideration needs to be given to the degree of motivation necessary as media materials seem to attract students more readily than printed materials. This leads to decisions on equipment for use in the center, e.g. filing cabinets, filmstrip projectors, slide projectors, film projectors, audiotape players, videotape players, computer terminals. Selection of media has to be made within the constraints of money and space available.

Choices need to be made about the necessity of having materials which can be used by groups (films, duplicate materials) or by teachers in planning curriculum units (lesson plans, career education materials). The specificity and reading level of the materials should be carefully selected. Age and grade levels of students can help determine this.

The last question the counselor may want to consider is the advisability of developing some local materials, e.g. community referral resources, taped interviews with people in various professions, or local occupational outlook briefs.

After consideration of personnel, materials, equipment, and materials development needs, the counselor should be able to present cost estimates for the various components of the career resource center.

It is at this point also that priorities need to be set. Assigning priorities to the goals enables the counselor to begin with limited resources, if necessary, or to modify his plans if sufficient resources are not available for the program as originally conceived.

At this point, the counselor should have assessed the needs and the environment, considered available resources and additional ones necessary, set his priorities, and determined the location, personnel, information and equipment needs. He is then ready to present his thoroughly-thought-out plan for a career resource center to the person or persons with the authority and resources to establish such a center.

ESTABLISHING THE CENTER

Having developed a plan for the career resource center and having obtained the necessary resources and administrative support, the counselor is ready to begin establishing the center.

After the designations of location, budget, and personnel have been made and existing equipment and resources have been identified, the next step is to identify sources of materials and equipment necessary.

Categories of information the counselor may want to consider are:

1. Briefs and pamphlets.
2. Books and monographs about specific careers.
3. Basic reference books such as the *Dictionary of Occupational Titles* and the *Occupational Outlook Handbook.*
4. Guides to colleges, universities, technical schools and graduate schools.
5. Career development books and books on special problems and/or opportunities for minority groups.
6. Salary information and occupational outlooks at the local, regional, and national levels.
7. Films and filmstrips which may be used by individuals or in group presentations.
8. Materials (printed and media) which may be used as part of the curriculum by teachers or counselors.

Equipment needs may include:

1. Filing cabinets
2. Display shelving or racks
3. Shelving for books, catalogs and other materials
4. Library tables (or study carrels), chairs
5. Listening-viewing carrels
6. Cassette tape players
7. Slide and/or filmstrip projectors
8. Sound on slide equipment by 3M or the Singer Graflex Caramate
9. 16mm film projector and screen
10. Monitor's desk
11. Bulletin boards
12. Card catalogs
13. Comfortable, lounge-type seating
14. Typewriter

Kunze (1967) describes a range of types of occupational information developed by Thompson which may be used as a guide to information which the counselor can provide. These types are arranged in order according to the degree of involvement (commitment) a student needs to have in order to use them.

1. Publications (books, monographs, etc.)
2. Audio-Visual Aids (films, tapes, slides, etc.)
3. Programmed Instructional Materials (books, workbooks, etc.)
4. Computer-based Systems (storage, retrieval, mechanized systems)
5. Interviews with Experts (direct questioning of occupational representatives)
6. Simulated Situations (career games, role playing, etc.)
7. Synthetically-created Work Environments (artificial reproduction of work settings)
8. Direct Observations (visits to work sites)
9. Directed Exploratory Experiences (work samples, evaluation tasks, etc.)
10. On-the-job Tryout (casual work or work-study programs)

Several of these categories involve programs which must be developed locally by the counselor (see Chapters 3 and 11 for additional comments on this topic) .

Identifying Sources of Information

Sources of occupational information are indeed numerous. A discussion of some recommended materials and sources of materials follows, and a more complete list of sources is included at the end of this chapter.

The *Dictionary of Occupational Titles* (DOT) is a standard reference for career information. Volume I offers descriptions of careers organized alphabetically. Volume II offers a way to identify related careers by numerical categories and worker trait groups. Isaacson (1971), Hoppock (1967), and Fine (1969) offer thorough discussions on the DOT and its use in counseling.

The *Occupational Outlook Handbook,* revised every two years, provides information on more than 800 occupations. The *Handbook* discusses the following topics for each occupation:

Nature of Work; Places of Employment; Training, Other Qualifications, and Advancement; Employment Outlook; Earnings and Working Conditions; and Sources of Additional Information.

Interesting articles describing occupational outlooks, the impact of national labor and economic trends on the job market, and the relationship between academic work and getting a job are found in the *Occupational Outlook Quarterly*.

Guides to colleges, universities, and technical schools include:

1. *The College Handbook,* College Entrance Examination Board
2. *Profiles of American Colleges,* Barron's Educational Series
3. *Guide to Two-Year Colleges,* Barron's Educational Series
4. *The College Blue Book,* Macmillan Library Services
5. *The Technical Education Yearbook,* Prakken Publishers
6. *The American Trade Schools Directory,* Croner Publications, Inc.

Several commercial companies publish libraries of occupational briefs. They include:

1. Science Research Associates, Inc. (SRA)
   259 East Erie Street
   Chicago, Illinois 60611
2. Chronicle Guidance Publications, Inc.
   Moravia, New York 13118
3. Careers
   Largo, Florida 33540
4. Vocational Biographies, Inc.
   P.O. Box 146
   Sauk Centre, Minnesota 56378
5. Houghton Mifflin Company
   110 Tremont Street
   Boston, Massachusetts 02107

Updating services—which provide revised occupational briefs, lists of new occupational materials and professional articles—are available through SRA, Chronicle, and Vocational Biographies.

Listings of sources of free and inexpensive career information

materials may be obtained through subscriptions to:
1. The National Career Information Center
   American Personnel and Guidance Association (APGA)
   1607 New Hampshire Avenue, N.W.
   Washington, D.C. 20009 ($25.00; $15.00 to members)
2. Counselor's Information Service
   B'nai B'rith Career and Counseling Services
   1640 Rhode Island Avenue, N.W.
   Washington, D.C. 20036 (10.00)

Other listings of free and/or inexpensive occupational information may be found in:
1. *A Starter File of Free Occupational Literature*
   B'nai B'rith Vocational Service ($1.25)
2. *Guide to Federal Career Literature*
   Superintendent of Documents
   U.S. Government Printing Office
   Washington, D.C. 20402 ($ .55)
3. *NVGA Bibliography of Current Career Information*
   American Personnel and Guidance Association
   1607 New Hampshire Avenue, N.W.
   Washington, D.C. 20009 ($2.00)
4. Current issues of *Vocational Guidance Quarterly*
   American Personnel and Guidance Association ($8.00
       yearly)
5. *Careers in Education: A Comprehensive Listing of Information Sources*
   National Center for Information on Careers in Education
   1607 New Hampshire Avenue, N.W.
   Washington, D.C. 20009 (free)

Membership in APGA and/or NVGA (National Vocational Guidance Association) can also be an asset in keeping current with career guidance materials. "Guidepost," a biweekly publication of APGA, carries an annotated listing of new guidance materials; a subscription to the *Vocational Guidance Quarterly* is included with membership in NVGA. Commercial publishers send advertisements of new materials to APGA members.

Books about specific careers may be purchased from companies such as:

1. Vocational Guidance Manuals
   235 East 45 Street
   New York, New York 10017
2. Richard Rosen Press
   29 East 21st Street
   New York, New York 10010

Audiotaped interviews with people in various professions may be obtained from the following companies:

1. Educational Progress Corporation
   P.O. Box 45663
   Tulsa, Oklahoma 74145
2. Jeffrey Norton Publishing Company
   145 East 49th Street
   New York, New York 10017
3. MacMillan Library Services
   255 B Brown Street
   Riverside, New Jersey 08075

Future career guidance programs, additional career and occupational information, career guidance materials for classroom use, films and film strips, job experience kits, and other materials may be obtained from commercial publishing companies. A list of these companies can be found at the end of this chapter. Catalogs may be obtained on request.

Professional organizations are a good source of occupational information. Of course, information from these sources must be evaluated to determine the degree to which it is recruitment literature and the degree to which it may be helpful to students. A list of professional organizations and labor unions may be found in the *Directory of National Trade and Professional Associations,* Garrett Park Press, Garrett Park, Maryland 20766.

Almost a dozen computer-based interactive guidance systems have been developed to aid students in selecting a career and/or a college. Several of these programs have been discontinued due to lack of funding; others are in various stages of development and refinement. Kroll (1973) provides a thorough discussion of the current status of four of these programs. At least one, the Computerized Vocational Information System (CVIS), is available for general use as of this writing (Harris, 1972). In addition, a nationally updated computer-based information retrieval system, the Guidance Information System, is available from Houghton Mifflin. Chick (1970) and Super (1970) offer extensive descriptions of the use of computers in guidance and counseling.

Layout

Different types of materials should be stored in areas which facilitate their use. Browsing materials and reading materials should be located in or near a lounge area or work table; media materials should be stored close to audio-visual carrels, tape recorders, or computer terminals. Jacobson (1971) provides examples of layouts in a secondary school setting.

Ordering and Filing

The actual ordering and filing of materials is a tedious but important process. Files and materials which are well-organized, cross referenced, and easily accessible encourage student use. Moreover, students are impressed by a complete, well-organized resource center and discouraged when information is lacking or out of place. Simply stated, if students can't find it, it may as well not be there.

Records need to be kept of materials ordered, date, and source. This enables the counselor to check up on materials which may not have arrived after having been ordered for an abnormally long time. These records are extremely important if the counselor works in an institution with no central purchasing department, but are not unnecessary even if there is a purchasing unit. A simple file of 3×5 index cards containing the required information and organized as "ordered" or "received" will suffice.

The overall filing plan for a career resource center must be adapted to local needs. There are, however, some general guidelines which may be helpful.

1. Separate locations need to be available for different types (occupational literature, guides to colleges and trade schools, classroom materials) and forms (briefs, books, films, audiotapes) of information.
2. Information needs to be indexed by both type and subject with the location indicated.
3. Materials should be cross-referenced so a student may locate all available information about a particular subject, e.g., choosing a college.
4. The system should, if at all possible, enable the students to use materials on their own, without having to request assistance in finding each piece or type of information.

Many plans for filing information and materials have been developed. Some of them are discussed by Hoppock (1967), Isaacson (1971), Norris, Zeran, Hatch, and Engelkes (1972), Michels and Kirk (1964), and Holland (1973). One of the most popular filing systems is that found in the *Dictionary of Occupational Titles* (DOT). It is easy for students to understand and use. Many commercial materials have the DOT number printed on them, saving the counselor or clerical worker time in filing them. Holland (1973) has even cross-indexed his occupational classification to that of the DOT.

Evaluating Materials

Materials may be evaluated on two criteria: the completeness of information presented and the accuracy of that information. To help the counselor evaluate completeness, NVGA has developed *Guidelines for Use in Preparing and Evaluating Career Information Media.*

The counselor must go to other sources for evaluation of the accuracy of information. These sources may include information compiled more recently or the counselor's personal knowledge and experience. When evaluating accuracy of information, especially occupational outlooks, the counselor may check the information about one or more fields with which he is personally familiar. If this information is consistent with the counselor's own knowledge and experience, he may be relatively sure that the information about other occupations is also correct. If the counselor knows that the information is incorrect, he may doubt the accuracy of other information in the same volume or published by the same company.

Counselors and students who use occupational outlook information need to be aware of its limitations. The counselor must convey to students the unreliability of some printed and media information about national occupational outlooks. This information usually describes the job market accurately as of the time it was compiled, and projects the future outlook based on current conditions. However, compilation and publication take a year or longer which frequently makes these statistics and outlooks outdated by the time they are printed. Further, a student who is interested in this information will frequently not be ready to enter the job market for two years or more. Thus, students should be cautioned against uncritical acceptance of occupational outlooks.

This should not be construed as discounting the value of national statistics developed by sources such as the Bureau of Labor Statistics, but as pointing up the fact that the student needs to understand the realities of the changing job market and to develop some flexibility in his goals.

Creating Materials

Local information is very important, especially to counselors in secondary schools, vocational schools, and junior colleges. Frequently it is necessary for the counselor to compile this information on his own. Local information needed would include job openings, occupational outlooks, and local training opportunities. Tolbert (1974) provides an excellent discussion of finding and organizing local information. Overs (1967) suggests that the counselor develop a more subjective type of occupational information, which he terms covert occupational information. He describes this information as a knowledge of "how it really is," and describes its sources as:

1. Reports from present and former clients.
2. Informal talks with significant administrators.

3. Observed employment outcomes.
4. Information from professional contacts.
5. Information from non-professional areas.

The counselor has a responsibility to develop reliable sources as to "how it really is" in order to best serve his clients.

OPERATION AND STAFFING

Beyond the information, stimulation, and exploration materials available in a career resource center, the most important aspect of the center is the availability of a professional staff member who might be termed a Career Information Specialist.

Scherini and Kirk (1963) describe the function of an Occupational Information Specialist at the University of California at Berkeley. This full-time staff member spends all of her time collecting information, consulting with other counselors, and gathering current local information. She also serves as a liaison with both the placement office and the faculty of the university. She arranges special presentations to the counseling center staff concerning topics such as summer job opportunities, graduate school admissions, and overseas careers.

Hoppock and Novick (1971) conducted a survey of counseling agencies and identified the following duties for the person they call an Occupational Information Consultant:

1. Determines what occupational information teachers and counselors need in order to make instruction and counseling more relevant to the world of work;
2. Identifies entry-level jobs in the community;
3. Serves as a liaison between school and business and industry;
4. Develops opportunities for students to obtain career information;
5. Explores and interprets possibilities in the area of computerized career counseling services;
6. Maintains a library of materials on careers and employment opportunities;
7. Provides teachers with career information to incorporate

in their course content;

8. Assists the guidance staff in organizing and conducting career guidance activities;
9. Organizes and prepares research studies relating to students' career choices and placement;
10. Develops and implements effective ways of publicizing occupational information to all students.

As indicated earlier, the career resource center needs one or more staff members available to help students whenever it is open. This may necessitate the use of paraprofessionals, including student assistants. Each person who works in the center should be well-trained in the availability and use of materials. Clerical assistance is also necessary to maintain the accuracy and currency of information and to order materials.

One part of the operation of a career resource center should be a continuous evaluation of all phases of operation. A formal or informal evaluation of the frequency of use of various materials would help determine what materials are most helpful and should have highest priority for replacement when outdated or lost.

SUMMARY

The first step in the process of developing a career resource center is the setting of goals. Important considerations in planning include 1. using the systems approach to develop a well-thought-out plan; 2. determining the most useful available location; 3. determining personnel, materials, and equipment needs; and 4. setting priorities. Establishing the center includes 1. identifying sources of materials and equipment, 2. ordering, 3. setting up a filing system, 4. determining the physical layout, 5. evaluating and creating materials, and 6. selecting and training the staff.

BIBLIOGRAPHY

Biggers, J.L. Use of information in vocational decision-making. *Vocational Guidance Quarterly*, 1971, *19*, 171-176.
Brammer, L.M., Williams, M.H., Jr. Organization and operation of a vocational library. *Occupations*, 1950, *29*, 177-181.

Capwell, J.E. Information materials used by counselors. *Occupations,* 1950, *28,* 535.

Chick, J.M. *Innovations in the Use of Career Information.* Boston: Houghton-Mifflin, 1970.

Dobberstein, W.F. Free occupational information: How much? How good? *Vocational Guidance Quarterly,* 1963, *11,* 141-142.

Fine, S.A. The 1965 edition of the *Dictionary of Occupational Titles:* Content, contrasts, critique. *Vocational Guidance Quarterly,* 1969, *17,* 162-172.

Harris, J.A. Willowbrook computerized vocational information system (CVIS). *Career Education and the Technology of Career Development.* Palo Alto, California: American Institutes for Research, 1972.

Holland, J.L. *Making Vocational Choices: A Theory of Careers.* Englewood Cliffs, New Jersey: Prentice-Hall, 1973.

Hoppock, R. *Occupational Information.* New York: McGraw-Hill, 1957.

Hoppock, R., and Novick, B. Occupational information consultant: A new profession? *Personnel and Guidance Journal,* 1974, *49,* 555-558.

Hosford, R.E., and Ryan, T.A. Systems design in the development of counseling and guidance programs. *Personnel and Guidance Journal,* 1970, *49,* 221-230.

Isaacson, L.E. *Career Information in Counseling and Teaching.* (2nd Ed.) Boston: Allyn and Bacon, 1971.

Jacobson, T.J. Career guidance center. *Exchange,* 1971, *1* (5), 1-4.

Kroll, A.M. Computer-based systems for career guidance and information: A status report. *Focus on Guidance,* 1973, *5* (10), 1-15.

Kunze, K.R. Industry resources available to counselors. *Vocational Guidance Quarterly,* 1967, *16,* 137-142.

Laramore, D. Career information center: An approach to occupational information on a university campus. *Personnel and Guidance Journal,* 1967, *45,* 821-823.

LeMay, M.L., and Warnath, C.F. Student opinion on the location of occupational information on a university campus. *Personnel and Guidance Journal,* 1967, *45,* 821-823.

Mathis, H.F., and Mathis, L.R. Occupational literature published by professional societies and trade associations. *Vocational Guidance Quarterly,* 1961, *10* (1), 70-72.

Michels, E., and Kirk, A. *California Plan for Classifying Occupational Information* (Part I). Palo Alto, California: Consulting Psychologists Press, 1964.

Norris, W., Zeran, F.R., Hatch, R.N., and Engelkes, J.R. *The Information Service in Guidance: For Career Development and Planning.* Chicago: Rand McNally, 1972.

Odle, S.G. Student information center as an educational resource. *Vocational Guidance Quarterly,* 1967, *15,* 217-220.

O'Hara, R.P. Theoretical foundations for the use of occupational information in guidance. *Personnel and Guidance Journal,* 1968, *46,* 636-640.

Overs, R.P. Covert occupational information. *Vocational Guidance Quarterly,* 1967, *16,* 7-12.

Peters, H.J. Riddle of occupational information. *Vocational Guidance Quarterly,* 1963, *11,* 253-258.

Peters, H.J., and Angus, S.F. New challenges in the riddle of occupational information. *Vocational Guidance Quarterly,* 1965, *13,* 179-183.

Purcell, F.E. Helping students use occupational information files. *Vocational Guidance Quarterly,* 1961, *10* (1), 55-56.

Rauner, T.M. Occupational information and occupational choice. *Personnel and Guidance Journal,* 1962, *41,* 311-317.

Reardon, R.C., Domkowski, D., Burkhart, M.Q., Minor, C.W., and Smith J.D. The curricular-career information service (CCIS): Development and evaluation of the pilot project, 1972-1973. *Programs and Practices In Life Career Development.* Ann Arbor, University of Michigan: ERIC/CAPS, 1974, 180-191.

Scherini, R., and Kirk, B.A. Keeping current on occupational information. *Vocational Guidance Quarterly,* 1963, *11,* 96-98.

Splaver, S. What high school students want in occupational books. *Personnel and Guidance Journal,* 1954, *33,* 15-18.

Super, D.E. (Ed.) *Computer-Assisted Counseling.* New York: Teachers College Press, Columbia University, 1970.

Tolbert, E.L. *Counseling for Career Development.* Boston: Houghton-Mifflin, 1974.

ADDITIONAL SOURCES

American Personnel and Guidance Association
1607 New Hampshire Avenue, N.W.
Washington, D.C.   20009

Barron's Educational Series, Inc.
113 Crossways Park Drive
Woodbury, N.Y.   11797

Bellman Publishing Company
P.O. Box 172
Cambridge, MA   02188

B'nai B'rith Career and Counseling Services
1640 Rhode Island Avenue, N.W.
Washington, D.C.   20036

Careers
Box 135
Largo, FL   30540

Catalyst
6 East 82nd Street
New York, N.Y.   10028

Charles A. Jones Publishing Co.
4 Village Green, S.E.
Worthington, OH   43085

Charles E. Merrill Publishing Co.
1300 Alum Creek Drive
Columbus, OH   43216

Chronicle Guidance Publications
Moravia, N.Y.   13118

College Entrance Examination Board
Publications Order Office
Box 592
Princeton, N.J.   08540

College Placement Council, Inc.
P.O. Box 2263
Bethlehem, PA   18001

Consulting Psychologists Press, Inc.
577 College Avenue
Palo Alto, CA   94306

Cowles Education Corporation
Look Building
488 Madison Avenue
New York, N.Y.   10022

Croner Publications, Inc.
211-03 Jamaica Avenue
Queens Village
New York, N.Y.   11428

Educational Progress Corporation
P.O. Box 45663
Tulsa, OK   74145

E.P. Dutton and Company, Inc.
201 Park Avenue, South
New York, N.Y.   10003

Garrett Park Press
Garrett Park, MD   20766

Guidance Associates
41 Washington Avenue
Pleasantville, N.Y.   10570

Harper and Row
51 East 33rd Street
New York, N.Y.   10016

Houghton Mifflin Company
666 Miami Circle, N.E.
Atlanta, GA   30324

H.Z. Walck, Inc.
19 Union Square, West
New York, N.Y.   10003

Jeffrey Norton Publishers
145 East 49th Street
New York, N.Y.   10017

Julian Messner, Inc.
One West 39th Street
New York, N.Y.   10018

The MacMillan Company
60 Fifth Avenue
New York, N.Y.   10011

MacMillan Library Service
255 B Brown Street
Riverside, N.J.   08075

McGraw Hill Book Company
1221 Avenue of the Americas
New York, N.Y.   10020

New Careers Development Center
184 Fifth Avenue
New York, N.Y.   10010

Pilot Books
347 Fifth Avenue
New York, N.Y.   10016

Prakken Publishers
416 Longshore Drive
Ann Arbor, MI   48107

Rand McNally and Company
405 Park Avenue
New York, N.Y.   10022

Richard Rosen Press
29 East 21st Street
New York, N.Y.   10010

Science Research Associates, Inc.
259 East Erie Street
Chicago, IL   60611

Ten Speed Press
Box 4310
Berkeley, CA   94704

Viking Press
625 Madison Avenue
New York, N.Y.   10022

Vocational Biographies
Box 146
Sauk Centre, MN   56378

Vocational Guidance Manuals
235 East 45th Street
New York, N.Y.   10017

Vocations for Social Change
4911 Telegraph
Oakland, CA   94609

Chapter Eleven

USING COMMUNITY RESOURCES

WILLIAM L. OLIVER

THE CAREER COUNSELOR CAN no longer afford to be office-bound. Maximum effectiveness in facilitating career development depends not only on a knowledge of the psychological needs of a particular individual, but also on a knowledge of the world in which the contemporary youth lives, or will live. Counselors and other helpers must become active, get out of their offices and experience the world of work. As a fledgling psychiatrist undergoes analysis, career counselors should personally experience career decision-making, the job search, placement interviews, and different kinds of work as a part of their preservice or inservice training. Many of these experiences can be obtained vicariously as the counselor proceeds into the community to develop its resources for facilitating career development. Career counselors must become resource brokers.

The purpose of this chapter is 1. to explore some of the barriers which have hindered the counselor's use of community resources, 2. to identify some benefits from changed counselor practice, and 3. to describe possible strategies the counselor might use to increase community involvement in facilitating individual career development.

ANALYZING THE PROBLEM

There appear to be several longstanding, deep seated reasons for counselors losing touch with the broader community as a resource for helping persons develop careers. It is ironic that Parsons and the early founders of the vocational guidance movement were almost totally community oriented—they were largely interested in social change. Specifically, they were social reformers interested in improving the life of the urban poor, finding training and jobs for immigrants, correcting abuses of child labor, etc. (Stephens, 1970). Contemporary career counselors have largely lost this legacy, and are more concerned with choice than placement, more interested in the psychology of the person than the conditions of the workplace.

Although an entire book could probably be written to fully analyze this problem, there appear to be four identifiable factors which help to explain why and how counselors have lost touch with the community. First, many counselors have a negative attitude toward business and industry. They are suspicious of the profit motive, and frightened by some of the negative values ascribed to businessmen. They believe most workers dislike their jobs and are sometimes fearful that many workers are oppressed. Although it is true that some industrial workers are dissatisfied and alienated (*Work in America,* 1973), it is also true that most workers like their jobs and are not anxious to change (Sorensen, 1973; *Newsweek,* 1974). As S. Norman Feingold, current president of APGA, has said, "Industry and education can work together in new and different ways. Industry is not the enemy" (*Guidepost,* 1974a, p. 6). He went on to say that "job placement is one of the key elements in school programs. Training without placement is a rip-off. We have to move to help students with innovative, cooperative programs. The time is later than you think" (1974a, p. 6).

Second, the development of community resources and the development of cooperative programs necessitates a strong, active counselor role. The creation of effective career development programs requires knowledge and skills previously identified by Bonar (see Chapter 8). It also requires a great deal of hard work, e.g., meetings, planning, telephone calls, letters, position papers or proposals, field trips, supervision of support staff, coordination of other personnel, typing and collating papers, etc. Bernard Novick (*Guidepost,* 1974b, p. 5) recently credited success in building a comprehensive career guidance program to an activist philosophy, not polite dialogue. School people under

Novick's leadership learned how to relate subject areas to the world of work and how to use industry resources. Industry responded by sending out resource people for making speeches, planning programs, giving field trips, and being more open and cooperative about placement and apprenticeship or work study programs. Thus, as Novick and others might view the problem, it is time for the counselor to stop being a "woman" (Farson, 1954).

Third, many counselors seem to be wearing conceptual blinders—they are unable to develop a "beyond counseling perspective" on facilitating career development. Holland, for example, has observed that vocational and avocational experiences and involvement are probably more influential and cheaper than personal counseling in helping the person make career decisions (Holland, 1973). Family members, peers, teachers, employers, and other significant persons have the greatest impact on one's vocational choice, but many counselors are not able to conceptualize how they might use these resources to facilitate career development. As Robert Strotz, President of Northwestern University recently observed, "We need increasingly to tap the counseling resources of the broader community; to bring into our schools people with experience in a broad range of personal and career choices to talk to students . . ." (*Activity,* 1974, p. 5).

Fourth, and finally, many counselors have a negative view of job placement which has served to artificially limit their effectiveness in facilitating career development. Tolbert (1974) has recently reviewed this problem and concluded that "it appears that counselors neither feel job placement to be their responsibility nor devote an appreciable amount of time and effort to it" (p. 260). Job placement functions, e.g. job listing and referral, employability skills training, follow-up, etc. provide a link between the school and the larger community. From a systems perspective it provides both a feedback loop to the school and a way to promote a reality experience which the counselee can share with his counselor. Working up to counselee choice and wishing to drop out at the time of implementation is a "cop out" on the counselor's part. As Tolbert says, "Some counselees seem to feel that the counselor has walked out on the 'hard part' of the helping process" (1974, p. 261). There is little doubt that this aspect of career counseling will change as more and more states—seventeen to date—legislatively mandate job placement responsibilities in the high school (*Career Education News*, 1974).

These four factors appear to be significant in explaining how and why career counselors have lost touch with the community. However, they also set the stage for the remainder of this chapter by identifying counselor beliefs, attitudes and behaviors which must change. Each practitioner will have to make his own choices in this matter. Before describing possible new strategies, a brief review of possible benefits of changed counselor practice is presented.

BENEFITS OF SCHOOL-COMMUNITY COOPERATIVE EFFORTS

The cooperative efforts between school and community may be viewed in terms of benefits to (1) the student, (2) the school, and (3) the community. In a real sense, no one loses through increased cooperation built around career development themes.

Student Benefits

An exposure to the workaday world is valuable to students in that it can provide for several significant educational experiences which are not usually available through traditional classroom activities. First, observation, visitations, volunteer work, work-study arrangements and the like can provide a testing ground for trying out a career before the student commits valuable time to it. Second, the student can come to appreciate the dignity of many kinds of work and thereby gain a greater appreciation of other workers. Third, the student often experiences an increased motivation as he sees a relationship between academic coursework and possible lifetime careers. And fourth, the student may see that a career is not merely a means for earning a livelihood, but is life itself. Student benefits, then, primarily involve an opportunity to directly experience the consequences of various career decisions under controlled conditions.

School Benefits

Since the school is shaped and supported by the community, almost all efforts toward increased cooperation are beneficial to it. Placement and other career guidance activities can serve as the schools' outside window to the community. It can help the school function as a realistic and integral part of the community rather than as an isolated entity (possibly as an "ivory tower").

Ideally, the placement process serves as a student product evaluation for the school through a feedback mechanism. If demand is strong for the services of its graduates, the feedback signal to the institution may be positive and reinforcing. If there is little demand for the services of a school's graduates, this lack of interest of prospective employers should signal the need for certain modifications in the school program. The ultimate success of the job placement program can be partly measured by the success it has in providing its users with appropriate skills with which to serve the larger community. Thus, the placement program serves as the decisive pivotal point between the policy of the school and the needs of the community.

The school also benefits from placement and related programs through the community's increased interest in the school and its activities. While such benefits may lead to financial returns and some votes on a local bond issue, the psychological boost to both students and administrators can bring even more positive results.

Community Benefits

Finally, there are benefits to the larger community. First, the school, if attuned to the needs of the outer world, can help provide the immediate and larger community with workers who may prepare themselves to meet community needs. Conversely, a lack of knowledge concerning emerging careers can help lead to a shortage of workers in some categories and an oversupply in others. Second, if the student has a greater awareness of the various available career options, his broader perspective of the functions of the community may help to promote an increased sense of citizenship. And, third, cooperative programs can help reform the community by improving the quality of life at the work place;

by providing new encouragement for previously disenfranchised groups, e.g. Blacks, women, handicapped, veterans; and by involving sometimes isolated community agencies and groups in a total community activity.

POSSIBLE STRATEGIES

Now that the problems and benefits of community involvement in facilitating career development have been analyzed, the possible strategies for improved professional practice can be described.

Prerequisites

Assuming that a school has made a decision to develop community centered activities to facilitate career developments, certain basic resources are required to insure its success. The program activities described on the following pages would all require an adequately furnished office, especially a conference room; a reliable working staff composed of two or more professionals supported by a secretary and paraprofessionals or volunteers; numerous books and multi-media materials; local, regional, and national directories; and adequate funding to cover expenses. In the beginning stages a minimal working staff and limited budget could launch an effective pilot program if there was a long range plan and realistic outlook for a continued increase in support. A strong commitment to this type of program by the school administration is an essential precondition.

In many respects, the professional counselors and paraprofessionals involved in the program must be information specialists. (The creation and use of covert information described in Chapters 3 and 10 is relevant here.) The counselor needs to be in contact with key persons in the local and larger community who can provide accurate and up to date information. Specific information sought might include such facts as the number of persons employed in non-agricultural occupations, a three to five year projection of occupational needs for certain occupational categories, and the educational prerequisites for a particular job. In assisting students, the career or placement counselor will be concerned with job specifications, training requirements, conditions of work, and names of key persons in different employment areas.

As the school-community career development project grows from a pilot phase it is sometimes vital to designate a special counselor to assist employer groups. Responsibilities of this counselor include visiting job sites, observing and interviewing workers, conferring with personnel directors, reviewing selection procedures with management, etc.

Besides physical resources and a completed staff, the formation of an advisory committee is another prerequisite. Even the earliest planning activities must involve community members outside of professional education. The scope and function of an advisory committee should be carefully planned, and the report by the Cashmere Public Schools is an excellent reference (*Advisory Committee for Career Education,* 1973) .

While there are an unlimited number of strategies which might be effectively employed, this chapter analyzes five which have proven to be both reliable and effective: 1. placement services; 2. an occupational survey; 3. a resource directory; 4. alumni participation; and 5. career conferences.

Job Placement Service

Earlier sections of this chapter identified and described problems and issues associated with counselor involvement in job placement activities. The actual function and administration of a career placement center would be too lengthy to describe in this chapter, and excellent references are available on the subject. These include Burks, Pate and Simpson (1971) ; *Career Counseling and Placement Guides* (1972) ; *The Journal of College Placement;* Simpson and Harwood (1973) ; Stephens (1970) ; Tolbert, 1974; and other materials produced by The College Placement Council (P.O. Box 2263, Bethlehem, PA 18001). In addition, most basic guidance tests have at least one chapter on placement.

Perhaps some reconceptualization of the placement function along the lines identified earlier would be helpful to counselors and make such professional activity more palatable. It is suggested, therefore, that counselors view placement as a dynamic process by which individuals are helped at the ultimate, critical point in a career decision. Placement is also a key process in which a school becomes accountable to the larger community interest.

In helping individuals, placement can be more than simply helping one find a job. It can include brief, temporary placements in settings where the student learns first hand about work. Such placements could include: 1. "shadowing," where students spend time at the job site with the worker on the job, observing, and where possible, doing; 2. volunteer work, e.g. teacher aide, candy striper, etc.; and 3. cooperative education or work-study arrangements. In this sense, placement is a continuing process wherein the student is successively presented with opportunities to learn about work.

The notion of job development is also relevant here. This involves the counselor in working to change jobs as they are listed in order to make them available to more varied applicants. It involves becoming an advocate and persuading employers to meet special needs of persons seeking placement. Facilitating one's career development through dynamic placement is the goal.

Finally, placement and the related followup function provide a feedback loop in the school system for changing curriculum and other policies or procedures. Placement and follow-up activities can provide the career counselor with information which may be used to help change social institutions and to make them more humane and liberating.

Occupational Survey

Many communities derive benefits from the development of comprehensive local job information systems. There have been numerous resources for general career information, but much of it is rarely related to the local situation. A school-community effort in collecting and organizing local occupational information is a valuable resource for both the school and the employers of the area. In acquiring occupational information, resources could include school personnel, the state employment service, city and county offices, and the Chamber of Commerce among others. Such groups can often provide the leadership to accomplish such a survey. Several exemplary systems have been identified by Tolbert (1974) and Elder (1969).

Resource Directory

A key element in any effort to utilize community resources to promote career development is a referral or resource directory. Reports on the procedures used in creating a directory are available in the professional literature (Barbarosh, 1966; Powers, 1973; Vineyard and Brobst, 1962). While a particular directory should meet local needs, typical information would include the following for each occupation listed: 1. name, address, and phone of the referral contact; 2. employer; and 3. type of assistance available, e.g. willing to be interviewed by individuals and/or small groups, "shadowing," work-study, provision of free information materials, available for classroom presentations. The updating of such a complex information resource is probably best done through an automated data processing system.

Guidance personnel could meet with chamber of commerce groups, civic clubs, and school-community organizations in order to obtain support for this project. Local radio and television stations and newspapers may assist in informing the community of the purposes of the program. A news story may be run in the local newspaper encouraging prospective and willing employers to complete an application, furnishing their names, addresses, telephone numbers, job titles, and signatures. Many communities report unusual success following this procedure. No matter what techniques prove to be most workable, it is clear that much leg work, perhaps done with the help of volunteers and paraprofessionals, will be required to implement this project.

Alumni As Resources

The use of school alumni as resource persons is similar to the occupational survey and resource directory previously described, but is unique in that a more particular group of employers and workers are involved.

In utilizing alumni for help in career guidance, a time should be selected when alumni can meet either individually or in groups with interested students. It is important that the alumni have terminated their educations within the past five years and are presently employed in occupations in which the students are interested. Selected alumni should have been employed in their present jobs for at least one month. In order to appeal to a variety of student interests, representative groups of alumni might include those whose occupations require training beyond the high school level and also those whose occupations require no post secondary training. In group meetings, prospective resource persons would not be expected to make speeches since question and answer responses will probably best serve the purpose of the interface between student and alumnus. While there are several possible plans which may be used, the following system has been effective for group meetings.

(1) Design a standard set of questions for group conferences with employed alumni.

(2) Take this list to the group conferences of students and alumni.

(3) Arrange a time and place for the group conferences and bring the participants (students and alumni) together.

(4) Explain to those participating that the purpose of the meeting is to afford students an opportunity to learn about occupations in which they are interested. (The significant advantage to this system is that the student will gain first hand information from a person who is actively employed in a particular occupation and who was a student in the same school.)

(5) Circulate the previously prepared set of questions for student-alumni conferences to the students. Ask the students to study the list of questions and sort out those questions which interest them most and allow them to identify questions of special interest.

(6) Provide sufficient time for students to ask their questions. Finally, summarize the questions and comments covered

during the meeting, and note the need for follow-up contacts with individual students.

The following questions are taken from a list reported by Hoppock (1970).

(a) What school (s) did you attend?

(b) Did you graduate? When?

(c) What was your first job?
How did you get it?
What three things did you like most about it? Least?
How long were you there?
Why did you leave?

(d) Describe other previous jobs (same questions as above).

(e) Regarding your present job:
What time did you go to work this morning?
Describe your activities during a typical day.
Are the activities similar or varied over a week?
What is the usual starting salary?
Does your work affect your family life or general life style?

(f) What qualifications are needed for your job?
Age? Sex? Physical requirements?
License? Personal tools? Union membership?
Capital?

(g) Are there other important questions we should ask or you should ask us?

There are obvious benefits to this type of program, including a feeling among alumni that they can provide helpful information to younger people. The school, of course, can be helpful through improved support and employers can get early contacts with potential job applicants.

Career Conferences

Career conferences are designed to provide information which will enhance the student's planning related to both curriculum and vocational goals. Students need an opportunity to compare careers, and a conference can provide the opportunity for numerous comparisons in a single setting and in a relatively short period of time. As students proceed through the career conference it is desirable to encourage them to inquire about career options to which they had not previously given serious consideration. This procedure may assure an exploration of many occupational possibilities of which students may not be aware.

PLANNING A steering committee, composed of representatives from school, business, industry, and government, decides on the scope of the proposed conference. Special effort is exerted to insure a proper balance in the various employment fields. Key employer categories include social action agencies, government, civic, business-industry, and religious organizations. It is important not to exclude labor, professional groups, and state employment agencies. The conference may be aimed at a target group or it may be open to interested students regardless of age or interest.

A comprehensive career conference requires the presence of employer representatives who are able to advise and counsel students concerning current employment trends and long range outlooks within their respective fields. If the particular location does not provide a favorable balance of industry and government, the counselor can contact the nearest U.S. Civil Service Inter-Agency Board. Professional staff members of the Board are especially prepared to assist in career conferences and they may provide a broad expertise regarding various federal careers. The local bar association, medical association, and other similar organizations probably can be expected to be helpful in seeking a balance among employer representatives.

Students should be encouraged to become actively involved in the planning and implementation of the program in order to assure more active participation and a larger attendance. For instance, one might involve the student government organization in arranging the physical setting of the conference, or ask the student newspaper to provide for publicity and public relations aspects of the conference. School clubs and organizations could be invited to provide other conference related services.

Selecting a date for the career conference is most important. Avoid dates which fall on or near local, regional, or national holidays. Likewise, Mondays and Fridays are less desirable, because out-of-town resource people generally do not like weekend travel.

Invitations to the conference should be extended approximately two to three months before the announced date, and reminders sent at a couple of intervals.

It is desirable to designate a variety of subcommittees for special conference related projects. One subcommittee could be named to promote the event. Faculty, students, and employers having the expertise in the techniques of advertising and public relations can be asked to serve on this committee. Broad coverage, both in advance publicity and news stories relating to the conference activities, are highly desirable. A second subcommittee may be asked to arrange the physical layout. This is no small assignment. Chairs, tables, special lighting, overhead signs for each occupation represented, public address system, wide aisles and walkways, and other props must be arranged in advance. A third committee may be designated to identify hosts and hostesses for the event. These guide persons can prove of great benefit to the success of the event by assuring that all requests for direction and special assistance are appropriately handled. A fourth committee may be used to design and produce signs and other directional materials for the conference. Additionally, a scale model of the entire conference lay-out would facilitate a more orderly traffic pattern. An alphabetical listing of occupational titles with a notation regarding location of each occupational exhibit on the floor plan is very helpful. A fifth committee could provide security to protect persons and property involved in the conference. A special three to five day insurance policy should be purchased to cover liability for personal damage and loss of exhibitor materials.

An orientation session for employers is desirable to achieve an understanding of how they can best respond to student inquiries. It is especially important not to assume employers will accurately anticipate the total scope of student response, or be able to properly respond to their questions or concerns regarding various career opportunities.

The format of the career conference may involve many employer exhibitions in a large convention hall or school gymnasium where students, parents and others are at liberty to "shop around" among those exhibits which interest them. Another possibility may involve five to ten employers presenting workshops or mini-seminars regarding various careers or a combination of each.

EVALUATION An evaluation questionnaire should be submitted to each participating employer and random questionnaires given to students. The questionnaire will provide an effective tool for evaluation of the conference and prove beneficial for subsequent conference planning. Career conferences can produce positive results in these ways: 1. increasing interface and coordination between school and the employment community; 2. increasing student and faculty awareness of the employment world; 3. increasing awareness to many school subjects because careers can be related to most things students learn in school; and 4. increasing employer awareness of student interest in various career categories. It is of interest to note that student requests for career-vocational information usually show a marked increase following well-planned conferences.

The steering committee, after evaluating the questionaires, may seek answers to these and other questions:

1. What did the career conference achieve?
2. Were the career resource speakers all satisfactory?
3. Which career areas were the most popular?
4. What educational-vocational guidance needs were highlighted by the conference?
5. What peculiar educational and vocational problems of the school and community were identified?

The career conference has been shown to be an effective means of stimulating student interest in career planning and involving the community in career development activities. Further information can be obtained from Cimino (1973).

SUMMARY

The task of the career counselor can no longer be confined to an office. Successfully promoting career development depends upon a knowledge of the needs of the student and the world of work. Career counselors must come to view themselves as community resource brokers who can use an extensive variety of people and situations to facilitate a person's career development.

Such an activist counselor will seek to build a greater working relationship between the school and the community whereby each helps and serves the other. With a minimal budget, a limited staff may begin a career oriented program in which the school and community can become more interrelated. This chapter briefly described five strategies in which a counselor could identify and use community resources. They were 1. a job placement service, 2. a local job survey, 3. a resource directory, 4. alumni as resources, and 5. career conferences.

BIBLIOGRAPHY

Activity. Predict changes in counseling "demands". May, 1974, Vol. *12* (3), p. 5. Iowa City, Iowa: American College Testing Program.

Advisory Committee for Career Education. Cashmere, WA.: Career Education Project, 1973.

Barbarosh, B. Developing a community vocational resource directory. *Vocational Guidance Quarterly,* 1966, *14,* 179.

Burks, H., Pate, R., and Simpson, L. Preparing counselors for the college placement service: a training manual. Report of a demonstration project to the ESSO Education Foundation, Charlottesville, VA., Nov., 1971.

Career Counseling and Placement Guides. Bethlehem, PA.: The College Placement Council, 1972.

Career Education News, January 1, 1974, Vol. *3* (1), p. 4. Chicago: McGraw-Hill.

Cimino, E.R. Steps to success with your career fair. *Journal of College Placement,* 1973, *33,* 59-63.

Elder, L.A. An inservice community occupational survey. *Vocational Guidance Quarterly,* 1969, *17,* 185-188.

Farson, R.E. The counselor is a woman. *Journal of Counseling Psychology,* 1954, *1,* 221-223.

Guidepost. Business and counseling meet. May 17, 1974, Vol. 16 *(7),* p. 6. Washington, D.C.: American Personnel and Guidance Association. (a)

Guidepost. Counselor successful with career education program. May 17, 1974, Vol. *61* (7), p. 5. Washington, D.C.: American Personnel and Guidance Association. (b)

Holland, J. Some practical remedies for providing vocational guidance for everyone. Report No. 160. Baltimore, MD.: Center for Social Organization of Schools, The Johns Hopkin's University, 1973.

Hoppock, R. How to conduct an occupational group conference with an alumnus. *Vocational Guidance Quarterly,* 1970, *18,* 311-312.

Newsweek. Blue-collar blues? April 29, 1974, p. 90.

Powers, K. People in careers: a resource directory. *Career Digest,* 1973, *5,* 2.

Simpson, L.A. and Harwood, R.K. Placement: From employment bureau to career development center. *National Association of Student Personnel Administrators Journal,* 1973, *10,* 225-230.

Sorensen, T. Do Americans like their jobs? *Parade,* June 3, 1973, pp. 14-16.

Stephens, E.W. *Career Counseling and Placement in Higher Education: A Student Personnel Function.* Bethlehem, PA.: The College Placement Council, 1970.

Stephens, W.R. *Social Reform and the Origins of Vocational Guidance.* Washington, D.C.: National Vocational Guidance Association, 1970.

Tolbert, E.L. *Counseling for Career Development.* Boston: Houghton-Mifflin, 1974.

Vineyard, E.E. and Brobst, H.K. Vocational interviews by lay resource persons. *Vocational Guidance Quarterly,* 1962, *10,* 35-36.

Work in America. Cambridge, Mass.: M.I.T. Press, 1973.

```
┌─────────────────────────────────────────────┐
│                                             │
│              Chapter Twelve                 │
│                                             │
│     CAREER DEVELOPMENT FOR WOMEN            │
│                                             │
│            MARY QUINN BURKHART               │
│                                             │
│                                             │
└─────────────────────────────────────────────┘
```

A T THE PRESENT TIME, most counseling programs are delivered basically in the same manner for all members of society; there usually is no differentiation made between the sexes in a conscious, organized response to the unique needs of each group. Many counselors may question the need for any separate programs, and may indeed feel that to have different kinds of programs might be discriminatory. It is true that such programs could prove to be discriminatory if so conceptualized. However, denying that the process of career decision-making is a particularly complex one for women is to deny women the support and information they need to develop to their greatest potential. The purpose of this chapter is to bring to the attention of counselors and counselors-in-training the problems women have in developing career identities, and the particular areas which should be of special interest for those who counsel women in career decision-making.

The special needs of women in career planning and career development are covered in four sections of this chapter. The first discusses the scope of the problem, previous research on career decision-making and development, the socialization process from early childhood through the adult years, and the role conflicts women suffer when attempting to make and stand by career decisions. A second section reviews the inadequacy of traditional approaches, with references to counselor biases, the lack of role models, problems in using a popular interest inventory, and the limitations of counseling on an individual basis. The third and fourth sections deal with what ideal programs in career development could include and what has been done in three representative college-level situations.

SCOPE OF THE PROBLEM

Previous Research on Career Decision-Making and Development

A number of research studies have been conducted which give evidence of the fact that women have more trouble than men of the same age in deciding who they are vocationally (Madison, 1969; Katz, et al., 1968; Katz, et al., 1969; Bardwick, 1971; Burkhart, 1973). Boys begin to define themselves in relation to some planned future vocational goal very early. In contrast, girls less often think about careers and often see the role of homemaker as their primary option (Madison, 1969).

Very often, women define their lives in relation to the men near to them instead of on the basis of their own identities. This conception is perpetrated by our social system. For example, in a vocational interest inventory frequently used by high school and college counselors (*Strong Vocational Interest Blank,* 1969) girls are asked if they would rather be the wives of farmers or the wives of executives. While the occupation of a spouse usually influences the style of life led by a couple, it is inappropriate to ask such a question in an inventory about the girl's own vocational interests.

Girls are often taught to see their high school, college and working careers as vehicles for finding a man (Katz, 1969), not as valuable experiences in and of themselves which should be used to aid them in making a career decision. Changing attitudes such as these can best be done by preventing such attitudes from developing in the first place. In the case that this cannot be done, counselors can have profound effects on young women by exposing them to new ideas, more information and additional alternatives.

Osipow (1968) stated that differences in patterns of vocational development occur for psychological and biological reasons. Using Super's developmental scheme, he compared the vocational decision-making behavior of men to women by stages. For the Tentative period, he found that girls' behaviors were not very different from those of boys of the same ages (11-15). All were making choices based almost entirely upon interests. Both groups remained similar in their change to more concern about abilities as they matured. The first significantly noticeable difference between the sexes showed in the Capacity Stage. Girls of 17 were much more heavily oriented toward marriage and homemaking. Boys were becoming much more concerned about making sound vocational choices based on their interests, abilities, and ideas about work.

The Socialization Process

Early Childhood

From the earliest days of a woman's life, she has been treated differently than men. Even as an infant, the emphasis for a female child is an attractive appearance and pleasant manner. Harmon (1970) found that by age two, little girls are less likely to engage in independent exploration and more likely to call for their mothers. This kind of early differentiation in behavior is due to different expectations of parents. Boys are encouraged to be competitive, independent, physically active and aggressive; girls are encouraged to behave in the opposite manner (Barry, Bacon, and Child, 1957; Sears, Maccoby, and Levin, 1957).

Female children, when asked what they want to be when they grow up frequently answer "A mother." Very few boys of the same age will answer that they want to be a father. Boys are not socialized to view parenthood either as their only adult role nor as a full time occupation. Girls are rarely given mechanical or manipulative toys with which they might develop their ideas of adult, non-housework tastes. The differences in the toys given children—trucks, guns, chemistry sets and other scientific equipment for boys, nurses kits, dolls, and toy stoves for girls—suggest the kinds of interests they should have (Bem and Bem, 1970).

Children's literature (Weitzman, et al., 1972) presents a very biased view of women. Little girls in these books model dependent, passive behaviors. Adult women are rarely shown in work situations outside the home. A woman growing up in our society has had very few exposures to role models of adult women in stimulating, responsible jobs. It is, therefore, often difficult for a woman to think of herself in such a situation.

High School and College

By the time women reach high school and college, their expectations of themselves as individuals and potential workers may have been severely limited by the socialization process. The counselor who does not take extra steps will be limiting these women by an act of omission.

Religious doctrine, Christian, Jewish and Moslem alike, states and restates the proposition that women are less than men, subservient or inferior to men (Bem and Bem, 1970). These teachings permeate every area of society. Another kind of doctrine stated by Bem and Bem is the myth of free will in choice of life style. An idea that an adult woman has the freedom to choose whatever she wants to do is a myth when the kind of training given her for the first part of her life is reviewed. It is not so much that women are denied the right to choose a variety of careers as they are trained not to *want* very many of the ones available.

Young women are often treated in a different manner than young men by their parents, teachers, professors, and counselors. Parents of girls may encourage and reward so-called feminine behavior: quietness, dependency, interest in domestic activity, passivity. Boys, on the other hand, are generally rewarded for exploratory behavior, aggression, independence, interest in physical activities, interest in mechanical toys. The behavior rewarded in girls may make for a good student in the sense that the pupil is quiet, neat and undemanding, but rewarding such behavior is not likely to encourage and facilitate the growth of a creative and serious scholar. Neither is it likely to help a girl develop those skills which she can use to succeed in the working world.

Role Conflicts and Confusion

Girls and young women often have a more difficult and complex process of decision-making because they often do not feel they have the ability to make decisions until they know what variables will be present. Ginzberg (1966), in the book *Life Styles of Educated Women,* points out that women sometimes do not feel they can make any decisions about their vocational futures until they know the man they will marry and have some understanding of the form the marriage relationship will take.

Research studies seem to indicate that the task of developing an identity is more complex for women. Madison (1969) states that a woman may define herself in terms of her boyfriend and marriage plans, while a male college student defines his identity in relation to what he does while in college and what he plans to do as an occupation when he completes his education. Katz, et al., (1969) also found that for women the greatest energy is spent not in trying to decide what they themselves are or want to do, but with finding their potential marriage partners. Even those women who are more oriented to careers choose traditionally feminine careers.

Most young women will say they plan to work full time before they are married, or until they have children (Katz, et al., 1969). Few, however, plan to work while they have young children at home. Since most women do think they will marry and bear children, it means that women, in making career decisions, have to plan on some period of interruption.

There are a number of factors which seem to contribute to problems in the amount of information women have on which to base their career plans. First, women are not adequately exposed to the idea of women working. As stated earlier (Weitzman, et al., 1972), children's literature rarely shows women in occupations other than full-time mother, teacher, or nurse, all traditional fields for women.

Second, women themselves limit their thinking about careers since they have the perception that men are threatened by intelligent women (Matthews, 1960; Matthews and Tiedeman, 1964; Horner, 1969). Others will not consider occupations which they feel are incompatible with marriage and family concerns (Matthews, 1960). They may not have any evidence that these areas are in fact incompatible with marriage and family; it is rather that these have traditionally been viewed in such a manner.

A third reason for the lack of information given to women about careers is that those people who give out information about careers (counselors, teachers, parents, peers) are themselves often biased or uninformed. Those who are biased may, either consciously or unconsciously, withhold information on areas which they feel are inappropriate or not suitable for their female clients. Those who are uninformed will obviously not be able to encourage women to explore the career options in depth. For example, a counselor cannot successfully prepare a girl for a college program in engineering if he or she does not know the course requirements and skills needed.

In many cases, women students have conflicting desires. As stated earlier, women may fear that men will find them unattractive if they are successful in careers (Hawley, 1971). Often, the options are seen as mutually exclusive: either a home and a family or a career. Statistics show that this is rarely the case. Most women will marry; most will also work at some time in their lives. Women who plan to have careers and families must deal with the difficulties of combining two activities comfortably. Counselors need to be aware of areas of concern such as these and be willing to discuss them, possibly assisting students in working out life plans incorporating these areas.

Bright young women are often torn between two desires: either to succeed and accomplish to the best of their abilities, or to be popular and well-accepted by their peers and men. They fear both failure and success (Horner, 1969).

INADEQUACY OF TRADITIONAL APPROACHES

Women have special needs for help and guidance from counselors. Astin and Panos (1969), for example, found that sex was one of the best predicators of final career choice. In the past, people could guess at birth that most girls would grow up to be housewives. Hopefully, this has changed. Almost all young women today will work at some time in their lives (Astin, 1968). More than 60 percent of working women are married (Astin, 1967). Women with young children are working more often than ever before (Bird, 1970), with 26 percent of the mothers of preschool children working outside the home.

However, there remain many problems with the kinds of jobs women obtain. Generally, they are not encouraged to develop all their potentialities nor to use their talents. Some women find themselves leading quiet but vaguely unsatisfying lives as a result of having been guided by tradition and socialization into mindless routines. These do not challenge their intelligence and their sense of the power of their abilities is diminished (Drews, 1965). Even if the women who work do find their jobs satisfying, they may have many other demands on them. For example, the working mother is expected to keep her home and raise her children without slighting her domestic duties; perform her out-of-the-home job; and continue to remain pleasant in appearance and disposition (Lundberg and Farnham, 1947).

Counselor Bias

Counselors, being human, have opinions about how the world should be ordered. If a counselor feels the primary purpose in a woman's life is to be a wife and mother, he or she is not likely to encourage the woman student to select a demanding career. If a counselor feels that women are best at certain jobs and shouldn't go into others, it is probably the accepted areas which will be given the most attention by the counselor. Pietrofesa and Schlossberg (1970) found that counselors in training showed definite biases when talking to a female client about the options for entering an area traditionally thought to be masculine and one traditionally thought to be feminine. Counselors of both sexes reported women clients who had expressed unusual or non-traditional career interests to be more in need of counseling (Thomas and Stewart, 1971). These findings, in view of the research on the inculcation of the value systems of counselor to client (Rosenthal, 1955; Welkowitz, Cohen, and Ortmeyer, 1967), point to serious problems in career counseling for women.

Another pervasive bias in our society is one shared primarily by psychologists, psychiatrists, social workers, and other counselors: the definition of a healthy, well-adjusted man is in fact, very close to that of a healthy, well-adjusted *person,* while the definition of a healthy, well-adjusted woman turns out to look not very healthy at all (Broverman, et al., 1970). Women are viewed as over-emotional, inferior, emasculating, and dependent by most currently popular personality theories. Some theories state that assertion in women is a neurotic striving to become male, others that assertive behavior is not a natural characteristic of the female personality (Barrett, et al., 1974).

Lack of Role Models

Women often see the idea of having a career as unfeminine (Horner, 1969). The career role may be seen as being in conflict with or different than that of being a woman. In a study of attitudes of married working women, Baruch, Segal, and Handreck (1967) found that the subjects identified with men and showed their working problems in a way similar to men. These conflicts and misperceptions could be alleviated by having more role models. If young women were able to see that successful working women are not necessarily unfeminine "old-maids" or hardened characters, they might be able to see the ways in which other women have ordered their lives, and their relative satisfaction with those life styles, they may be able to make more satisfying choices for themselves.

Bias In An Interest Inventory

The *Strong Vocational Interest Blank* (Strong, 1966) is an interest inventory used frequently in counseling high school and college students about careers. At the present time, the *SVIB* has separate booklets for men and women. Each asks different questions and yield some occupational categories and basic interest scores which are different. The test for women has more occupations such as sewing machine operator, nurse and a variety of teaching areas but does not have veterinarian, architect, or public administrator. The men's form also has certain occupations not listed on the women's form but does not include some that are. The questions asked to derive these scales are very different for women. Many seem to reflect the belief that a woman to a great extent defines herself in relation to the occupation of her husband. This is a weakness of the test and should be taken into account when counseling women on the results it returns. The *SVIB* is currently being revised and the forms for both sexes are being combined. It is highly recommended that counselors use the new combined form as soon as it is available.

Limitations of Individual Counseling

In an individual counseling session, one counselor and one client interact. As stated previously, counselors do have biases about how women should act or about what kinds of roles are appropriate for them. In the one-to-one situation, the woman counselee may feel she is peculiar or unreasonable if her decisions or interests differ radically from those the counselor feels are best for her. The woman facing career decisions alone may feel she is the only one having difficulties, the only one who feels confused or unsure of her options.

Most counselors have extremely high case loads and are not able to spend as much time assisting individual women in career exploration as might be desirable. Constraints on resources forbid a comprehensive program for each counselee.

A way to alleviate some of the impact of the possible intentional or unintentional bias of a counselor, the time and the resource constraints, and the feelings of aloneness that many women have is to offer group counseling sessions or a career planning class.

BASIC CHARACTERISTICS OR ASSUMPTIONS OF AN OPTIMUM PROGRAM

A sensitive, informed counselor can have a profound and positive impact on the future of a young woman. Counselors in the public schools have an excellent opportunity to reach young women at the time in which the sexes begin to differ in expectations and planning (Osipow, 1968). It is at the time when girls are changing and beginning to react to the socialization process by narrowing their options that they are also having to make important decisions about their futures: what courses to take in high school; whether or not to continue education beyond high school; and, if so, where to go and what to study.

Douvan and Gold (1966) found that boys and girls differ in the relative importance they place on making vocational plans. Boys are more likely to feel that job preparation and job choice are extremely important than are girls. This difference is probably a result of a mistaken idea that few women will work except as a stop-gap before marriage or raising a family.

Women need to be exposed to non-traditional ideas about careers and life-styles. This is not to say that every woman should make a nontraditional life-style, but that the exposure will make them aware of the options available. Women in particular have felt that their sex alone was a very important determinant of which occupational areas were open to them. The sensitive concerned counselor usually wants all of his or her clients to realize their fullest potential and find the life-style which is most likely to continue the process of growth and satisfaction. By limiting women to certain restricted career choices, one large segment of their clientele is, therefore, less likely to be able to develop fully.

Counselors need to expose their women clients to more information about career options. Many students have a limited perspective about the alternatives available to them. Far too often, the girl who is good in science and likes working with people decides, perhaps as a result of outside pressure, to be a nurse. An introduction to other health related careers such as being a physician, a dentist, an optometrist, a physical therapist, an occupational therapist, etc. could give her more resources for choosing a training area better suited to her individual talents.

In order to present such information to students about the variety of careers available in any given area, the counselor has to take responsibility to be both personally informed and to be aware of personal prejudices which might color perceptions of what information should be given.

Many counselors agree there are certain strategies for helping women develop their potentialities. Two major goals to be included in any career development program are: 1. to increase and optimize self-understanding; and 2. to expand awareness of the career and life-style options available.

Self-Understanding

A program designed to facilitate self-understanding and self-awareness needs to include exploration of interests, abilities, and values.

Women in particular have been taught they should be interested in and adept at only certain skills and careers (Barry, Bacon, and Child, 1957; Sears, Maccoby, and Levin, 1957; Bem and Bem, 1970; Birk, Cooper, and Tanney, 1973; Bem and Bem, 1974). Women have also been taught what kinds of work and which life-styles they should value (Bem and Bem, 1970). Therefore, extra attention needs to be focused on how women are able to determine their interests, abilities and values.

Interests

Vocational interest inventories may be helpful in encouraging assessment of interests. Two vocational interest inventories used frequently for high school and college women are the *Strong Vocational Interest Blank* (Strong, 1966) and Holland's *Self-Directed Search* (Holland, 1970). As mentioned earlier, the *SVIB* has separate booklets with different kinds of questions and different occupational categories for men and women. This inventory is in the process of being revised and will be combined into one booklet for both sexes. Holland's *SDS* does not have separate categories, forms, or scales for the sexes. Men and women would derive the same three letter code and its resulting job titles if they had the same interests and competencies. However, in our society, men and women have been socialized to have different skills. This should be explored with women when discussing the results of the inventory. An immediate caution in using any standardized instrument is to screen out those tests which are based on sexual stereotypes, or at least be aware of their presence and explain the implications of them to users. Taking the warning into account, interest inventories may still be very useful in stimulating discussion or further exploration into different career areas (see Chapter 4).

Using existing games or worksheets, or developing and using games or role playing situations which fit the unique needs of a specific group can be useful. A typical worksheet would include statements or questions designed to stimulate discussion or questions. For example, questions relating to type of work enjoyed—working alone or with people, with supervision or without. Depending on the population, questions can be as varied as the problems facing the group. For high school women, questions about combining marriage and career, career and motherhood are appropriate. Since many people have strong opinions about mother-child relationships, these could be included.

One example of a worksheet for discussion with college women asks such questions as "I would have a great deal of difficulty changing diapers, scrubbing floors, twenty-four hours a day;" "I expect to move to a geographical area where my future husband's work takes us;" "I believe in quitting my career when I have a child;" "It is important to me to be self-supporting" (Bartsch, Frisbey, and Scott, 1973). Women indicate that they agree, disagree, or don't know how they feel about the questions. This type of stimulation may be used in counseling, in group discussions, in training groups, or in classes on career development.

Games can be very helpful in career development programs. Games such as "Be Married" (*Impact*, 1972) ask women to deal with profiles of life situations or hypothetical stresses. Some particularly useful aspects of games are: (1) they remove the student from the immediate situation and cause her to think about areas which may come up (this added perspective is frequently important for a woman who has not yet begun to think about her future); (2) they can also be a way to practice or try out various behaviors or styles; and (3) they can stimulate women to think about how they can order their lives, make their career decisions, in order to avoid situations similar to those in the games or to facilitate the ones they desire (see Chapter 5).

Aptitudes

The matter of abilities is a very important topic to discuss in career development counseling. For the woman student to be truly open to exploration of her options and potentials, she must have done a realistic (neither inflated nor underestimated) assessment of her abilities: academic, physical, social, or interpersonal. Women are likely to have *unrealistic* ideas about their abilities due to their perceptions of how they should act (Horner, 1969; Hawley, 1971). An excellent way to help a woman determine her abilities is to review in a group past successes and accomplishments, past failures, and difficult areas. Past experiences, especially when viewed objectively to see if they are indeed valid indicators of talent, can be very useful. Motivation and desire to succeed are probably the best predicators of future successes.

Aptitude testing, whether for a specific ability such as numerical or mechanical ability, or for a more general area, such as scholastic aptitude, can be useful if interpreted very carefully.

Values

Most women need information and guidance in clearing up the dilemma presented in choosing a career and making decisions about marriage and children. Our society has persuaded women into thinking that they should value a home, husband, and children above all (Bem and Bem, 1970). Those who have other desires or wish to combine a number of activities need a vehicle for exploring alternatives. Consciousness-raising groups in which women help each other think through the areas of concern are useful. Worksheets such as those developed by Amatea (1972) and Bartsch, Frisbey, and Scott (1973) are excellent.

Women also need to be aware of the prejudices existing in society: the difficulties they may have in implementing their choices of life-styles. This understanding is best built on an awareness of the socialization process that has shaped them into what they are at present. The purpose in knowing the problems which may be in store for them in the future is to encourage them to prepare to deal with them. The idea is not to discourage a woman about going into a field because she will meet with a great deal of resistance, but to counsel her so she is aware of the possibilities and can prepare to deal with them.

Awareness of Options

One of the counselor's most important functions can be to encourage women students to look into a variety of options, to help them develop a career plan which meets their immediate needs and gives them the flexibility for the future which is vital in a rapidly changing society. Exposure to information about career areas, career options, and people working in careers is vital. Career planning courses, in which literature about the total range of jobs available in any career area is explained, can encourage more individual choices and plans. For example, many women are aware of only a few of the dozens of job categories in the health sciences. Workshops in which women are exposed to a number of adult role models are productive. Also important is access to a career information library.

Both counselors and clients need to be aware of the range of options open to women. Exploration of non-traditional careers for women as well as the old standbys of nurse, teacher, and secretary is necessary.

DESCRIPTIONS OF STRATEGIES

In this section, some general ideas about what strategies may be used for facilitating a woman's career development will be outlined, with three specific program illustrations following.

General Delivery Systems

Women's Studies Programs

Women's Studies Programs are excellent settings for classes, seminars, and/or discussion groups for women about careers. The topics of career choice, career planning, or life-style planning can be separate classes or incorporated into appropriately related ones. For example, classes on women in psychology, women in society, women in medicine can be the settings for discussions about the careers involved in these areas and the problems and satisfactions of working in these areas.

Courses

Courses on the career development of women may be part of the regular curriculum. Such a course in general career decision-making offered in the College of Arts and Sciences, for example, may have a special unit devoted to the specific problems women have vocationally (see Chapter 9).

Women's Centers

Many high schools and colleges now have Women's Centers. From such a center, or from the Counseling Center, may come groups or classes which relate to women. Two kinds of groups that are particularly appropriate to career planning are assertion training and consciousness raising. Assertion training for women deals with the ability of women to stand up for their legitimate rights, while not violating the rights of others (Jakubowski-Spector, 1973). Most women have been trained to be non-assertive (passive, imposed upon, unexpressive of feelings in an open manner). Non-assertive behaviors do not help a woman "get ahead" in the world of work. Aggressive behavior (behaviors which result in the rights of others being violated) are also not productive. Jakubowski-Spector has developed a series of films and a training manual (available through the American Personnel and Guidance Association) which are appropriate for high school and college assertion training groups.

Conscious-raising may be helpful in encouraging career development if the groups and agendas for the groups are organized around the concerns women have for themselves in their roles as workers. Many women have a great deal of difficulty comfortably combining their roles as ambitious, self-actualizing people and as wives, mothers, or partners. As a result of the women's movement, a more open society, and a more open educational system, women are beginning to see their rights as people and this conflicts with traditional expectations. Participation in a supportive, concerned group may help the women deal with these conflicts, to see them as results of a changing society, and not as a personal inadequacy.

Career Planning and Placement Center or Guidance Offices

Career Planning and Placement Centers or Guidance Offices can take the initiative in exposing young women to adult women already in jobs. One manner in which this may be done is to have career days featuring women who are working in non-traditional areas. A good way to put on such a program is to contact professional women's organizations, professional organizations, local schools, universities and training programs, and ask for individuals who might assist. Students need to have adult role models who can advise them on the difficulties and rewards of particular careers and combinations of roles.

Examples of Specific Strategies

Three career development programs for women are outlined in this section. Many high schools, community colleges, and universities have career counseling programs for women but these are not discussed here. Some extremely innovative and exciting courses are being offered now for the mature or second career woman. These are not specifically appropriate here, but for those wishing more information on such courses, the following pamphlet is a starting point: *Continuing Education Programs and Services for Women,* Women's Bureau, Superintendent of Documents, U.S. Government Printing Office, Washington, D.C., stock number 2902-0052 ($.70).

Many other institutions have career counseling programs, which although not geared specifically to the needs of women students, may be adequate to meet these needs. These specific programs are presented to give ideas about what kinds of things may be done.

PENNSYLVANIA STATE UNIVERSITY: The Career Development and Placement Center at Pennsylvania State University has described a program of career counseling with elements designed specifically for women. The outreach program included a values clarification seminar called Choices for Women (Bartsch, et al., 1973). Women students were given a worksheet with statements about lifestyles and asked to react to them. The first segment of a two-part video tape was then shown. In the twenty-three minute segment, seven women, of differing life-styles and points of view who were all college graduates, talked of how they were integrating their lives and careers. After viewing the video tape, students wrote a paragraph on the same topic, having been asked to imagine they were on a similar panel. Then the second thirty minute segment of the video tape was played. In this part, the same panelists discussed and clarified with each other their earlier statements. Following the video tape, the students participated in a discussion about their reactions. Student comments following the seminar were that it helped them realize the kinds of problems they might face, that others have similar concerns, and that they had a better idea about how they felt about these questions after having verbalized them.

Birk and Tanney: Birk and Tanney (1973) have developed a model for a career exploration program for high school women. The authors' stated that their purpose in developing the model was to try to *prevent* many of the problems women would face in later life if they were not prepared to deal with the multiple roles they will probably have.

The program was in workshop form, three one-hour sessions. The purposes were to encourage the participants to think about the problems which exist in society regarding women's roles; the options they had in defining their own roles; and personal attitudes they had which would hinder them in their role development.

In the first session, the women were instructed to group themselves under a placard on the wall which was closest to what they expected to be doing in five years. The placards had job titles which were both traditional female jobs, such as teacher and nurse, and those typically non-female, such as electrician and college professor. After grouping, each woman explained why she had chosen that job title. Then the women discussed which placards had few people grouped under them, which had many, and why.

In the second part of the first session, the women were asked to complete an Opinionaire of questions as "women are absent from the labor force more than men. . . " (Birk and Tanney, 1973, p. 19). After these were completed, the responses were scored. Then, the statistical reality of the statement was discussed and the participants were given a summary sheet.

In the second session, the women were divided into small groups and asked to participate in a fantasy based on hypothetical situations given them. After completing the fantasy, they discussed with the entire group what they had come up with and why.

Next, the participants were divided into groups of three and instructed to take one of three roles, speaker, receiver, or observer. The speaker reacted to the receiver, telling her about what kind of non-traditional career she would be imagined in and why. The receiver responded to this while the observer coordinated and clarified the interaction. The participants then switched roles. When all three members had each role, they reported their reactions to the larger group.

In the third session, the students had role playing explained to them and were asked to volunteer to play roles. These roles were ones about a woman dealing with problems in her work, discussing career decisions with her family and others. Discussion followed the role playing situation.

All participants were asked to fill out an evaluation form. The purpose of the assessment was to measure informally the reactions of the students to the program and to determine what new information was learned. The students generally rated the experience as very positive.

CALIFORNIA STATE UNIVERSITY, SAN DIEGO: Ramsey (1973) at the Career Planning and Placement Center of California State University, San Diego developed a program to meet the career exploration needs of women on the campus. She worked in the planning of three career courses sponsored by the School of Education. Some of the classes were designed for women only. The goals stated for the classes was that the women would develop some understanding of their interests and talents, while also becoming aware of the forces in the social system which had shaped their personalities. A particular concern was that women would be given enough information and encouragement so that they would not self-select out of certain areas through unfamiliarity.

The class was offered for course credit and met for an entire semester. The first meetings were devoted to discussions in dyads about expectations and needs, films on the socialization of women, and career fantasies. Sessions in the middle of the term covered such topics as myths and realities about women as workers, the administration and interpretation of interest inventories and work values inventories, and career information presented in panel discussions, literature, and discussion groups. The last sessions were devoted to determining the unmet needs and dealing with those, hearing about the results of projects of career exploration, and evaluations of the course.

Ramsey recommended that larger groups of students, with one coordinator and several other facilitators, be used whenever possible. In this manner, the students can have more exposure and more variety. Another comment of particular interest was that she felt it is extremely important that the class leaders participate in the activities and assignments of the class—it is important that leaders do not present themselves as having been liberated and the women in the class not liberated.

SUMMARY

Programs designed specifically to meet the career development needs of women are long overdue. The problems faced by women in planning their lives are myriad and unique. Of particular concern are the conflicts of roles, the expectations of society which limit them, and their expectation of themselves which may also limit their options. Counselors need to be well informed of the areas which give the most difficulty to women in planning their lives. Counselors need to assume the responsibility for making the information necessary for good decision-making available to women students and encourage them to explore non-traditional life-styles and careers when appropriate.

The manner in which career development programs can be implemented are as many as the groups of women needing them. In some situations, workshops using exercises, media presentation and/or discussions may be the best methods. In other cases, programs designed to be on-going within the institution may be more suitable to the needs of the women participating.

BIBLIOGRAPHY

Amatea, E.S. A study of the effects of a career planning program for college women. Unpublished doctoral dissertation, The Florida State University, 1972.

Astin, H.S. Factors associated with the participation of women doctorates in the labor force. *Personnel and Guidance Journal*, 1967, *46*, 240-246.

Astin, H.S. Stability and change in the career plans of 9th grade girls. *Personnel and Guidance Journal*, 1968, *46*, 961-966.

Astin, H.S., and Panos, R.J. *The Educational and Vocational Development of College Students*. Washington, D.C.: American Council on Education, 1969.

Bardwick, J.M. *Psychology of Women: A Study of Bio-cultural Conflicts.* New York: Harper & Row, 1971.

Barrett, C.J., Berg, P.I., Eaton, E.M., and Pomeroy, E.L. Implications of women's liberation for the future of psychotherapy. *Psychotherapy: Theory, Research, and Practice,* 1974, *11,* 11-15.

Barry, H., III, Bacon, M.K., and Child, I.L. A cross-cultural survey of some sex differences in socialization. *Journal of Abnormal Psychology,* 1957, *55,* 327-332.

Bartsch, K., Frisbey, N., and Scott, G.J. An outreach program in career planning. Paper presented at American College Personnel Association convention, Cleveland, Ohio, April 1973.

Baruch, R., Segal, S., and Handrick, F. Career and family: Variation on a theme. Harvard Studies in Career Development, No. 52. Cambridge, Massachusetts: Harvard University, 1967.

Bern, S.L., and Bern, D.J. Case study of an unconscious ideology: Training the woman to know her place. In Bern, D.J. (Ed.), *Beliefs, Attitudes, and Human Affairs.* Belmont, California: Brooks/Cole, 1970.

Bern, S.L., and Bern, D.J. Training the woman to know her place: The social antecedents of woman in the world of work. Harrisburg, Pennsylvania: Pennsylvania Department of Education, 1974.

Bird, C. (with Briller, S.W.). *Born Female.* New York: David McKay, 1968.

Birk, J.M., Cooper, J., and Tanney, M.F. Racial and sex stereotyping in career information illustration. Paper presented at American Psychological Association Convention, Montreal, 1973.

Birk, J.M., and Tanney, M.F. Career exploration for high school women: A model. Paper presented at American Personnel and Guidance Association Regional Convention, Atlanta, 1973.

Broverman, I.K., Broverman, D.M., Clarkson, R.E., Rosenkrantz, P.S., and Vogel, S.R. Sex-role stereotypes and clinical judgments of mental health. *Consulting and Clinical Psychology,* 1970, *34,* 107.

Burkhart, M.Q. Vocational decision-making: A comparison of the rates of development for men and women. Unpublished doctoral dissertation, The Florida State University, 1973.

Douvan, E., and Gold, M. Modal patterns in American adolescence. In Hoffman, M., and Hoffman, L. (Eds.), *Review of Child Development, II.* New York: Russell Sage Foundation, 1966. Pp 469-528.

Drews, E.M. Counseling of self-actualization in gifted girls and young women. *Journal of Counseling Psychology,* 1956, *12,* 167-175.

Ginzberg, E. *Life Styles of Educated Women.* New York: Columbia University Press, 1966.

Harmon, L.W. *The Childhood and Adolescent Career Plans of College Women.* Milwaukee: Wisconsin University, 1970.

Hawley, P. What women think men think: Does it affect their career choice? *Journal of Counseling Psychology,* 1971, *18,* 195-199.

Holland, J.L. *The Self-Directed Search.* Palo Alto: Consulting Psychologist Press ,1970.

Horner, M. Fail: Bright women. *Psychology Today,* 1969, *3,* 36-62.

Impact. Woman in flux. Ann Arbor: University of Michigan ERIC/CAPS, Winter, 1972. Pp. 31-34.

Jacobowski-Spector, P. Facilitating the growth of women through assertive training. *Counseling Psychologist,* 1973, *4,* 75-86.

Katz, J., Korn, H., Leland, G.A., and Levin, M.M. *Class, Character, and Career: Determinants of Occupational Choice in College Students.* Palo Alto, California: Institute for the Study of Human Relations, Stanford University, 1969.

Katz, J., Korn, H., and Levin, M.M. *No Time for Youth: Growth and Constraint in College Students.* San Francisco: Jossey-Bass, 1968.

Lundberg, F., and Farhnam, M.F. *Modern Woman: The Lost Sex.* New York: Grossett and Dunlap, 1947.

Madison, P. *Personality Development in College.* Reading, Massachusetts: Addison Wesley, 1969.

Matthews, E. The marriage-career conflict in the career development of girls and young women. Unpublished doctoral dissertation, Harvard University, 1960.

Matthews, E., and Tiedeman, D.E. Attitudes toward career and marriage and the development of life style in young women. *Journal of Counseling Psychology,* 1964, *11,* 375-384.

Osipow, S.J. *Theories of Career Development.* New York: Appleton-Century-Crofts, 1968.

Pietrofessa, J.J., and Schlossberg, M.K. *The Counselor Bias and the Female Occupational Role.* Detroit: College of Education, Wayne State University, 1970.

Ramsey, S.E. Career exploration for women. *Journal of College Placement,* 1973, Feb.-Mar., 36-40.

Rosenthal, D. Changes in moral values following psychotherapy. *Journal of Consulting Psychology,* 1955, *19,* 431-436.

Sears, R.R., Maccoby, E.E., and Levin, H. *Patterns of Child Rearing.* Evanston, Illinois: Row and Peterson, 1957.

Strong, E.K., Jr. *Strong Vocational Interest Blank.* Palo Alto: Stanford University Press, 1966.

Thomas, A.H., and Stewart, N.R. Counselor response to female clients with deviant and conforming goals. *Journal of Counseling Psychology,* 1971, *18,* 352-357.

Weitzman, L.J., Eifler, D., Hokada, E., and Ross, C. Sex-role socialization in picture books for pre-school children. *American Journal of Sociology,* 1972, *77,* 13-26.

Welkowitz, J., Cohen, J., and Ortmeyer, D. Value-system similarity: Investigation of patient-therapist dyads. *Journal of Consulting Psychology,* 1967, *31,* 48-55.

Chapter Thirteen

CAREER COUNSELING FOR THE HOMOSEXUAL

DONALD A. BROWN

BASED ON THE MOST AUTHORITATIVE ESTIMATES, it appears that there are upward of several million men and women in the United States whose predominant interpersonal sexual relations are with members of their own sex. Because of the religious, legal and social sanctions condemnatory of homosexual practices, most homosexuals in the past have generally been very secretive about their sexual orientation; however, a growing liberalism and permissiveness concerning sexuality in general has contributed to a climate that is fostering sexual openness and expression. It is evident that an increasing number of homosexuals are surfacing from their anonymity and are beginning to overtly demand the freedom and rights afforded heterosexuals.

While we can only speculate regarding the ramifications of this overtness, it is evident that counselors are going to deal with an increasing number of acknowledged homosexual clients. More homosexuals are going to reject a covert, paranoid double life and, instead, will strive, as overt homosexuals, to lead productive and rewarding lives.

A counselor involved in helping a young homosexual choose a college or an occupation has little data which will enable the student to make an enlightened decision. Is a large university or a small liberal arts college more accepting of homosexuality? Is a secretarian or nonsectarian institution a better choice? Are some jobs closed to the overt homosexual? What industries are the most discriminatory? Is being gay ever an advantage vocationally? Is homosexuality an important consideration when making educational and vocational decisions? Information of the most basic and elementary nature is not available.

PROBLEMS ASSOCIATED WITH RESEARCH

Although much has been written about homosexuality, particularly in the past several years, it is particularly devoid of information based on research. It is difficult to investigate the "normal" sexual behavior of society and even harder to study behavior termed "perverted" and 'illegal."

The failure to research homosexuality is evidenced by the fact that, even though it dates back to antiquity, there is no agreement as to whether it is a moral, medical, social or psychiatric phenomenon. Furthermore, in the nearly half-century since Freud's first pronouncements about homosexuality, there has been little progress toward explaining basic questions pertaining to etiology, incidence and treatment. There has been virtually no research relating to its educational and vocational dimensions.

Examination of the existing homosexual literature reveals its limitations. Relatively few studies done prior to 1940 involved adequate statistical procedures. The quality of recent research appears improved; nevertheless, studies in general have been deficient in a number of criteria: in their systematic coverage of material, in the composition of the sample, in the methodological checks employed, and in their statistical analyses.

Understanding is further complicated because the counselor is confronted on one hand by a mass of clinical materials emphasizing pathology derived mainly from samples of patients institutionalized or in treatment, and on the other hand by autobiographical materials by homosexuals which tend to play on their plight or which are unrealistically laudatory of homosexuality. Somehow, the counselor must find his way through this maze of materials and develop a balanced perspective.

Because the educational and vocational dimensions of homosexuality involve the individual as a complex, total system reacting to his environment, any serious attempt to develop a broad understanding of these dimensions necessarily involves a multi-disciplinary investigation; therefore, it will be helpful to consider briefly the topic from several other vantage points.

HISTORICAL, RELIGIOUS, AND LEGAL FACTORS

Homosexuality can be traced back to prehistoric times. Cave drawings suggesting homosexuality and believed to date to the late Bronze Age can be found in the U.S.S.R. References occur in the Code of Hammurabi, the *Bible* and in other historical writings. It was practiced by the ancient Babylonians and Egyptians as well as the Greeks and Romans. Socrates, Plato, Alexander the Great, Virgil, Catullus and Julius Caesar were active homosexuals or bisexuals.

Homosexuality knows no geographic boundaries. The anthropologists, Ford and Beach, reporting in their book, *Patterns of Sexual Behavior* (1951), found that in 49 of the 76 societies studied homosexual activities were considered normal and socially acceptable.

Homosexuals in contemporary America have the traditional religious backgrounds of their heterosexual peers; however, the supportive and pallitive relief that the church could provide has generally been denied. Within the past several years a few churches have become more accepting of the homosexual and are taking positive actions. Homosexuals are beginning to found their own churches and often employ ministers who have been barred from more orthodox congregations because of their homosexuality. In the past, the homosexual's opportunity for public social contact has generally been limited to the gay bar or a homophile organization. The gay church is important because, in addition to meeting spiritual needs, it enables the homosexual to socialize with his peers in a socially respectable environment and thus relieves his feelings of guilt and denigration.

Historically, homosexuals have been victims of legal persecution. Until the middle of the 18th century, homosexuals in France were burned at the stake. Even into the 19th century, sodomy was punishable by death under English law; then the punishment was reduced to life imprisonment. It was not until 1967 in England that the report of the Wolfenden Committee led to the repeal of the laws against consensual sodomy. In the United States current penalties vary, but in more than thirty states a homosexual act could result in a maximum prison term of ten to twenty years. The homosexual who is flagrant in his behavior, e.g. who utilizes public restrooms and baths for sexual purposes, may very likely be arrested and convicted. Even in more permissive locales the homosexual cannot be free of fear because law enforcement tends to vary and is applied selectively. Police actions reflect the political climate and too often function expediently.

Police enticement and entrapment are still common and account for the majority of the arrests for homosexuality. In 1964 in Mansfield, Ohio, colored movie films were taken in a men's restroom for the purpose of apprehending homosexual offenders. Homosexuals are particularly bitter about the plain-clothes vice officer who engages them in conversation, makes some suggestive remark causing the homosexual to make a sexual proposition, and then arrests him using the proposition as evidence of desire to commit sodomy. Because of such police activities, the relations between police and the gay community are often openly hostile.

The homosexual has frequently been persecuted for what he is labeled rather than for what he has done. Kinsey states that "the homosexual has been subject to penalities involving cruelties which have not often been matched, except in religious and racial persecution." Documented cases run the gamut from that of a presidential advisor arrested, disgraced and forced to resign, to a complaint by the Connecticut Civil Liberties Union involving a homosexual denied a driver's license on the grounds that the admitted homosexual is "an improper person to operate a motor vehicle."

Homosexuals have become politically active. Politicians have been pressured to liberalize laws and modify practices that affect homosexuals. Police have been pressured to end persecutory practices. Homosexuals are beginning to seek public office. On occasion, homophile groups have joined with militant black and feminist groups to work against their exploitation by "the establishment." There have been no major legislative changes; however, politicians are becoming aware of their homosexual constituency and police militancy has frequently been tempered. Other governmental agencies such as Civil Service are beginning to reconsider hiring and firing practices in view of changing employment criteria.

VOCATIONAL IMPLICATIONS

A review of the literature indicates that there is relatively little which relates directly to the many vocational decisions a homosexual must make. Many references make some passing comment but only a few would be of immediate relevance to the counselor and his client and even fewer are based on the findings of research.

Many references perpetuate the homosexual stereotype. Textbooks frequently refer to their fondness of music, drama, ballet and painting, and references to employment generally emphasize aesthetic careers.

Homosexuals have lent credence to the stereotype. Some believe that they have unusual sensitivity, appreciation of the arts, and creativity. A homosexual teacher remarked that they possess "understanding, insight, patience, neatness, parental yearnings, and a wide range of interests and, consequently, may make outstanding teachers."

The belief that homosexuals are found primarily in certain occupations cannot be substantiated by research. This myth that employment is limited to the arts, hairdressing, or other aesthetically-oriented vocations, has been perpetuated in part because overt homosexuals were accepted in these vocational areas and would not face the censure and discharge which would result in business, education, the military and other less liberal vocations. The overt homosexual who wishes a minimum of conflict must seek employment in the above areas or else seek jobs where there are no considerations for employment other than the ability to perform satisfactorily.

Some research studies have indicated that homosexuals as a group are less masculine in their interests than heterosexuals. Because art, music and drama have traditionally been more feminine interests, it can be hypothesized that more homosexuals than heterosexuals enter these vocational areas; however, as the following studies indicate, some homosexuals have masculine interests and pursue traditionally masculine careers.

Henry (1948) studies 80 sexual variants divided into three groups—homosexual, bisexual and narcissistic—and collected data relating to the vocations of forty. Five were unemployed, but the remaining thirty-five were distributed in twenty-two occupations. About half of the individuals studied were not employed in occupations generally associated with homosexuality. Several, in fact, were in occupations considered very masculine.

A study by Lenzhoff and Westley (1956) illustrates the relationship between overtness, covertness, and the socio-economic level of employment. Their results indicate that an individual is less inclined to be overt as he moves up the socio-economic vocational scale. The individuals with the highest job status concealed their homosexuality at work. Those individuals at the bottom of the occupational scale, e.g. hospital attendant or waiter, could be overt because they had little to lose. A manager who had just been promoted was beginning to become more covert. Twenty of the homosexuals were secretive because of fear of dismissal from their jobs, or where self-employed because of a fear they might not get clients.

The record of the Federal Government in its treatment of homosexuals has generally been poor. During World War II homosexuals who were detected were discharged, generally as undesirables. Such a discharge caused them to forfeit their G.I. benefits and was an effective bar to many forms of civilian employment. It was often a real social stigma in a small community.

In 1950 a United States Senate Committee, investigating the employment of homosexuals in the government, concluded that homosexuals are not suitable for government employment because they are immoral and a security risk. This committee report made various government units more aware of the dangers of homosexuality.

Donn Teal (1971), an acknowledged homosexual, wrote, "They are scared of being fired. Many private and most public employers refuse to hire admitted homosexuals and fire people when they find out." Teal believes that discrimination in the area of employment is one of the major problems which homosexuals experience.

A Civil Service administrator, high in the echelon of the Federal Government, frankly admitted the discriminatory practices of the past, but felt that the governmental practices were a reflection of public attitudes and that any liberalization of practice would occur only as public attitudes changed. If this appraisal of employment trends is accurate, the homosexual cannot expect any drastic change in Federal employment.

The young homosexual considering a vocation needs to be aware of the unique problems which await him because of his homosexuality. If he hopes for a career in education at the public school level, business, industry, the military, Civil Service, the professions or the ministry, he generally must be secretive about his homosexuality. At any time he may be discovered and face the loss of his employment and career. The anxiety resulting from leading a double existence can be overwhelming. The overt homosexual finds that many vocations are closed to him. He must seek employment in those few areas which are accepting, develop some business of his own, or work at some job so menial that his sexual orientation is not a consideration.

Because traditional marriage is denied the homosexual and because our society is oriented toward the heterosexual couple, some of the usual satisfactions in life are denied the homosexual. He must find rewards in other areas. Dickey (1961), in her study of the feeling of adequacy in male homosexuals, found that the homosexual who is satisfied with his job tends to feel adequate. Winterstein-Lombert (1949), in his study of neurotic homosexual soldiers, found that helping them obtain a satisfactory job was an important step in their recovery.

Cannon (1973), after reflecting upon the emergence of homosexuality and its implication for counseling, states:

> There is good reason to reconsider employment in careers traditionally denied to homosexuals. A gay employee should be judged—as would a heterosexual employee—on the basis of his overt behavior. Other things being equal, there seems to be little reason to raise the matter of sexual preference at the time of employment.

Frequently, before an individual can benefit from career counseling, it is necessary to resolve more basic personal concerns. Thus, a consideration of counseling and psychotherapy is appropriate.

COUNSELING AND OTHER STRATEGIES

There are three broad possible objectives which may result from counseling or psychotherapy: 1. a change in the direction of sexual preference; 2. a better adjustment to problems resulting from homosexuality and to life in general; and 3. greater self-control over one's sexual desires.

There is lack of unanimity among experts regarding the degree to which an individual's direction of sexual preference may change as a result of counseling or psychotherapy. The Wolfenden Report (1963), which was based upon the testimony of a considerable number of authorities, stated, "Our evidence leads us to the conclusion that a total reorientation from complete homosexuality to complete heterosexuality is very unlikely indeed."

Various therapists such as Bieber (1962), Ellis (1956), Hatterer (1970), and Socarides (1968) cite their success in treating homosexuals; but, unfortunately, studies have not been conducted which would be conclusive in determining to what extent therapists in general are successful. Probably most authorities, if lacking unanimity regarding changing sexual direction per se, would agree that a better adjustment to problems associated with homosexuality or life in general may be expected from counseling or therapy. There would probably be little agreement regarding the part the therapist can play in helping the individual gain control over his sexual behavior.

Many counselors, in dealing with a homosexual, are inclined to place too great an importance on the individual's homosexuality. There is data which indicates that to most homosexuals their homosexuality is no more the primary motivating force in their lives than heterosexuality would be to most heterosexuals. It is obviously an important consideration, but it is only one of several which affect the life process. They feel that the major decisions of an individual's life should be based upon a number of criteria. The counselor can help the client explore all criteria and can help keep the homosexual behavior in a reasonable perspective.

Most counselors and student personnel workers have heavily biased heterosexual values and have had little experience with acknowledged homosexuals; consequently, they tend to overreact when they learn that an individual has had a homosexual experience. They may convey their own sexual concerns to the client. They may mistake either an isolated homosexual act or two or situational behavior (occurring in prison or a similar environment where heterosexual relations are impossible) with a definite homosexual preference. They may not be aware that Kinsey found that thirty-seven percent of American males had a homosexual experience between adolescence and old age to the point of orgasm. A young person having had an experience or two may need help in understanding the true significance of his behavior. The counselor can help the young person determine just what the experience means—whether it was transitory or whether it was more basic.

Many homosexuals report that by the age of four or five they knew that they were different from their peers. Often they could not articulate their feelings but they had a sense of being different. For others, this realization did not occur until adolescence, and for a few not until their early twenties or thirties. Generally, when awareness of their homosexuality develops or when they experience homosexual responses, many homosexuals feel unique and alone. They may feel guilty and believe that only they experience these emotions. The counselor can help them to realize that they need not be ashamed of their feelings—that homosexuality does not preclude a useful, socially productive life.

Some counselors report that they feel ill-at-ease when they learn that a client is homosexual. When this occurs it would be advisable for them to refer the client to someone else. The counselor who experiences these feelings can take several steps to become more at ease. By familiarizing himself with the literature, he may gain some understanding of homosexuality. He may meet with homosexuals and discuss homosexuality and the impact it has on these persons' lives. Most counselors respond favorably to this method and report that it has helped them to be more understanding. Most colleges now have homophile groups and representatives who generally are available upon request. Occasionally, this experience may not be positive for a counselor and may increase his anxiety. When this latter occurs, counseling should be considered.

A frequent response of parents and relatives is hostility when they learn that their child or loved one is a homosexual. Some will totally reject the child, others will resort to denial; few can accept the news with equanimity and compassion. Parents with traditional values hardly can be expected to immediately accept their child's homosexual feelings or behavior; however, the passage of time frequently moderates these negative feelings. The counselor, by facilitating catharsis and providing an objective perspective, often can prevent a tenuous situation from being tragic.

Even a counselor with very limited skills can help those concerned by supplying them with reading materials which will present the facts about homosexuality. The materials should help them realize that homosexuality is an ubiquitous phenomenon and that homosexuals can lead satisfying and productive lives. Books like Merle Miller's *On Being Different* and Martin Hoffman's *The Gay World* are interesting and informative sources.

Many homosexuals have traditional religious backgrounds and could get support and relief from guilt from their churches; but generally, in the past, institutionalized religions have been unsympathetic and condemnatory. Counselors with religious affiliations must become active in encouraging religious institutions to modify their generally unsympathetic attitude toward homosexuality and, instead, develop a more positive and helping relationship.

Frequently a counselor can be of real service to the young homosexual by providing him with information to help him avoid some of the serious problems which many homosexuals experience. A typical situation involves law enforcement agencies. The counselor should appraise the neophyte homosexual of police practices and help him to find ways of taking care of his sexual needs with a minimum of risk. To avoid arrest is important because entry into a number of educational programs and occupations is dependent upon "good moral character." Often this simply means no record of arrest and conviction.

The counselor can work politically to change state and national legislation pertaining to homosexuality which is persecutory in nature. At the local level effort can be expended to encourage law enforcement agencies to discontinue their policies of enticement and entrapment. Too frequently a legal conviction early in the young homosexual's life precludes certain educational or vocational opportunities. He can be taught how to be discreet with police and to pass as a heterosexual.

Individuals should not be intimidated by a homosexual overture. Women continually deal with heterosexual advances of the amorous male; thus to incarcerate the homosexual for a look or brief verbal overture constitutes a flagrant example of differential law enforcement.

Presently in the United States venereal disease is reportedly approaching epidemic proportions. Homosexuals are as likely to contract this disease as heterosexuals. They should be encouraged to have regular physical examinations and to be particularly careful if they engage in sexual activities with a variety of persons.

The counselor can help the homosexual explore the advantage of overt and covert life styles. The homosexual who chooses to be covert about his gayness probably has more career options than the overt and very likely can practice his career; however, he may have to appear heterosexual in order to keep his employment. He frequently learns various techniques for passing as heterosexual. These include taking women to heterosexual social functions, relating the incidents occurring on a date but not mentioning his date's sex, telling heterosexual "dirty jokes," pretending to have an interest in sporting events and avoiding effeminate mannerisms, clothing and speech.

The covert homosexual lessens the risk of possible rejection by family and friends; however, for these privileges he pays a heavy price. He lives with the constant fear of discovery, possible arrest and public disgrace. For some, each sexual encounter is at best an ambivalent experience. Homosexuals cite instances where a friend who has been discovered—usually a respected community member —chooses suicide rather than live with his secret known to his family and friends.

The individual who chooses to be open about his gayness may face many hardships. Rejection by parents, siblings and good friends is not uncommon. Harassment from police, finding certain professions and occupations closed to him, and general social ostracism are not infrequent experiences. There are certain advantages. He can be himself and need not fear the unknown. The homosexual must consider the advantages and disadvantages of overt and covert life styles and, assuming he can make a choice, choose the life style most appropriate for him.

Even though homosexuals generally experience vocational discrimination, the vocational outlook is not totally bleak. In some occupations homosexuality is not a disadvantage while in other occupations—for instance, those related to the theater or artistically-oriented careers—it may even be an advantage. The counselor should keep these facts in mind when working with a client who despairs over vocational discrimination.

The counselor can reassure employers that they need not fear that homosexuals will use their place of employment as a means of making sexual contacts. Most homosexuals report that they keep their sex lives and their work situation separate. Many observe that there are various risks involved in attempting to establish a relationship at work. They would not endanger their job.

Brown (1973), in his study of forty-three college-educated homosexuals, reported that at least four models of vocational adjustment can be identified:

1. *The "Successful Professional"*
   Most typical was the apparently well-adjusted and reasonably happy and productive executive or professional. They were pursuing successful careers and their gayness and sexuality seemed to play no greater a part in their lives than would heterosexuality in the lives of the majority of the general population.

2. *The "Under-Employed"*
   Another type which could be identified was the individual who had been trained as an educator or as a similar professional but who worked as a factory laborer or in some other menial job because his gayness caused him either to leave his profession or to terminate his education before becoming fully qualified.

3. *The "Craftsman"*
   The third type is the homosexual who is employed in some

craft or field which emphasizes aesthetic talents. Representatives would include a framer of expensive pictures and a restorer of old musical instruments.

4. *The "Professional Homosexual"*
    A fourth type is the overt homosexual who supports himself marginally with some menial or part-time job. His primary interest is the Gay Liberation Movement. His total being seems absorbed with the movement and personal and other considerations appear to be relatively unimportant.

Other models of vocational adjustment possibly exist; however, the four types discussed above are those which are readily apparent from those homosexuals observed by Brown.

SUMMARY

Discriminated against vocationally, frequently persecuted because his sexual needs are in conflict with the mores of society, denied the traditional family relationships, life is not particularly easy for most homosexuals. Many seek a permanent and stable relationship, but few achieve it. To most homosexuals their homosexuality is no more a matter of choice than heterosexuality is for the majority. Differential treatment and ignorance add to their burden. Counselors and other members of helping professions, through understanding and acceptance and example, can help the homosexual to become a respected and productive member of society.

BIBLIOGRAPHY

Bieber, I. *Homosexuality*. New York: Basic Books, 1962.

Brown, D.A. A study of the educational and vocational decision-making of four groups of homosexuals. Unpublished doctoral dissertation, University of Michigan, 1973.

Cannon, H.J. Gay Students. *Vocational Guidance Quarterly*, 1973, *21*, 181, 185.

Dickey, B. Attitudes toward sex roles and feelings of adequacy in homosexual males. *Journal of Consulting Psychology*, 1961, *25*, 116-122.

Ellis, H. *Studies in the Psychology of Sex*. Kingsport, Tennessee: Kingsport Press, 1941.

Ford, C.S., and Beach, F.A. *Patterns of Sexual Behavior*. New York: Ace Books, 1951.

Hatterer, L.J. *Changing Homosexuality in the Male.* New York: McGraw-Hill, 1970.

Henry, G.W. *Sex Variants: A Study of Homosexual Patterns.* New York: Paul B. Hoeber, 1948.

Hoffman, M. *The Gay World.* New York: Bantam Books, 1973.

Lenzhoff, M., and Wesley, W.A. The homosexual community. In Gagnon, J.H., and Simon, W. (Eds.), *Sexual Deviance.* New York: Harper & Row, 1967.

Miller, M. *On Being Different.* New York: Random House, 1971.

Socarides, C.W. *The Overt Homosexual.* New York: Grune and Stratton, 1968.

Teal, D. *The Gay Militants.* New York: Stein and Day, 1971.

Winterstein-Lombert, E. Observation on homosexuals. *Bulletin de la Faculté de Medecine de Istanbul,* 1949, *12,* 216-220.

Wolfenden Report. *Committee of Homosexual Offenses and Prostitution—Great Britain.* New York: Stein and Day, 1963.

Chapter Fourteen

CAREER DEVELOPMENT FOR ETHNIC MINORITIES

WINFRED O. STONE

MINORITY CAREER DEVELOPMENT is often viewed from many perspectives. The most frequent classifications used to present information evolve from groupings determined by race, sex, aspiration levels, educational settings, vocational choice and career-change decisions. Within the broad definition of minorities, the categories of Blacks, women, veterans and gay people are increasingly becoming the focus of career publications. Although minority group classifications appear to be distinctly different, the classifications accommodate common elements of need for career information, counseling, decision-making, equal opportunity, income and advancement, and job satisfaction.

Even though a mirage of common elements is apparent in minority classifications, minority career development can assume many forms as the state of career employment practices currently exists. The racial variance which exists between minority access to vocational/technical education and job placement is seemingly historical and inherent. Subsequently, career development for ethnic minorities is adversely affected in unique ways by the practice of racism. In view of this unique practice in our education and free enterprise systems, it is imperative that career development for ethnic minorities is presented in the context of the "real world" in order to be of maximum value to readers in search of help.

While attending to some relevant factors that can make a difference in the "real world," this chapter will consider four counseling and career development issues pertinent to minorities and aforementioned conditions: (1) Minority Classifications and Implications; (2) Minority Counseling; (3) Minority Testing and Evaluation Reconsidered; (4) Career Development Systems for Minorities.

MINORITY CLASSIFICATIONS AND IMPLICATIONS

Before preceeding with the text of this chapter, the minority terms should be discussed and defined in perspective. Today it is fashionable to hear a variety of White Americans proudly identify themselves as ethnic minorities. This reference, most often, alludes to European Anglo-Saxon heritage. The meaning of the term minority has also expanded in usage by governmental agencies, business and educational institutions. At one time, minority was almost a code word used primarily to identify Blacks when one was uncertain of the appropriate racial descriptor (i.e. Negro, colored, Black). However, as the U. S. Congress passed legislation and appropriated funds to alleviate the disadvantaged conditions of Black citizens, the level of awareness (political, social, economic) created by Black protest was soon espoused by other citizens of foreign extraction and color. Subsequently, legal statutes were officially amended in order to promote equal opportunity conditions in employment, education and housing for all minorities.

On October 13, 1968, pursuant to Executive Order 11246 as amended by Executive Order 11375, two significant revisions occurred concerning minority designations. The first revision addressed phrases in federal government regulations which read "without regard to race, creed, or national origin." The phrases were revised to read "without regard to race, color, religion, sex or national origin." The second revision effected by the Executive Order was more profound. The term "minority group" was designated to include females.

Numerous legal and budgetary problems have developed in funding minority programs as a result of the decision to include women as minorities. Specifically, the recent development of special offices and positions for the women's movement has contributed to the slowing of progress for ethnic minorities. Women studies, Women Affairs Offices, court suits and equalization of salaries now constitute a progressive impetus which exceeds that for ethnic minorities in government and educational institutions.

The Equal Employment Opportunity Commission recognizes the gamut of minority designation problems. It currently considers the following minorities within the concept of race for federal reports (Proposed EEOC Regulations, 1973) :

1. The category "Black" should include persons of African descent, as well as those identified as Jamaican, Trinidian and West Indian.
2. The category "Spanish Surnamed" should include all persons of Mexican, Puerto Rican, Cuban, Latin American or Spanish descent.
3. The category "American Indian" should include persons who identify themselves or are known as such by virtue of tribal association.
4. The category "Asian American" should include persons of Japanese, Chinese, Korean or Filipino descent.
5. The category "Other" should include Aluets, Eskimos, Thais, and others not covered by the specific categories. . . .

It is apparent from the categorical designations that numerous ethnically different groups, as well as women, may be included in the definition or concept of "minority groups." It is imperative that personnel in helping professions truly understand that inter- and intra-group minority characteristics vary significantly. However, there is a tendency to erroneously globalize certain attributes to all ethnic minorities. Typically, such generalizations traverse educational and socio-economic strata within each racial minority population.

With the classifications of minorities as defined, a title such as Minority Career Development is, indeed, global and can be somewhat misleading. In deference to this recognition, the term "minority" or "minority groups" in this chapter will have reference only to the racial classifications of minorities. Most often, research, publication trends and concerns relative to Black Americans will be cited in this chapter. It is obvious that such citations point to the need for similar publications and research information pertaining to each ethnic minority group.

MINORITY COUNSELING

It is time for minority counseling to come of age and interface the fourth major development in the brief history of counseling—that of self-sufficiency via a variety of developmental experiences.

Ethnic minorities in the last decade virtually demanded advocate behavior from their counselors. Today, advocacy as a counseling service remains an essential function in working with minorities in ways that are unique to their respective cultures. However, minority counseling must consist of more than advocacy which has been mistaken for ethnic rapping and relating. Proficiency and self-sufficiency, in terms of attainment of specific skills to live and work more effectively, are also desirable minority counseling outcomes.

Increasingly, minorities are plagued with problems of anxiety, racism, employment and education. These problems which complicate career development appropriately identify cogent areas to unfold specific self-sufficiency skills.

Some of the appropriate skills needed may be identified as relaxation, exercise, constructive leisure time activities, understanding racism, rational thinking, decision making, career interest evaluation, career exploration, application and interview preparation, and interpersonal relations.

The practice of minority counseling during the next decade must focus on development and modification of a variety of counseling techniques appropriate and effective with different ethnic minority groups. Perhaps it is the cultural modification of existing theories and techniques that will prove most helpful in addressing these essential areas where skills are needed to facilitate achievement and fulfillment of self-sufficiency goals.

In counseling minorities, a critical issue continues to surface regarding the counseling dyad. The issue considers the question, "Who should counsel minorities?" While some social progress is evident, Johnson (1974) proposes that the race of the counselor is still a significant factor. He suggests that it may be a contradiction of the basic principles and objectives of career counseling to have a white counselor telling a Black student about career opportunities open to him. This position is held because the impact of principles associated with modeling behavior are absent in the minority counselee/non-minority counselor dyad.

Additional factors facilitative to the minority counseling relationship and affective-domain are reported by Carkhuff (1969a, 1969b) (1972), Carkhuff and Berenson (1967), Truax (1970) and others. However, there may be no common critical factor in counseling for other minorities as the race factor is for Blacks. Even within racial classifications, the female counselor may be able to establish more positive and lasting rapport with the Black male counselee (Vontress, 1971). On the basis of available research trends, the following hypothesized outcomes would seem to suggest that minority counselees with a good self-concept and intra-group identity will probably respond maximally in the extended dyadic counseling relationship in this order:

1. To a trained counselor of own race.
2. To a trained minority counselor.
3. To a trained white counselor.

Initial reactions to this minority hypothesis of maximal counseling response may include rejection, denial and subsequent dismissal by counselors who refuse to recognize the significance of the racial factor. However, the fact of the matter is that racism exists. The effective counselor, regardless of race, should recognize the inherent role and effect of racism in our systems. It is a factor that can significantly dictate the outcome of counseling and, in essence, minority career development.

Theories that adequately explain and account for the existence of racism have not existed in abundance in academic disciplines. However, one of the most recent theories, the Cress Theory of Color-Confrontation and Racism (White Supremacy), explains this phenomenon in psycho-genetic terms within a world outlook framework (Welsing, 1970). Welsing interprets racism as white supremacy behavior. She defines it as, "The behavioral syndrome of individual and collective color inferiority and numerical inadequacy which includes patterns of thought, speech and action as seen in members of the white organization (race)."

Counselors and minority counselees, alike, must understand this and other theories of racism. Both must comprehend the historical, present and future impact upon minorities. For it is only with this kind of knowledge and futuristic insight that a minority student can truly perceive and know how the practice of racism may affect his education, chosen career and total life.

In discussing our model (Stone and Harper, 1973; 1974) of Transcendent Counseling, we propose the following considerations in working with Black clientile:

1. The counseling approach should be flexible and comprehensive such as to be useful with counselees of different ethnic backgrounds. A combination of individual and small group techniques should be used for maximum effectiveness.
2. The goals of counseling Blacks should be: (a) satisfaction of basic needs; (b) modification and/or development of new life style; and (c) transcendence of personal and environmental obstacles.
3. The effective counselor must manifest: (a) affective and cognitive personality traits of effective counseling; (b) humanistic qualities of mental health and self-actualization, and (c) experiential knowledge of the social sciences of ethnic minorities.
4. In the counseling process, the being of the counselor is more important than the techniques employed.
5. The counselor should initially establish priority for using supportive, directive, and informative techniques in quickly bringing the counselee to a level of awareness and taking some appropriate action.
6. The counselor should employ action-oriented and responsibility-oriented techniques which are developmental in nature.
7. In the counseling relationship (especially with Blacks), the counselor should be about assessing: (a) needs of the counselee; (b) life style of the counselee; (c) behavior of the counselee; and (d) the dynamics of the counselee as he operates in his environment. Subsequently, the counselor should prescribe and generate action for positive change and growth of the counselee.
8. Such a counseling approach can be labeled as "Transcendent Counseling" or "APAT Counseling," i.e., counseling via *assessment, prescription,* and *action* for *transcedence* of self and culture.

Counseling and career development for ethnic minorities

should be programmatic over an extended period of time. The skill and levels of awareness which must be created are, indeed, evolutionary in nature and may require a minimum of 10-30 developmental education sessions.

There are shortcomings in counseling for career development in relationship to career education that the counselor should understand. Some minority authors have made penetrating extensions about the concept of career education because it cannot be separated from future career development trends in society.

Career Education

Much has been said and written, pro and con, about career education, the proposed system for career development for all students, including ethnic minorities. Career education is supposed to be a systematic method of making education and training more meaningful for students, more rewarding for teachers, more available for adults, more relevant for the disadvantaged and more productive for the country (Nixon, 1972; Marland, 1973). The inclusive suppositions of this broad definition of career education have varied somewhat in response to criticism. Informed minority educators are skeptical of career education and have outlined their concerns in precise terms.

Johnson (1974) warns Black Americans in *Black Agenda for Career Education:*

> . . . the Black American must critically analyze all the hidden agendas which career education, as conceived and implemented by some administrators, will inhere. Those hidden agendas must be counterattached by a well-thought out, well researched, and well-implemented black agenda . . . (p. 17-18).

Johnson (1974), Davenport and Petty (1973) and other Black authors repeatedly recite the mistrust held by minorities regarding federal programs, none of which has ever solved or significantly alleviated a major minority problem. It is not that minorities are disinterested in career education and career development. As proposed, the problem is that career education may lead to the detriment of minorities in professional, scientific, technical and managerial occupations because of early tracking in school. The Carnegie

Commission (1973) has already predicted that employment of minorities in higher education will not reach fifteen percent until the year 2000 or even beyond. This percentage is only proportional to the number of minorities in the total labor force. Appropriately, minorities are forced to reason at this point, if equal opportunity and affirmative action will not work in our institutions of higher education, how can we expect citizens with less education to fairly train, employ and advance minorities. In addition to the career education questions posed at this juncture, ethnic minorities must insist upon responsible and responsive answers to the list of questions raised by Davenport and Petty (1973) which also are crucial to career development:

1. How does the concept prevent tracking of students that could occur on the local level?
2. Can a school really guarantee job placement to students?
3. Are the manpower statistics reliable enough to make projections on the local level?
4. To what extent will the social behavior which is taught be controlled by businesses which control jobs?
5. What role will schools play in breaking down job discrimination?
6. Should career education be important to minorities when basic education is still lacking?
7. How will career education be tied into remedial education?
8. To what extent can local schools realistically give a wide range of career choices, given present financial limitations?
9. How does career education mesh with the need of minorities for ethnic awareness?
10. Given the present educational segregation along social class lines, will not a student in a wealthy district tend to have more occupational choices at his disposal than one from a poor district?
11. Will the curriculum revision called for by career education be made at the expense of the humanities?
12. If in the future man is expected to spend less time earning a living, should not the use of leisure time be given more emphasis (pp. 13-14)?

Only by implementing goal oriented program changes toward minorities will responsible federal and state departments of education adequately answer the outstanding list of questions raised above. Equal Opportunity and Affirmative Action policy statements in education and employment have not proved to be grossly important in bringing about significant advancements. Therefore, until specific programs are implemented to assuage practices of racism in education and employment, career development expectations for ethnic minorities may continue to be less than those for non-minorities in the foreseeable future.

MINORITY TESTING AND EVALUATION RECONSIDERED

In a survey of the literature of three professional counseling journals (Stone, 1973), publications by minorities concerning IQ and achievement tests were found to be very sparse for a period of three years (1969-1972). It was general knowledge during the period of the survey that most tests needed improvement in terms of cultural bias and appropriate norms for minority groups. This knowledge coupled with the demand for revolutionary economic, social and educational changes spurred by riots, student protest and demands for minority community control of schools, significantly, influenced decisions to abandon testing of minorities.

After assessing the obvious abandonment of testing for Blacks, Sowell (1973) offers this proposition for reconsideration: "The practical question at any given point in time is, what are the alternatives? Other selection devices and criteria ranged from ineffective to disastrous. Moreover, it is precisely the Black students who need IQ tests most of all, for it is precisely with Black students that alternative methods of spotting intellectual ability have failed." This discussion of testing is not limited to IQ tests. Clark (1972) recommends the use of standardized tests for diagnostic purposes to facilitate improved academic achievement in minority education settings. In general, it is the broad scope and usage of testing which must be reconsidered.

In this regard Flaugher (1973) believes that four points of confusion exist in discussing the testing of Black students which has delayed improvement in the understanding that testing is not a source of unfairness for minority students:

1. The assumption underlying most of our psychometric manipulations are often not acknowledged or understood;
2. The extent of the objectivity of psychometrics is frequently exaggerated;

3. The meaning of certain terms, particularly 'validity' (largely because it has both a technical and common usage), is quite confused; and
4. The understanding of just what function the tests are serving shifts from one function to another, unnoticed by those concerned.

Traditionally, testing and evaluation instruments have cast a negative aura on the self-concept of minorities. This and other negative test associations are related to cultural bias, inadequate norms, interpretation methods, and typically, a pronouncement of disqualification from achieving a desired goal or objective. Most test developers and users are aware of the wrong ways in which tests have been used and cultural bias elements. However, problems continue to exist. The systems in which test users are employed remain fixed in terms of assessment alternatives available instead of tests. Likewise, policy often dictates and restricts test users to established courses of action once results are available. Unfortunately, many educational systems still do not possess the capability of developing individualized learning prescriptions on the basis of secured test results.

Although the above conditions are present, some encouraging steps are being taken. Emphasis provided by the Fund for the Improvement of Post-Secondary Education in allocating funds to encourage development of modular and competency-based programs in a variety of academic and vocational areas will help the situation. Through the development of competency-based and modular programs, a closer relationship can exist between diagnosis and learning. Self-paced learning modules can help remove deficiencies indicated by tests in a short period of time without first attempting to change the life style of the minority learner.

Vontress (1971) contends that, ideally, an impressionistic approach to assessing Blacks should be used by an experienced psychologist. In lieu of such an assessment specialist, seven minimal testing guidelines are recommended for minorities:

1. Informally determine the degree to which the individual is assimilated in the American culture before administering standardized tests.

2. Establish rapport with the examinee whether he is being tested individually or in a group.
3. Examiners with regionally different accents should not be used.
4. Determine formally or informally the reading level of the examinee before administering tests.
5. Since motivation affects test behavior and results, it is recommended that Blacks be prepared for test sessions.
6. To insure optimum testing conditions, it is recommended that the size of the testing group be kept small.
7. The duration of testing sessions should be segmented whenever possible into single short period administrations (pp. 58-59).

As the age of accountability in teaching, learning and counseling gains momentum, it seems imperative that minority testing and evaluation for diagnostic purposes must be *cautiously* reconsidered. Individualized personal assessment based upon extensive experience and impressionistic knowledge can continue to exist and play a major role in minority student evaluations and decision-making. The reliable methods of assessment which do not use testing must be translated into meaningful training formats. This translation will facilitate development of other trained minority assessment specialists. Subsequently, appropriate research models concerned with in-put, process, outcome and follow-up data relative to testing and evaluation may be made applicable or adaptable to career development for ethnic minorities.

CAREER DEVELOPMENT SYSTEMS FOR MINORITIES

Federal funding patterns and program priorities have significantly influenced developments in the counseling profession. Within the last decade, at least seven major job training programs have been initiated and designed to enhance minority employment and career development. The programs have emphasized a variety of services and counseling approaches. The titles are rather descriptive of the missions: 1. Job Corps; 2. Neighborhood Youth Corps (NYC); 3. Manpower Development and Training Act (MDTA); 4. Concentrated Employment Program (CEP); 5. Work Incentive

Program (WIN); 6. Opportunities Industrialization Centers (OIC); and 7. National Alliance of Business (NAB). OIC and NAB represent private and business efforts aimed at work and career rehabilitation.

Career development services as performed by professional and paraprofessional personnel in these programs have been admirable in combating skill deficiencies in out of school, unemployed and under-employed participants. Although the services are admirable, they largely constitute after-the-fact career development efforts.

In view of such pervasive needs, the documented superiority of any set of career development systems for minorities versus other systems is an unfulfilled desire on the part of many educators. However, invaluable lessons and insight can be gleaned from existing career techniques and programs. The absence of extensive research data concerning minority career development systems is somewhat a reflection upon the commitment of practitioners in the field to declare war on this problem. More especially, the absence of such systems may prevail because it has primarily been perceived as a Black or minority problem.

The problems involved in modifying and designing systems for minority career development are indeed complex. Karnes, Zehrback and Jones (1971), outline the task ahead as follows:

> The approach to the guidance of disadvantaged youth must be viewed not as singular but as plural, not as individual oriented but as process and group oriented, as existing not in a static situation but in a variety of changing situations, each of which may cause or require changes in the individual's behavior.

Menacker (1971) has suggested that the first step for assisting minority students is to establish meaningful communication. Secondly, he proposes that negative self concepts may exist in two primary forms—the defeatist self-image (inner-directed) and the hostile self-image (outer-directed). Menacker further explains that both self-perceived deficiencies are equally destructive to the individual but require different treatment strategies from a sensitive counselor or specialist.

This section has alluded to multiple concerns that should be considered and appraised in a counseling system for minority career development. An effective system also must possess facets of career techniques which are corrective and developmental in nature. Logically, to adequately consider the list of concerns, a systems approach to career development must be devised which identifies objectives, techniques and measurable-behavioral outcomes. The career development system, as stated previously, should encompass aspects of a treatment-training model (Stone and Harper, 1973) for the counselee as well as the counselor. This model is deemed appropriate because counselors are not immune to the pathologies of society (Beck, 1973).

The primary focus of the career development model should be competency based. It should consist of three major types of counseling services: (1) academic; (2) career and informational; and (3) personal and interpersonal skills development. For optimum results a modular achievement learning format is suggested in individualize and small group settings. An outline of the suggested model follows:

A Systems Approach to Career Development

1. Orientation to modular learning for career development
   a. purpose
   b. goals
   c. objectives
   d. expectations
   e. contingencies
2. Diagnosis (administration of evaluation and career interest instruments)
3. Counseling regarding results of diagnosis
4. Select modules (academic, personal, interpersonal, career, developmental)
   a. sign learning contracts for modules
   b. receive explanation of modules, achievement levels, and alternatives
   c. assignment of tutors (peer-staff), instructors, schedule of modules, group meetings, etc.
5. Work through modules and progress tests
6. Complete module and proficiency test

7. Staff-student evaluation of objectives and outcomes
8. Proceed to selection of next module
9. Repeat steps 3, 4, 5, 6, 7, and 8

With this systematic approach, the counselor must constantly strive to personalize and humanize his services. Flexibility as well as the generation and application of alternative techniques are essential.

To facilitate career development, the following resources and systems are suggestive of available items that may be used with minorities. Again it is advisable to remember that adaptation and modification must characterize the counselor's implementation of these resources that this author has utilized or studied:

1. *Decision Making*
   a. *Decision and Outcomes:* This exercise was developed by the College Board to help students to: "learn how to make decisions that will bring about more desirable outcomes, discover more about themselves and their environment, increase the chances of achieving what they want in life" (Gelatt, Varenhorst, Carey and Miller, 1973). The program contains sections entitled: 1. The Starting Point; 2. The Deciding Self; 3. Before Deciding; and 4. Applying Skills. It is appropriate for older teenagers and adult minorities with modifications. It may be used in a variety of classroom, counseling and community agency settings (see Chapter 9).
   b. *Vocational Exploration Group (VEG):* "VEG is a structured group approach that helps members learn career decision making skills, move toward appropriate career goals and become actively involved in the steps necessary to reach their goals" (Elster, 1973). VEG is effective in working with students who possess negative attitudes toward counseling and have no stated career goals (see Chapter 7).

2. *Vocational Planning*
   a. *The Self-Directed Search* (SDS): A self-administered, self-rating guide to facilitate educational and vocational plan-

ning. SDS correlates with the *Vocational Preference Inventory* and helps a person assess his resemblance to six occupational personality types: 1. realistic; 2. investigative; 3. artistic; 4. social; 5. enterprising; and 6. conventional. *The Occupations Finder* which accompanies SDS contains 456 of the most common occupations. General educational development levels and six digit DOT numbers are provided for the occupations listed. High and low level reading ability forms of SDS are available (Holland, 1970; 1972a; 1972b; 1973b). Blacks tend to choose social service occupations more often on the SDS; therefore, there are implications for counseling in helping Blacks understand this pattern. Nevertheless, it is an appropriate instrument for Blacks and, perhaps, other minorities (Kimball, et al., 1971).

b. *Planning: Your Post-High School Career (Student's Booklet):* This is a six part booklet to help students with career planning in these ways: 1. The Career Development Journey; 2. Decision Making; 3. Using Your Student Report In Career Planning; 4. Information Under The Flap; 5. Finding Out What Jobs Are Like And How To Prepare For Them; and 6. Where To Get More Information About Careers. This booklet is prepared for usage with the Student Report of the American College Testing Program. It will help students explore information about abilities, interests, needs, goals and a better understanding of self (The American College Testing Program, 1972; 1973). Again, although this is a good booklet, maximum involvement of the minority student in activity and small group oriented sessions will add to its effectiveness.

3. *Racism and Racial Understanding*
   a. *The Cress Theory of Color-Confrontation and Racism (White Supremacy):* Within the framework of psychogenetics and a world outlook, the theory analyzes the universal behavioral phenomena of white supremacy. Inherent dynamics between "whites" and "non-whites" are placed in the context of theoretical formulation. This ap-

proach provides "non-white" people with a rational basis for understanding the motivational nuances of individual and collective white behavior (Welsing, 1970).

b. *Situation Attitude Scale* (SAS): A measure of the attitudes of whites toward Blacks. SAS is useful in measuring attitudes (racism) about race related programs and misunderstanding about the needs of minority students (Sedlacek and Brooks, 1972).

c. *Encounter Tapes for Black/White Groups:* An audiotape program for a racially mixed group interested in seeking a structured opportunity to experience directly the meaning of racial differences with understanding. Groups may range from eight to twelve people with no more than 60% or 40% racial composition. Learning and interpersonal growth occurs within a self-directed or "leaderless" format (Human Development Institute, 1974-75 catalog). Other minority training programs and films are available.

4. *Group Teaching Techniques*

a. *Information Intermix (IM):* Information intermix is a group approach to maximize human learning. It is effective as a group guidance technique for the classroom teacher and school counselor. The technique is effective with large and small groups ranging from the fifth grade to graduate students.

Information intermix is an organizational process by which individuals who seemingly represent disparate concepts are mixed and blended in a humane and congenial way so that all members learn many times the amount they brought to the mix (Rapp and Capuzzi, 1973).

IM is an enjoyable way to learn and apparently effective.

b. *Learning Thru Discussion (LTD):*

Any classroom program intended to maximize learning will benefit from the technique of this method. Utilizing this method will increase understanding and retention of any material: (1) by encouraging the correlation of materials being discussed with what has already been learned through previous experience of the group's members, and (2) by guiding their interaction toward the sharing of new and acquired knowledge. This scheme replaces authority with clarity, both in its own formulation and in its recommendations. It may be used as a detailed outline, a set of flexible guidelines, or simply as a model of a productive group (Hill, 1962 and 1969).

The LTD Group Cognitive Map consists of 9 outlined steps to facilitate direction and progress in learning. Flexibility is a key word in utilizing this effective discussion and learning technique.

5. *Personal Growth and Developmental Systems*

    a. *Transcendent Counseling:* This model of counseling employs training as a mode of treatment in facilitating behavioral change. The system involves implementation of training modules from existing theories and practices. It is designed to convey experiential knowledge and skills about the following discerned elements of transcendence: (1) The Psychology of Transcendent Behavior; (2) Racism; (3) Rational-Emotive Principles (Thoughts); (4) Relaxation Training (Feelings); (5) Personal Growth Group Experiences (Behavior); (6) Science of Creative Intelligence; and (7) Practice of Transcendental Meditation (TM). This comprehensive growth oriented system implements the concept of multiple treatment. Diet orientation and exercise are also areas of concern in assisting the client to transcend personal and environmental obstacles (Stone and Harper, 1973 and 1974).

    b. *Systemic Counseling:* Gunnings (1972) proposes Systemic Counseling as a methodology to facilitate Black and minority students in developing skills that will effectively and successfully enable them to negotiate situations and institutions within our system that are thwarting because of racism. The counselor works actively to help change both the system and minority students.

Although the proposed counseling models are in their embryonic stage, they recognize the universal problem of truly understanding and dealing with racism as it affects Blacks and other minorities. Both approaches merit consideration for inclusion in counselor education programs and implementation in career development training for ethnic minorities.

In conclusion, we must recognize that development of special interventions and models for minorities is a strategy that can result in positive as well as negative outcomes (Holland, 1974). Nevertheless, intensive efforts to reduce systematic bias and racism in education and employment must continue endlessly.

SUMMARY

Through the effective use of career development systems and techniques, career specialists can positively influence the life style, education and employment trends of ethnic minorities. These outcomes are intricately related to implementation of improved training programs for career specialists, initiation of short and long term minority research programs, and more intensive efforts to reduce the practice of racism in employment.

We have seen that the term minority is, indeed, global. The meaning of the term now includes these designations: 1. Blacks; 2. Spanish-Surnamed; 3. American Indian; 4. Asian American; and 5. Other. For some purposes, the term now includes females. However, the term was used only in reference to the ethnic classifications of minorities in this chapter.

Present and future achievements pertinent to career development for ethnic minorities will focus on the elements of concern considered: 1. Minority Classifications and Implications; 2. Minority Counseling; 3. Minority Testing and Evaluation; and 4. Effective Career Development Systems for Minorities.

BIBLIOGRAPHY

Beck, J.D. *The Counselor and Black/White Relations.* Guidance Monograph Series, No. VIII. Boston: Houghton-Mifflin, 1973.

Carkhuff, R.A., and Berenson, B.G. *Beyond Counseling and Therapy.* New York: Holt, Rinehart, and Winston, 1967.

Carkhuff, R.A. *Helping and Human Relations.* Vol. I, Selection and Training. New York: Holt, Rinehart, and Winston, 1969 (a).

Carkhuff, R.A. *Helping and Human Relations.* Vol. II, Practice and Research. New York: Holt, Rinehart, and Winston, 1969 (b).

Carkhuff, R.A. Credo of a militant humanist. *Personnel and Guidance Journal*, 1972, *51*, 237-242.

Clark, K.B. *A Possible Reality.* New York: Emerson Hall, 1972.

Davenport, L., and Petty, R. *Minorities and Career Education.* Columbus: ECCA, 1973.

Elster, W.L. Vocational Exploration Group. *Guidepost,* 1973, *6,* 5.

Equal Employment Opportunity Commission. Proposed EEOC Regulations. *Labor Relations.* Englewood Cliffs, N.J.: Prentice Hall, 1973.

Flaugher, R.L. *Some Points of Confusion in Discussing the Testing of Black Students.* Paper prepared for a Symposium of the American Educational Research Association Annual Meeting, New Orleans, Louisiana, February, 1973.

Gelatt, H.B., Varenhorst, B., Carey, R., and Miller, G.P. *Decisions and Outcomes.* New York: The College Entrance Examination Board, 1973.

Gunnings, T. A systematic approach to counseling disadvantaged youth. *Journal of Non-White Concerns,* 1972, *3,* 1.

Hill, W.F. *Learning Thru Discussion.* Beverly Hills: Sage, 1962 and 1969.

Holland, J.L. *The Self-Directed Search.* Palo Alto: Consulting Psychologists Press, 1970.

Holland, J.L. *The Occupations Finder.* Palo Alto: Consulting Psychologists Press, 1972 (a).

Holland, J.L. *The Occupations Finder.* Palo Alto: Consulting Psychologists Press, 1972 (b).

Holland, J.L. *The Self-Directed Search.* Palo Alto: Consulting Psychologists Press, 1973.

Holland, J.L. Some guidelines for reducing systematic biases in the delivery of vocational services. *Measurement and Evaluation in Guidance,* 1974, *4,* 210-218.

Human Development Institute—1974-75 catalog. *Encounter Tapes for Black/White Groups.* Human Development Institute. A division of Instructional Dynamics Incorporated, 166 E. Superior St., Chicago, Illinois.

Johnson, R. *Black Agenda for Career Education.* Columbus: ECCA, 1974.

Karnes, M.B., Zehrback, R.R., and Jones, G.R. *The Culturally Disadvantaged Student and Guidance.* Guidance Monograph Series, No. V. Boston: Houghton-Mifflin, 1971.

Kimball, R.L., et al. *Black and White Vocational Interests on Holland's Self-Directed Search (SDS).* Report No. CSC-RR-6-71. College Park, Maryland: Cultural Study Center, Maryland University, 1971.

Marland, S.P., Jr. Career Education and the Minorities. Speech before a national convention on Career Education: Implication for Minorities, Sheraton-Park Hotel, Washington, D.C., February, 1973.

Menacker, J. *Urban Poor Students and Guidance.* Guidance Monograph Series, No. VI. Boston: Houghton-Mifflin, 1971.

Nixon, R.M. The State of the Union Address by the President of the United States, 92nd Cong., 2nd sess., *Congressional Record,* January 1972, *118,* 494-509.

Perkins, J.A., et al. *Priorities for Action: The Final Report of the Carnegie Commission on Higher Education.* New York: McGraw-Hill Book Co., 1973.

Planning: Your Post-High School Career (Student's Booklet). Iowa City: The American College Testing Program, 1972, 1973.

Rapp, D.W., and Capuzzi, D. Information intermix: A group approach to maximize human learning. *The Guidance Clinic,* 1973, *5,* 1-4.

Sedlacek, W.E., and Brooks, G.C., Jr. *Race as an Experimenter Effect in Racial Attitude Measurement.* Report No. CSC-RR-1-71. College Park, Maryland: Cultural Study Center, Maryland University, 1971.

Sowell, T. The great IQ controversy. *Change,* 1970, *5,* 33-37.

Stone, W.O. *Black Publication Trends in Three Counseling Journals.* Paper presented at the American College Personnel Association Annual Convention, Cleveland, Ohio, April, 1973.

Stone, W.O., and Harper, F.D. *Transcendent Counseling for Blacks: A Modular-Conceptual Theory.* A paper presented at the American Personnel and Guidance Association Regional Convention, Atlanta, Georgia, May, 1973.

Stone, W.O., and Harper, F.D. *A Treatment-Training Model for the Transcendent Counselor and Counselee.* A program presented at the 1974 American Personnel and Guidance Association Convention, New Orleans, Louisiana, April, 1974.

Truax, C.B. An approach to counselor education. *Counselor Education and Supervision,* 1970, *10,* 4-15.

Vontress, C.E. *Counseling Negroes.* Guidance Monograph Series, No. VI. Boston: Houghton-Mifflin, 1971.

Welsing, F.C. *The Cress Theory of Color-Confrontation and Racism (White Supremacy).* Washington, D.C.: Howard University, 1970.

Chapter Fifteen

ACCOUNTABILITY IN PROGRAM EVALUATION: A HYPOTHETICAL CASE STUDY

GARY W. PETERSON

A FUNDAMENTAL TREND in career development activities will likely hallmark the mid 70's: there will be a need for a broader perspective in service programs relating to the career decision-making process while financial support for such programs will be held at current levels or reduced. Consequently, institutional administrators will rely on results from evaluation studies to help them allocate resources wisely to meet institutional goals or clientele needs. The present chapter takes the Stufflebeam (1971) view of program evaluation which is to assist decision-makers by providing reliable evidence regarding the effectiveness of service programs in accommodating clientele needs. The intent of this chapter is to present a process for evaluating service programs and to acquaint the reader with some of the major issues in accountability in program evaluation.

HISTORICAL PERSPECTIVE

During the mid and latter 60's, service programs were often supported by rather plentiful supplies of financial resources from federal, state and local governmental coffers. Programs were often justified under the rationale of helping a disadvantaged population cope with a rather vaguely defined problem, usually described in emotionally laden rhetoric. Even though program goals were ambiguously defined, as long as people were carrying on some activity, no one really questioned the merits of such efforts. However, due to such pressing national problems in the early 70's as the balance of payments deficit, rising inflation, the growing national debt, etc., which resulted in the attrition of fiscal surpluses, the availability of external funds to support innovative service programs began to decrease. As a result, institutions were compelled to assume larger costs from internal resources which in turn necessitated the examination of their programs more carefully in terms of results relative to costs. These events provided underlying conditions for what is now often referred to as the accountability movement. Accountability may be defined as *who* is directly responsible for promoting *what* discernible outcomes by *which* set of legitimate means (Henry, 1972). Given limited fiscal resources to support service programs, the issue of accountability in program evaluation is now regarded with increasing importance.

A Sample Problem

To illustrate important procedures and issues regarding accountability in program evaluation, a hypothetical example of a career development program at Middleberg High School, USA, will be used throughout the remainder of the chapter for purposes of clarification. Often, service programs may arise out of either the implementation of existing institutional objectives or from a proposal to meet a new institutional need. For example, at Middleberg High School an under-representation in college parallel courses and a disproportionate drop-out rate existed for minority groups. This phenomenon was attributed to low vocational aspiration levels and expectations held by members of these groups. At the same time an institutional goal stated that: the school shall provide opportunity for the maximum fulfillment of individual potentialities. When evidence of inequalities in college parallel representation and in attrition rate was presented to leaders of these minority groups, pressure was placed on the county school board and the high school principal to develop programs which might have an impact on rectifying these discrepancies.

DOCUMENTATION OF NEED

An important aspect in the development of any service program is the precise documentation of the need for it. Many programs have been doomed to failure from the accountability standpoint because they were founded on a false problem or championed by one or two individuals. In the case of Middleberg High, it would be extremely important to know the number and the distribution of minority and majority students among occupational levels (see Tables 15-I and 15-II). These data provide not only a necessary baseline for performance goals, but they can also be used to promote the program and estimate its required resources. Documenting a need is commonly alluded to as a *needs assessment.* A well conducted needs assessment enables the setting of clear and reasonable performance goals upon which the program will be held ac-

TABLE 15-I
OCCUPATIONAL AND EDUCATIONAL PLACEMENT OF MIDDLEBERG HIGH SCHOOL SENIOR MALES

		MAJORITY		*MINORITY*	
		N	%	N	%
I	COLLEGE OR UNIVERSITY	400	40.0	30	15.0
II	COMMUNITY COLLEGE OR				
	TECHNICAL SCHOOL	250	25.0	50	25.0
III	CLERICAL	200	20.0	30	15.0
IV	UNSKILLED LABOR	100	10.0	50	25.0
V	DROP-OUTS FROM ORIGINAL				
	10TH GRADE POPULATION	25	2.5	20	10.0
VI	UNEMPLOYED	25	2.5	20	10.0
	TOTAL	1000	100.0	200	100.0

TABLE 15-II
OCCUPATIONAL AND EDUCATIONAL PLACEMENT OF MIDDLEBERG HIGH SCHOOL SENIOR FEMALES

		MAJORITY		*MINORITY*	
		N	%	N	%
I	COLLEGE OR UNIVERSITY	300	30.0	30	15.0
II	COMMUNITY COLLEGE OR				
	TECHNICAL SCHOOL	200	20.0	30	15.0
III	CLERICAL	100	10.0	20	10.0
IV	UNSKILLED LABOR	175	17.5	80	40.0
V	DROP-OUTS FROM ORIGINAL				
	10TH GRADE POPULATION	25	2.5	10	5.0
VI	UNEMPLOYED	200	20.0	40	20.0
	TOTAL	1000	100.0	200	100.0

countable. The needs assessment for the Middleberg High project provided the following information about twelfth grade educational and occupational placement of minority and majority groups.

The results of the needs assessment revealed that there were major differences between minority and majority groups in terms of level of occupational and educational placements for both males and females. These data provided comparisons with which to document the need for a career development program and to establish a baseline against which to evaluate its effectiveness.

THE PROGRAM

Upon the presentation of these findings to the Middleberg County School Board, a program leader and two associates were designated to formulate a career development program to address the issue of lower occupational aspirations and placement levels of minorities. A program, directed to the 10th grade, was planned during the following summer and instituted in the fall with three full-time professionals. Goal statements and behavioral objectives were formulated. Activities to attain these goals included career exploration groups, individual aptitude and personality assessment, field trips to work settings and to schools, and career exploration sessions for parents of participants. Facilities included a conference room with an educational-vocational library and three individual counseling offices. A secretary was appointed for typing, record-keeping, testing and receptionist activities. A requirement of the program was that evaluations of the program would be submitted annually to the Middleberg County School Board. The program was supported on a pilot basis the first year and included working with 200 tenth graders from minority populations. Each year afterward for three years, the program was to be open to all who wished to participate on a voluntary basis.

Stage 1: Purpose of the Evaluation

At the first stage, four issues should be resolved at the beginning of the evaluation process. First, in any accountability system, it is important to know *who* will make *what* kinds of decisions or take *what* kinds of action. Decisions are made at a number of levels. At the practitioner level, the instructors may wish to evaluate impact of each activity on individual participants, so as to improve the quality of the activities. The Middleberg High School principal may wish to know the extent of the impact the program has had on all participants, and participants' parents or non-participants as well, for the purpose of making decisions regarding space utilization or teaching assignments. At the next level, the County School Board may wish to know how effective the program is in relation to its costs in order to determine whether to disseminate the program to other schools, maintain the *status quo,* or to discontinue support of the program.

A second issue is the *criteria* on which decisions will be made. In all likelihood decisions will be made on the basis of the interaction among several overt and covert criteria. It is the evaluator's task to identify the overt and covert criteria as explicitly and as operationally as possible. In the case of the Middleberg Career Development program, an overt criterion on which the program is held accountable may be cost-effectiveness in achieving its goals, but a covert criterion may be whether the program receives notoriety in the local press as a showpiece of educational concern. In order to produce an effective evaluation for decision-making, the evaluator should become cognizant of criteria operating at both of these levels.

A third consideration is the conclusion which decision-makers might wish to draw from an evaluation study. Examples of conclusions stated in research form may be: (1) Program A is more effective than no program; (2) Program A is more effective than Program B; (3) There is a highly probable cause-effect relationship between participation in Program A and a change in behavior Y; (4) Program A is more efficient than Program B; etc. The exact nature of the desired conclusion governs the nature of the research methodology employed in the evaluation.

Finally, the kinds of data decision-makers comprehend or consider credible should be identified. Some individuals believe that numbers never lie while others abhor statistical data because it never tells the whole truth. Furthermore, the decision-makers may possess a wide degree of knowledge regarding research methodology and statistical techniques. Therefore, if the final product of an evaluation is a report, it ought to communicate necessary information concisely, comprehensibly and reliably to the readership.

Stage 2: Setting Performance Indicators

The second stage of the evaluation process is the task of defining valid performance indicators upon which to hold the program accountable. In the case of the Middleberg High program, the county school board wished to know *how much* it cost to produce *what kinds* of effects. Before the implementation of the program, the board wished to know the performance indicators on which the program would be assessed.

Performance indicators may be derived from a number of sources: program goals, results of a needs assessment, theoretical rationales, life styles analyses of target populations, etc. The general aim of the Middleberg High Career Development program was stated as follows: to facilitate the realization of individual productive potentials. Examples of two program goals edifying this general aim are:

1) To identify occupations consistent with each student's abilities and interests.
2) To relate minimal educational requirements and entry-level skills to at least five occupations which are consistent with a student's abilities and interests.

Using these goal statements, an evaluator may observe the following performances: the accuracy with which students recall results of tests; given an expectancy table students assess their chances for gaining admission to several colleges; given five occupations, students state educational requirements for those occupations, etc.

A complete program evaluation should contain two basic sets of performance indicators. The first set of performance indicators should evaluate the effectiveness of each individual program activity while the second set should assess the effects on the target population resulting from the *total* program. Examples of indicators for the first set (program activities) may include: percentage of students or parents attending given activities; performance on short content quizzes on occupational study units; recall of results from a diagnostic testing unit; attitudes about an occupation after an on-site visitation; etc. Examples of the second set of indicators (effects from total program) may be: changes in drop-out rate; change in grade point average; change in percentage of students continuing their education; changes in aspiration levels for educational or vocational attainment; changes in attitudes toward school; etc.

As a general rule, the smaller the program in terms of participants, the more indicators should be observed. When judgments are made from smaller population samples, more information is required from each subject in order to draw inferences about the impact of the program. A program such as the Middleberg High School program with 200 students per year may require several indicators, while programs with 20-30 participants would require more. Finally, attention should be paid to the validity of the performance indicators. Individuals who read an evaluation report must believe that an indicator relates directly to the program goals and to the problem the program addresses.

Stage 3: Selecting the Data

The third stage in the evaluation process involves the determination of the kinds and quantities of data to collect. One axiom in evaluation is that the evaluator should collect no more data than he can effectively manage. Much effort is wasted if incomplete or inaccurate data are collected in the attempt to assess too many outcomes. The simplest, least expensive, and most easily accessible indicators are most often the best. Among the types of data one could collect are the following: 1. behavioral data; 2. attitudinal assessments; 3. published psychological tests, inventories and questionnaires; 4. descriptive statements or testimonials; and 5. monetary expenditures.

Stage 4: Analyzing the Data

The fourth stage is the application of basic research procedures for the manipulation and analysis of data. The selection of possible research designs depends upon a number of factors, e.g. at what stage in the development of the program the evaluator is consulted, whether control or comparison groups are accessible for testing, the sample size, the institutional policies toward testing, the conclusions one wishes to draw from the study, etc. (An in-depth treatment of research designs is not deemed appropriate for this writing. However, if the reader is interested, basic research designs are described in Tuckman, B.W., 1972.)

Three examples of basic research designs which could be used in the evaluation of the Middleberg High School project include: 1. one group pretest-posttest design, 2. posttest-only control group design, 3. a co-relational study. The *one group pretest-posttest design* may be used to assess the knowledge a subject gains about an occupation from a field trip. This design makes use of a measure before an experience, a similar measure after the experience, and the notation of the difference. The second, the *posttest-only control group design* assesses differences in attitudes or performance (e.g. grade point average, drop-out rate, credits earned) between an experimental group and one or more control groups. It assumes that the experimental and control groups are drawn at random from the same general population. That is, if one control group is used, the experimental population of minority students and the control sample would both be drawn from the same general population of minority students. Since the experimental group and the control group would then possess the exact same characteristics at the outset, differences in behavior or attitudes taken after an experimental treatment can be attributed to the effects of the treatment. The third, a *co-relational* study may be used to demonstrate the relationship between the number of interviews a student conducts with workers from a variety of job settings and the degree of change in occupational aspirations. This analysis assesses the strength of a relationship between two continuous variables such as the number of interviews versus the degree of change. Using the co-relational design one investigates whether the more of one variable (number of interviews) is associated with the more of the other variable (amount of change). An important characteristic of co-relational studies is that one cannot conclude a causal relationship between variables, only an association. The choice of design enables the evaluator or decision-maker to draw certain conclusions or inferences about the effects of programs and the validity of those conclusions. For instance, without control groups, cause-effect relationships can never be reliably affirmed but only inferred.

A final issue in analysis of the data is the matter of cost of the program in relation to its impact. Ultimately, the fundamental purpose of an accountability system is to optimize the relationship between resources and results (Knezevich, 1973). The ratio between outputs (results) and resources (costs) may be referred to by the term *cost-effectiveness* (C/E). Returning to the Middleberg High School Career Development program, the school board wished to know the impact of the program on the minority student drop-out rate. Table 15-III summarizes the results for males relative to a comparison group from a previous year.

TABLE 15-III
COMPARISON BETWEEN THE DROP-OUT RATE OF PARTICIPANT
MALES AND NON-PARTICIPANT MALES

		PARTICIPANTS *n=200*		*NON-PARTICIPANTS* *n=200*	
		N	%	N	%
10th grade		3	1.5	7	3.5
11th grade		4	2.0	7	3.5
12th grade		3	1.5	6	3.0
	TOTAL	10	5.0	20	10.0

Three years after the program, it was observed that there were 10 (5%) dropouts among those who participated in the program and 20 (10%) drop-outs among the control group from the previous year. If the experimental program had no effect, one would expect approximately the same number of drop-outs in both groups. Therefore, the program likely had an impact of decreasing the drop-out rate by 5 percent $\left(\dfrac{10 \text{ "saved"}}{200 \text{ original population}} \right)$

To conduct the program for the first year, the costs for planning, personnel, clerical assistance, expenses, renovations, travel, supplies, etc., amounted to $30,000.00. This amounted to an expense to the school system of $3,000 per student who would have dropped out $\left(\dfrac{10 \text{ "saved"}}{\$30,000.00} \right)$. The C/E is therefore $3,000 per student drop-out saved. The cost-effectiveness ratio (C/E) in this instance is useful in comparing the efficiency of similar programs at different settings in terms of expenses relative to output. Remember that planning costs and renovations were included in the first year C/E ratio. Given the same performance in the following years, the program will appear to be more efficient since these costs are spread over a longer period of time.

Another ratio used in evaluating the worth of a program is a *cost-benefit ratio* (B/C) —output value/output cost. In the Middleberg High School Career Development program, the cost-effectiveness analysis revealed that ten students achieved a high school diploma who might not have under the pre-existing conditions. This outcome could represent a considerable contribution to the society in terms of increased productivity. If these ten students were able to earn at least $1,000 more than drop-outs in the first year after graduation, then an increase in productivity of $10,000 to society in one year would result. The cost-benefit ratio for the program is .33 for one year.

$$B/C = \frac{\text{output value (\$10,000 in increased earnings)}}{\text{output cost (\$30,000 for cost of the program)}}$$

One can note in the example that in the period of one year, the program does not realize its investment, i.e. program costs exceed return values in the time period. However, if the cost-benefit time period is extended for three years, the ratio would accrue 1.0 or the break-even point. However, it is likely that increments in wages are divergent when comparing wages of high school drop-outs to high school graduates as time progresses. Therefore, the break-even point would likely occur at less than three years. The cost-benefit analysis is helpful in assessing the net worth to society in relation to expenditure. To reiterate, in this example, costs included planning and renovations which are one-time expenses. Assuming similar performance, the cost-benefit ratio becomes higher as the time interval is extended. The C/E and B/C ratios will probably be used more often in the future as institution implement Program Planning and Budgeting Systems where programs are funded on the basis of costs required to attain specific performance goals. These ratios provide concise accountability measures from which to make difficulty monetary decisions about programs. However, the complexities of deriving the coefficients may be more intricate than is described here.

Stage 5: The Decision-Making Process

Ultimately, a decision will be made concerning whether to expand, to maintain the status quo, to cut back resource allocations, or to phase out the program. The decision will likely be made on the basis of evidence of performance and intuitive impressions of the decision-makers. Furthermore, not all judgments about the program will be based on empirically substantiated outcomes. Cryptic criteria may exist in such forms as an attitude held by a member of a policy board who happened to hear of an unfavorable incident associated with the program or that the program inopportunely became a political football or bargaining chip among high level administrators attempting to invoke territorial imperatives. Sometimes existing programs must compete for survival with innovative proposals. A school administrator might be required to apportion resources between an existing career development program and a proposed remedial reading program and weigh the observed benefits of the former with anticipated benefits of the latter. However, if reliable and comprehensive evidence exists about the effects of the former, chances are increased that the program may not only be continued but improved as well. Hopefully, the trend will continue where decisions are based on evidence from reliable performance measures over subjective or intuitive impressions.

SUMMARY

The issue of accountability in program evaluation is only a beginning in the development, improvement and survival of a good program. The procedures and issues covered in this chapter are intended to help the practitioners in both determining areas for improving the program and in justifying its place among other service programs in light of limited or diminishing financial resources. For the administrator or decision-maker, the chapter pointed out procedures and information that could be used for making decisions and for establishing priorities regarding programs which most effectively serve the needs of the institution or the community.

BIBLIOGRAPHY

Bloom, B.S., Hastings, J.T., and Madaus, G.F. *Handbook on Formative and Summative Evaluation of Student Learning.* New York: McGraw-Hill, 1971.

Henry, D.D. Accountability: To whom, for what, by what means? *Journal of Educational Research,* 1972, *53,* 287-292.

Knezevich, S.J. *Program Budgeting (PPBS).* Berkeley, California: McCutchan Pub. Co., 1973.

Stufflebeam, D.I., et al. *Educational Evaluation and Decision-making.* Bloomington, Indiana: Phi Delta Kappa, Inc., 1971.

Tuckman, B.W. *Conducting Educational Research.* New York: Harcourt, Brace and Jovanovich, 1972.

APPENDIX

A CAREER DEVELOPMENT MODEL IN A UNIVERSITY SETTING

Camille W. Ashcraft

T HE PURPOSE of this appendix is to present a career development model designed to provide an overview of the knowledge, skills, and attitudes students need to facilitate their own career development at the university level. Although the model will be defined specifically in terms of those services provided by units in the Office of Undergraduate Advisement and Counseling at Florida State University, it might be extended to include a description of all career development services offered to students within any college setting. It can also be used by counselors elsewhere who need to develop goals and objectives for a career development program at their own institutions.

Having a model to work from is important because it provides a framework for the identification, development, implementation, and evaluation of career development programs. By providing a comprehensive conceptual framework for career development activities, the model allows both staff and students the opportunity to identify the variety of services available to them and permits them to select the activity which most appropriately satisfies their needs in the career development area. In addition, the model provides a format for the evaluation of services by focusing on numbers and types of students served. It also provides for the coordination of services by identifying areas of unnecessary repetition and/or gaps. It supplies a blueprint for the development and implementation of new programs. And finally, through the process of continual revision and refinement, the model can remain flexible and responsive to the career development needs of students.

The model presented in the following pages is an adaptation of the Career Conscious Individual Model reported by Norman C. Gysbers and Earl J. Moore (1974). Their model was designed primarily for grades K-12. The adapted model lacks the developmental aspects stressed in the Career Conscious Individual Model, but appears to be none-the-less applicable to a college setting. The adapted model consists of three basic domains which serve as organizers for present and future career development programs. These domains are highly similar to the four domains established by Gysbers and Moore. The three basic domains are (1) Self-Knowledge and Interpersonal Skills, (2) Educational and Occupational Knowledge and Preparation, and (3) Knowledge and Implementation of Life Career Planning Skills. These domains are discussed briefly in the following paragraphs.

In the *Self-Knowledge and Interpersonal Skill Domain,* activities focus on helping the student understand himself and others. The major concepts involve the student's awareness and acceptance of himself and others, the development of interpersonal skills, and the awareness of environmental influences on career development. Within this domain the student begins to develop an awareness of his personal characteristics: interests, aspirations, aptitudes, abilities, and values. He learns techniques for self-appraisal and analysis of personal characteristics in terms of present and future development. The student also becomes knowledgeable about the interactive relationship of self and environment in such a way that he develops personal standards and a sense of purpose in life. As a consequence of experiences in this domain the student will utilize self knowledge in life career planning and become self-directed by accepting responsibility for his own behavior.

In the *Educational and Occupational Knowledge and Preparation Domain,* emphasis is placed on knowledge and understanding of the structure and dimensions of the educational, work, and leisure worlds. The student is encouraged to relate educational course work and plans to future occupational goals. The student becomes aware that there are many occupations and industries which comprise the world of work, and that these occupations and industries can be grouped in a number of ways. Emphasis is placed on the student's learning of selected associations among specific occupational requirements and characteristics and personal skills, interests, values, and aspirations. The rapidity of social and technological change and other factors affecting the flux of the work force and the work situation are elements considered in this domain. Emphasis is also placed on the student becoming involved in actual work experiences which can increase his knowledge of a specific occupation and the realities of the work world. In addition, this domain focuses on the development of employability skills which may facilitate the job seeking, obtaining, and maintaining process.

In the *Knowledge and Implementation of Life Career Planning Skills Domain,* the student is encouraged to understand that decision-making and planning are important tasks in the life career planning process. One focus of this domain is the mastery of decision-making skills related to career planning. The student begins to develop skills in this area by identifying the elements of the decision-making process. He is encouraged to develop skills in gathering materials from relevant sources both external and internal and to learn to utilize the collected information in making informed and reasonable decisions. As a consequence of activities in this domain the student will begin to engage in planning activities and to accept responsibility for making his own choices. Ultimately he will implement his career planning skills by selecting a specific job from a number of alternate choices. Another dimension of this domain includes the concept of change as it affects career planning. The student is encouraged to foresee alternatives which he might choose and to determine the implication of these alternatives in terms of his present planning. The purpose of activities in this domain is to facilitate the development of students who value planning and who formulate and implement reasonable career plans.

Each domain contains important concepts, goals, and objectives derived from needs statements. Activities have been identified for each objective in the model. In constructing the activity section it was recognized that each activity could fulfill from one to several of the listed objectives. In order to avoid over-generalization and confusion, an effort was made to place each activity with the objective it fulfilled most appropriately. Therefore, the focus was placed on the primary purpose of each activity rather than on the secondary goals it might also fulfill in movement toward the primary goal(s).

The following pages represent a model description of some of the career development activities at a large, State supported university. The model consists of concepts, goals, objectives, and activities. Each activity is identified with the unit providing the service. Additional information includes the number and type of students served as well as a description of the activity. Ideally, the model would include a statement of the specific outcomes expected at the termination of each activity. Although the present model does not include specific outcomes, the statement of outcomes would be an important undertaking in future refinements. It should be noted that the model is incomplete in several areas and restricted to the description of only some of the possible career development activities available at the college level. However, it does provide a starting point for the description and categorization of career development activities within a particular model, which can serve several important functions for organizing an effective career development program at the university level.

BIBLIOGRAPHY

Gysbers, N. and Moore, E.J. *The Career Guidance, Counseling and Placement Project*. Columbia: University of Missouri, 1974.

DOMAIN I: SELF KNOWLEDGE AND INTERPERSONAL SKILLS

A. Concept: An individual is unique. That is, individuals differ in their interests, aptitudes, abilities, values, and attitudes.

    Goal: The student will realize and utilize in his own planning the fact that his personal characteristics are unique and will influence his career related decisions.

    Objective: The student will become aware of his unique personal characteristics which he can utilize in his career planning.

Unit: Curricular Career Information Center

    Activity: CCIS Module III: Self Assessment

    For: All students

    Serves:

    Descriptions: This activity enables the student to examine himself in terms of his interests and values related to career decision making. A self-administered test, the Self Directed Search, is included in the module and permits the student to relate his personal characteristics to potentially satisfying majors and occupations.

Unit: University Counseling Center

    Activity: Career Development Lab (Proposed) : Assessment

    For: All students

    Serves:

    Description: The Lab will provide the student with information concerning his own unique interests and abilities through appropriate standardized tests.

B. Concept: As members of society, people interrelate.

    Goal: The student will develop adequate interpersonal skills.

C. Concept: Self development is a personal responsibility.

    Goal: The student will understand that he alone is responsible for implementing his goals.

        Objective: The student will develop confidence in his ability to be autonomous and self-directed.

        Unit: University Counseling Center

           Activity: Personal Counseling

             For: Students with Inadequate Self Concepts

Serves:
Description: Counseling at the University Counseling Center provides assistance to the student who is anxious, depressed, confused, or alienated over his lack of direction. Counseling can help him find a sense of direction and purpose in his search for a career. By helping the student to understand the underlying causes for his feelings, the counselor helps the student to become more confident in his ability to become an autonomous, independent adult who can contribute to the world of work.

D. Concept: An individual is influenced by his environment.
   Goal: The student will understand how different environmental factors may affect his career development.
   1. Objective: The black student will be aware of factors which may influence his career development.
      Unit: CCIS Curricular Career Information Service
      Activity: CCIS Module V—Special Opportunities for Blacks
      For: All Black Students
      Serves:
      (1) Periodicals
          Description: The periodicals include materials on equal opportunities for minority group college graduates in the areas of locating, recruiting, and employment.
      (2) Planning Guide for Graduate School and Graduate and Professional School Opportunities
      (3) Videotapes
          Description: The videotapes include

information on job placement interviews and techniques, careers for
Blacks, and specific career opportunities for Blacks in the navy, business, postal service, and the theater.
(4) Articles
Description: Articles are available
describing employment outlooks for
Blacks in specific fields.

Unit: University Counseling Center
    Activity: Career Information for Black
        Students
    For: Black Students
    (1) Black Career Week
        Serves: Approximately 75
        Description: Black Career's Week is
        designed to make black students
        aware of career opportunities avail-
        able to them in the 70's and 80's.
        Blacks representing various career
        fields speak to the students serving
        as career development models for
        them. Printed career information
        for Blacks is also distributed to the
        students.
    (2) Black Careers Club
        Serves: 50
        Description: The purpose of the
        club is to research, compile and com-
        municate career opportunities for
        Blacks.
    (3) Career Raps for Blacks
        Serves: 75
        Description: The career raps focus
        on vocational opportunities, inter-
        ests, and employability skills for
        Blacks.

(4) Athlete Career Rap for Black Athletes (Proposed)
For: All Black Athletes
Serves:
Description: The purpose of these raps will be to enhance and instill in the black athlete the desire to obtain a B.A. or B.S. degree as opposed to aiming toward reaching the Pro's only.

(5) Employability Skill Workshop
For: Blacks and Whites
Serves:
Description: The workshop is designed to provide the student with insights and skills in the interviewing process. It concentrates on appropriate dress, communication skills, writing applications and resumes, and the importance of appearing poised and confident.

(6) Interest Assessment
Serves: 130
Description: By providing the black student with a vocational interest inventory, the black student is given additional insights about his expressed interests. It is given to Horizon Unlimited Students and others.

1. Objective: The female student will be aware of her role in society and of factors which may facilitate or inhibit her personal and career development.
   Unit: Curricular Career Information Service
   Activity: CCIS Module V: Career Guidance Materials for Women
   For: Women Students

Serves:

(1) Books about Women and Careers
Description: These books include information on careers for women in the 70's: the women doctorate, the woman in management, developing women's potential, and day care facts.

(2) Career Guidance Materials
Description: These materials provide guidance and occupational information for women who want to re-enter the labor market.

Unit: University Counseling Center

Activity: Women's Programs Relates to Career Development.

For: Women Students

(1) Women's Discussion Group Program
Serves:
Description: Groups of 10-12 women meet together for 10 two hour meetings. Discussion guides and exercises allow the women to deal with issues which tend to hinder their career development. Emphasis on understanding such feelings and irrational ideas which might interfere with optimal vocational development, the members are encouraged to practice new behaviors and explore a wider range of career options.

(2) Course, Psy 399, Psychology of Women
Serves: 80-90 yearly: mostly women
Description: The course covers a wide range of theoretical and empirical literature on women and

their roles in society. Students become familiar with problems women encounter in educational and vocational endeavors, as well as attitudinal and affective variables significant in women's career development. Students are encouraged to apply these ideas to an understanding of their own personal development.

(3) Dormitory Consultation and Programming

For: Lower Division Women Students

Serves: Approximately 100

Description: Discussions held with women's dorm counselors and RA's regarding problems of women students which reflect the influences of irrational social forces on the young women. In this manner lower division women are introduced to attitudinal and behavioral issues which need to be dealt with if they are to progress optimally in educational and career development.

3. Objective: The homosexual student will be aware of factors which may facilitate or inhibit his career development.

Unit: University Counseling Center

Activity: Gay Peer Counseling

For: Homosexual Students

Serves:

Description: Gay Peer Counseling attempts to help homosexuals with career problems specific to their minority status through one-to-one peer counseling.

DOMAIN II: EDUCATIONAL AND OCCUPATIONAL KNOWLEDGE AND PREPARATION

A. Concept: Education and work are interrelated.

    Goal: The student will understand that educational experiences are related to applied experiences in a chosen field.

        Objective: The student will be aware of educational paths which lead to specific occupations.

           Unit: Curricular Career Information Service
Activity: CCIS Module IV

              (1) Relate Personal Characteristics to Majors
For: Freshmen and Sophomores
Serves: Approximately 900 yearly
Description: Module IV provides the student with data concerning college majors related to his profile on the Self Directed Search (SDS).

              (2) FSU Catalog
For: Freshmen and Sophomores
Serves: Approximately 900 yearly
Description: After identifying a major or several majors related to his personal characteristics, the student may read a summary of the major in the FSU Catalog.

              (3) File on Majors
For: Freshmen and Sophomores
Serves: Approximately 900 yearly
Description: A file containing information on specific majors is available to the student.

              (4) Recorded Interviews with Professors
For: Freshmen and Sophomores
Serves: Approximately 900
Description: Recorded interviews are provided so that the student can

view what it is like to be a student
in a particular department or area.
(5) Curricular and Career Resources
Directory
For: Freshmen and Sophomores
Serves:
Description: This Directory provides
the names of faculty members in
various departments whom the student can contact for additional information about majoring in their area
of specialization.
Unit: Center for Academic and Career Exploration for Undecided Majors
Activity:
(1) Counseling Service for Undecided
Majors
For: Freshmen and Sophomores
Serves: Projected 800-1,200 yearly
Description: The counseling service
for undecided students encourages
the student to consider past and present experiences when considering career options. After the student has explored options available to him and
narrowed his field of choices, the
counselor helps him to relate the
educational programs available at
FSU to his career choices.

B. Concept: Knowledge of the structure of the world of work is
important.
Goal: The student will understand that there are a wide
variety of occupations available to him.
1. Objective: The student will be aware of existing
and emerging career opportunities.
Unit: Curricular Career Information Service
Activity: CCIS Module IV

(1) Occupations Finder
For: All Students
Serves: Approximately 900
Description: The occupational information provided in Module **IV** allows the student to match his personal characteristics derived from a Self Directed Search with occupations which might interest him. Using his SDS code and the Occupations Finder he will be able to identify a list of occupations which interest him.

(2) Dictionary of Occupational Titles
For: All students
Serves:
Description: The student may choose one or more occupations which interest him and investigate them further through the use of the *DOT.* The *DOT* provides information on qualifications, requirements, working conditions, salary, and employment outlook.

(3) Audio taped Interviews
For: All students
Serves:
Description: Audio-tapes of interviews with persons in different careers are available to provide the student with specific information on specific careers.

(4) Books and References to Materials in Strozier Library.
For: All Students
Serves:
Description: Books on specific career

areas and related materials available in Strozier Library also provide information on specific occupations.

Unit: Cooperative Education

Activity: Occupational Information

(1) Vocational Counseling

For: All students

Serves: Approximately 600 yearly

Description: Vocational counseling in the Coop Unit provides the student with information concerning various career areas open to him and associated entrance requirements.

(2) Annual Career Week

For: All students

Serves: Approximately 250

Description: During one week each year representatives from five nationally acclaimed career areas (advertising, government, education, insurance, and social action agencies) visit the campus and participate in a workshop where they speak to students about career opportunities in their area of specialization.

(3) Career Seminars

For: All students

Serves: Approximately 400 yearly

Description: Career scpecialists visit the campus as speakers throughout the year with the purpose of acquainting students with different career areas.

(4) Guest Speakers from the Coop Unit

For: All Students

Serves: Approximately 300-400 yearly

Description: Representatives from the Coop staff serve as guest speakers and resource persons for classes, dorm residents, minority groups, and others in order to provide information about existing and emerging career opportunities.

(5) Coop Career Library

For: All students

Serves: Approximately 200 yearly

Description: The Coop Library contains current information from recruiters concerning job opportunities, salaries, and geographical locations.

Unit: Career Planning and Placement

Activity: Occupational Information

(1) Vocational Counseling

For: All students

Serves: 2,800 students yearly

Description: Vocational counseling in the Placement Unit provides the student with information concerning various career areas and associated entrance requirements.

(2) Guest Speakers

For: All students

Serves: Approximately 150 yearly

Description: Guest speakers representing various employers describe job opportunities available in various career areas.

(3) Placement Library

For: All students

Serves: Approximately 4,500

Description: The Placement Library provides reading materials concerning various general career fields and specific employers as well as graduate school catalogs.

(4) College Placement Council Salary Survey

For: All students

Serves: Posted on bulletin board outside Placement Office.

Description: This survey consists of a collection and reporting of salary offers to recent FSU graduates.

2. Objective: The student will become involved in work experiences which will further his capacity to identify and choose between particular vocations suitable to his personal goals, abilities, and interests.

Unit: Cooperative Education Unit

Activity: Cooperative Education Placements

For: All students who have completed two quarters of academic study and have a 2.0 GPA.

Serves: 220 placements yearly

(1) Alternate Quarter Work Experience

Description: The student can investigate different employment areas while continuing his academic studies on a traditional schedule which alternates one quarter of full time work with one quarter of academic study on campus.

(2) Concurrent Work and Study Experience

Description: Concurrent work and study allows the student to have a parallel work and study program where students work in the Tallahassee area on a part-time basis and go to school at the same time.

(3) Six Month Placement Experience
Description: The six month placement allows students to be employed for two consecutive quarters. The model is particularly advantageous to students employed outside the Tallahassee area.

Unit: Career Planning and Placement
Activity: Summer Employment Program

(1) Summer Employment Program
For: All students
Serves: 500 students inquire
Description: This program provides assistance to students in obtaining summer jobs primarily outside the Tallahassee area. The Tallahassee area is handled by the Office of Student Financial Affairs.

Unit: Curricular Career Information Service
Activity: Module V — Information on Work Experience Opportunities

(1) Student Community Interaction
Description: A list of volunteer experiences available through SCI is located in the CCIS Module V file. SCI offers volunteer work experiences, mostly in the area of helping other people.

(2) Volunteer Placement and Human Needs Service
Description: CCIS Module V file identifies volunteer experiences that are available in the Tallahassee area through this service.

(3) Volunteer Organizations in Tallahassee

Description: CCIS Module V file lists volunteer organizations in Tallahassee which would provide students with a variety of work experiences.

Unit: University Counseling Center

Activity: Apprenticeship Opportunities

For:

Serves:

Description: The Counseling Center provides opportunities for undergraduates to gain a first-hand look at career opportunities in the mental health profession through a variety of professional and pre-professional programs such as the Telephone Counseling Service, Project Alteract, and group training programs.

C. Concept: Occupational skills are necessary in the world of work.

Goal: The student will be aware of employability skills which are useful in seeking, obtaining, and maintaining a job.

Objective: The student will develop skill in seeking, obtaining, and maintaining a job.

Unit: Cooperative Education

Activity: Develop Employability Skills

(1) Work Experience

(2) Class Presentations

(3) Vocational Counseling

Unit: Career Planning and Placement

Activity: Develop Employability Skills

(1) Interviews with Recruiters

(2) Career Planning Course

(3) Vocational Counseling

Unit: University Counseling Center
Activity: Develop Employability Skills
(1) Career raps for blacks
(2) Employability skills workshop

DOMAIN III: KNOWLEDGE AND IMPLEMENTATION OF LIFE CAREER PLANNING SKILLS

A. Concept: Awareness of resources is necessary for effective career planning and development.

Goal: The student will be aware of resources in the university which will facilitate his career planning and development.

Objective: The student will be aware of the major career development services available in the university and will be able to identify the service most appropriate for his particular needs.

Unit: Curricular-Career Information Service
Activity: CCIS Module V—Referral Source
For: All students
Serves: Approximately 800 yearly
(1) Referral Source for Career Planning and Placement: video-tape description
(2) Referral Source for Cooperative Education Program: video-tape description
(3) Referral Source for the University Counseling Center: printed materials
(4) Rerferal Source for the Center for Undecided Majors: printed materials
(5) Referral Source for Financial Aid Resources: printed material
(6) Placement Faculty Referral Directory:

Unit: University Counseling Center
   Activity: Career Development Laboratory
      (Proposed)
   For: All students
   Description: The CDL is proposed as a clearing house for all career related services offered through the University Counseling Center. In addition to administering tests such as the SVIB when appropriate, it will serve as a referral source for career related services. At the time of referral, the staff will make arrangements with the student to provide specific feedback on his experience. In this way the Lab will be able to identify problems in service delivery, help the student get additional or more appropriate help, and, at the same time, personalize the student's experience.

Unit: All Units

   Activity: Orientation Programs
   (1) Career Planning and Placement: Orientation programs before various student groups and brochures distributed throughout the university.
   (2) Cooperative Education: Orientation programs before various student groups and brochures distributed throughout the university.
   (3) Curricular Career Information Service: Orientation programs before various student groups and distribution of brochures throughout the university. Other orientation activities include radio spots and interviews, articles in the Flambeau, and posters on campus.

B. Concept: Competency in decision-making skills allows an individual increased freedom to control his own life.

　Goal: The student will be aware of decision making and career planning skills.

　　1. Objective: The student will develop competence in decision making skills.

　　　Unit: Curricular Career Information Service

　　　Activity: Career Decision Making

　　　　(1) CCIS Module II—Career Decision Making

　　　　For: All students

　　　　Serves:

　　　　Description: This activity identifies improper assumptions students often make when selecting majors. It also provides an outline of a method to use when making curricular or career decisions.

　　　　(2) CCIS Module V—Educational Career Plan

　　　　For: All students

　　　　Serves:

　　　　Description: This plan consists of a questionnaire designed to help the student focus on possible directions for his education and/or career. It helps the student identify personal factors and other forces which influence his decisions. It enables the student to state specifically what is involved in his area of investigation and encourages him to outline a schedule of action which will help him to reach his goals.

　　　Unit: University Counseling Center

　　　Activity: Future Groups

　　　For: All students

Serves:

Description: Future groups are personal growth career development groups designed to help members explore assumptions underlying career decisions.

Activity: Mini-Future Groups

For: All students

Serves:

Description: The Mini-Future Group is a one-shot experimental group designed to begin people on the process of exploring assumptions underlying career decisions. It can serve from 200-300 at one time.

Activity: Academic Improvement Training Groups

For: All students

Serves:

Description: These groups are designed to assist in career and academic goal setting, motivation, and scheduling of time.

2. Objective: The student will learn the techniques of career planning and job search.

   Unit: Career Planning and Placement

   Activity: Career Planning Course

   For: All students

   Serves: 80 yearly

   Description: The Career Planning Course offered in cooperation with the School of Business is designed to familiarize the student with the career planning process. The course provides the student with information on interviewing skills and occupation seeking skills, in addition to requiring the development of a written career plan.

   Unit: Cooperative Education

Activity: Class Presentations
For: All students
Serves: 600 yearly
Description: Several class sessions devoted to a discussion of the techniques of interviewing and where to look for jobs after exhausting university resources are conducted by representatives of the Coop Program at the invitation of professors.

C. Concept: There are a variety of life-styles
    Goal: The student will understand the relationship between occupations and life styles.

D. Concept: Leisure time is important to an individual's well-being.
    Goal: The student will understand the function of leisure time in his life.

E. Concept: Healthy career development leads to implementation of career plans.
    Goal: The student will integrate past knowledge and experience into a planned career.

    1. Objective: The student will participate in on-campus recruitment programs.
       Unit: Career Planning and Placement
       Activity: Placement Programs
       For: Seniors and Graduate Students

       (1) Annual Placement Conferences
          Serves: 2,700 students
          Description: These conferences are organized each year to bring large numbers of similar employers to the campus simultaneously for one or two days for recruiting.

       (2) Career Placement Assistance
          Serves: 9,500 student interviews yearly

Description: This assistance involves campus visits by employer representatives from educational systems, government, business, industry, and social action agencies who interview interested students.

(3) Placement Credentials File

Serves: 7,670 yearly

Description: The credentials file contains a resume, letters of recommendation, and a course listing sheet which is sent to prospective employers. The file is maintained by the student and facilitates his employment.

2. Objective: The student will be aware of job vacancies which do not involve on campus interviews.

   Unit: Career Planning and Placement

   Activity: Position Vacancy Listing

   For: All students, particularly seniors and graduate students.

   Description: This listing provides notification to students of specific job openings through bulletin board posting, notification of deans, department heads, and instructors.

3. Objective: The student will be aware of graduate school opportunities available to him.

   Unit: Career Planning and Placement

   Actitvity: Graduate School Information

   (1) Career Library: Graduate School Catalogs

   (2) Periodic campus visits by graduate school recruiters.

4. Objective: The alumni of the university will be aware that continuing assistance is pro-

vided for them in furthering development of their individual career plans and interests.

Unit: Career Planning and Placement

Activity: Alumni Placement Service

(1) Bi-weekly publication

For:

Serves:

Description: This service consists of a bi-weekly publication in cooperation with the Alumni Affairs Officer containing nationwide position vacancies.

(2) Career Planning and Placement Services

For: Alumni

Serves: 800 yearly

Description: All regular career planning and placement services are available on a continuing basis to alumni.

AUTHOR INDEX

A

Abt, C. C., 74, 75, 78
Adkins, W. R., 80
Allen, T. W., 91
Amatea, E., 225
Anastasi, A., 4-12, 53
Anthony, W., 158
Astin, H. A., 218

B

Bacon, M. K., 215, 223
Bandura, A., 75
Banning, J. H., 127, 144
Barbarosh, B., 205
Bardwick, J. M., 214
Barrett, C. J., 226
Barry, H., 215, 223
Bartsch, K., 224, 228
Baruch, R., 220
Beach, F. A., 236
Beck, J. D., 260
Bem, D. J., 215, 216, 220
Bem, S. L., 215, 216, 220
Berenson, B. G., 251
Bernard, H. W., 14
Bieber, I., 241
Biggers, J., 44
Bird, C., 218
Birk, J. M., 223, 229
Birney, J., 117, 119
Blau, P. M., 30
Blocher, D., 13, 155, 174
Boocock, S. S., 77, 78
Borow, H., 154, 158
Brammer, L., 37
Brewer, J., 5
Brobst, H., 205
Brooks, G. C., Jr., 267
Broverman, I. K., 220
Brown, D. A., 245
Brown, W. F., 145, 146

Buehler, C., 27
Burck, H. D., 8
Burkhart, M. Q., 177, 180, 214
Burks, H., 203

C

Calvert, R., 158
Cannon, H. J., 240
Capuzzi, D., 263
Carey, R., 176, 261
Carkhuff, R. A., 251
Carney, C., 159
Carroll, M. R., 146
Carter, E., 158
Chick, J. M., 142, 188
Child, I. L., 215, 223
Cimino, E. R., 210
Clark, K. B., 256
Clark, R., 79
Cochran, D., 107, 119, 139
Cohen, J., 219
Coleman, J. S., 72
Conyne, R. K., 139
Cooper, J., 223
Cramer, S. H., 20, 52, 65
Crawford, J., 74
Crites, J. O., 65
Cronbach, L. J., 53
Cunha, J. E., 139, 170

D

Daane, C., 110, 111
Davenport, L., 254, 255
Davis, J., 5
Dawson, R. E., 71, 74
Devlin, T., 154
Dewey, C. R., 61
Dickey, B., 240
Dolliver, R. H., 62
Domkowski, D., 177, 180
Douvan, E., 222

Drews, E. M., 219
Dugan, W., 155, 174
Dunphy, P. W., 41
Dustin, E. R., 155, 174

E
Edwards, D., 176
Egan, G., 86, 87
Eisenberg, S., 73
Elder, L. A., 205
Ellis, H., 241
Ellis, R. A., 20, 94
Elster, W., 115, 261
Engelkes, J. R., 189
Erikson, E., 153
Espich, J. E., 143

F
Farnham, M. F., 219
Farson, R. E., 199
Feingold, S. N., 198
Fine, S. A., 184
Falugher, R. L., 256
Ford, C. S., 236
Freud, S., 235
Frisbey, N., 224, 225
Fuhriman, A., 159
Fullmer, D. W., 14

G
Gagné, R. M., 71
Gelatt, H. B., 79, 109, 156, 261
Ginzberg, E., 7, 27, 217
Gold, M., 222
Goldman, L., 39, 47, 56, 65
Greer, N., 117
Gunnings, T., 265
Gustad, J. W., 30
Gysbers, N. C., 284

H
Haimowitz, M. L., 87, 88, 89
Haley, J., 93, 94
Hamilton, J. A., 139
Handreck, F., 220
Harmon, L. W., 215
Harper, F. D., 253, 260, 264
Harren, V. A., 66, 67

Harris, J. A., 188
Harwood, R. K., 203
Hatch, R. N., 189
Hatterer, L. J., 241
Hawley, P., 218, 225
Hays, D. G., 139
Helms, S., 176
Henry, D. D., 269
Henry, G. W., 239
Herr, E. L., 20, 65
Hewer, V., 19, 102, 103, 115, 117
Hill, W. F., 264
Hinkle, J., 117, 118
Hoelting, F. B., 144
Hoffman, M., 243
Hoffman, S. D., 85, 119, 122
Holcomb, J., 153, 156
Holland, J. L., 11, 23, 60, 62, 64, 163,
    189, 199, 223, 262, 265
Hollifield, J., 176
Hollis, J., 43
Hollis, L., 43, 176
Hoppock, R., 184, 189, 191, 207
Horner, M., 217, 218, 220, 225
Hosford, R., 127, 132, 139, 167, 180
Houston, R., 172
Howe, L., 108
Hoyt, D., 115
Hurst, J., 127

I
Isaacson, L., 40, 47, 184, 189

J
Jacobson, T. J., 188
Jakubowski-Spector, P., 227
Jessor, R., 30
Johnson, L., 160
Johnson, R. H., 76, 251, 254
Jones, G. B., 139
Jones, G. R., 259
Jones, H., 176
Jones, J., 109

K
Karnes, M. B., 259
Kass, E., 160

Katz, J., 214, 217
Keen, S., 120
Kelly, G. A., 76
Kimball, R. L., 262
Kinsey, A., 237, 242
Kirk, A., 189
Kirk, B. A., 189, 191
Kirschenbaum, L., 108
Knezevich, S. J., 276
Korn, H., 127
Kroll, A. M., 101, 188
Krumboltz, J. D., 49, 50, 75, 85, 170
Kunze, K. R., 183

L

Laramore, D., 176
Lasser, B., 170
Lee, J., 158
Lemay, M. L., 178, 180
Lenzhoff, M., 239
Levin, H., 215, 223
Levine, L., 79
Lewis, J., 127
Lippset, L., 20
Lowrey, B., 176
Lundberg, F., 219

M

Maccoby, E. E., 215, 223
Madison, P., 214, 217
Mager, R. F., 139
Magoon, T. M., 80, 165
Mahler, C., 103
Marland, S. P., 254
Martin, A., 44
Martin, R., 160
Maslow, A. H., 21, 153
Matheny, K., 76
Matthews, E., 217
McHolland, J., 108
Meehl, P. E., 65
Menacker, J., 259
Mencke, R., 119
Mezzano, J., 153
Michels, E., 189
Miller, G., 109, 176, 261
Miller, M., 243

Minor, C. W., 44, 77, 180
Mitchell, A., 176
Montgomery, A., 89
Montgomery, D., 89
Moore, E. J., 284
Morrill, W. H., 127, 144
Murphy, I., 158
Myrick, R. D., 76

N

Nafziger, D., 176
Nixon, R. M., 254
Noble, V., 160
Norman, R. P., 44
Norris, W., 189
Novick, B., 191, 198, 199

O

Oetting, E., 127
O'Hara, R. P., 66, 100
O'Hare, R., 170
Ortmeyer, D., 219
Osipow, S. H., 28, 214, 221
Osmond, M. W., 78
Otto, H., 120, 121
Overs, R. P., 46, 190

P

Pace, A., 176
Packard, T., 159
Palomeras, V. H., 127
Panos, R. J., 218
Parker, C., 127, 155
Parnes, H. S., 30
Parsons, F., 5, 37, 197
Pate, R., 203
Patterson, C. H., 39, 47
Perkins, J. A., 267
Perrone, P. A., 142
Perry, W., 101
Petty, R., 254, 255
Pfeiffer, J., 109
Pietrofessa, J. J., 219
Powers, K., 205
Prediger, D. J., 7, 52, 53, 54, 61
Putsell, T .E., 8

R

Ramsey, S. E., 161, 230
Rapp, D. W., 263
Reardon, R. C., 154, 155, 162, 180
Roe, A., 11, 21
Rogers, C., 102
Rosenthal, D., 219
Rusalem, H., 40, 45
Ryan, T. A., 127, 132, 139, 167, 180

S

Samler, J., 39
Sanz, D., 119
Sauber, R. S., 75
Scates, A. Y., 142
Scherini, R., 191
Schild, E. O., 78
Schlossberg, N. K., 219
Schroeder, W., 50
Scott, A. M., 74
Scott, G. J., 224, 225
Sears, R. R., 215, 223
Sedlacek, W. E., 267
Segal, S., 220
Shearn, R. B., 139
Shostrom, E. L., 37
Simon, S., 108
Simpson, L., 203
Sinick, D., 37, 47
Smith, J. D., 177, 180
Smith, P. M., 127
Smith, T., 176
Socarides, C. W., 241
Sorenson, T., 198
Sowell, T., 256
Sprague, H. T., 72
Sprague, J., 116
Steiner, C., 87, 88, 92
Stephens, E. W., 203
Stephens, W. R., 198
Stewart, N. R., 49, 219
Stoddard, K., 159
Stone, W. O., 253, 256, 260, 264
Strong, D., 116
Strong, E. K., Jr., 220, 223
Strozt, R., 199
Stufflebeam, D. I., 268
Sullivan, H., 170
Super, D. E., 11, 27, 28, 67, 68, 188

T

Tanney, M. F., 223, 229
Teal, D., 239
Thomas, A. H., 219
Thomas, L., 117, 118
Thompson, A., 43, 183
Thoresen, C. E., 49, 50, 75
Thrush, R. S., 142
Tiedeman, D. V., 11, 66, 199, 217
Tobiason, R., 160
Tolbert, E. L., 190, 200, 203, 205
Truax, C. B., 251
Trueblood, J., 108
Tuckman, B. W., 275
Twelker, P. A., 73, 74
Tyler, L., 20

V

Varenhorst, B. B., 49, 77, 79, 176, 266
Vineyard, E., 205
Vinitsky, M., 107
Volsky, T., 102, 103, 117
Vontress, C. E., 252, 257

W

Walz, G., 157
Warnath, C. F., 178, 180
Warren, P., 107
Warsaw, P., 159
Webb, E., 161
Weitzman, L. J., 215, 217
Welkowitz, J., 219
Welsing, F. C., 252, 263
Wesley, W. A., 239
White, S., 176
Wilcock, R. S., 30
Williams, B., 143
Winterstein-Lambert, E., 240
Wooley, D., 176

Y

Yabroff, W., 79
Yankelovich, D., 10

Z

Zehrback, R. R., 259
Zeran, F. R., 189
Zytowski, D. G., 19

SUBJECT INDEX

A

Ability, 19
Accountability defined, 269
ACT Interest Inventory, 60
  Interest Map, 61
  World of Work Map, 61
Administering counseling programs, 147
Adolescent, 9
Advisory committee for career education, 203
Affirmative action, 249, 255
Age
  interest development and, 19
  self-concept theory and, 27
Alumni resources, 205, 206
  representative groups, 205
American College Testing Program, 60
Assessment
  counselor bias in, 55
  criticisms of, 53
  of minorities, 54, 256-258
  objective, 107
  subjective, 108
  trait-and-factor approach in, 53
  of women, 54
  (see also *Non-Sexist Vocational Card Sort,* Tests, Needs)
Assessment of vocational maturity, 65
Attrition, 110, 122

C

California State University, San Diego, 161, 230
Career, ix
Career conference, 207-210
Career Counseling & Placement Guides, 203
Career sources, 132, 154, 156, 158, 171
  for women, 161, 226, 230
Career development, ix
  for ethnic minorities, 248-267

for homosexuals, 234-247
for women, 213-233
implication regarding, 31
model, 283-305
relationship to assessment, 52
theories of, 17-32
  (see also Domains)
Career Development Group, 106-110
Career Development Systems, 258-260
Career development theories, 11, 17-33
  nature of changing, 11
Career education, ix, 154, 254-256
Career Education News, 200
Career guidance, 53
Career information, 183
  sources, 184-187
Career Pattern Study (CPS), 28
Career Resource Center
  equipment, 181
  goals, 178
  layout, 188
  location, 180
  materials, 181, 194, 195
    development, 190
    evaluation, 189
  organization, 191
  personnel, 181, 191
Carnegie Commission, 254
Case-Conference Group, 115-117
College Placement Council, 203
Community Resources, 197-211
Comparative Guidance & Placement Program, 58
Competency based instruction, 143
Conceptual framework
  of occupational choice, 30
Contracts
  advantages, 87
  behavioral goals, 90
  carrying out, 93
  characteristics of, 88

313

client "shoulds" vs "wants", 89
confrontation, 92
evaluating, 94
game playing, 87
partial transcript, 94-98
steps in negotiating, 90-93
uses, 85-99
Cooperative education, 200
Cooperative efforts, 197-200
Cost-benefit ratio, 277
Cost-effectiveness ratio, 276
Counseling *(see* Contracts, Information, Groups)
Counseling and psychotherapy, 241
homosexuals, 241
limitations of, for women, 221
Counseling as instruction, 132
Counselor anxiety, 38, 39, 46, 242
Counselor role, 8, 35, 45-50, 127-129
Covert information, 46, 190
Covert-overt behavior, 240
Cress Theory, 252
The "cube", 127
Curricular approaches
defined, 152
described, 156, 171
California State University, San Diego, 161
Deciding, 156
Decisions and Outcomes, 157
Florida State University, 158
Langley High School, 160
Life/Career Development System, 157
Phoenix College, 159
University of Utah, 158
design of, 170
goals, 155
history, 153-156
women, 226
Curricular-Career Information Service, 162, 172
CVIS, 188

D

Deciding, 156, 171
Decision-making, 41-42, 76, 79, 81, 100,

156, 163, 165, 278
Decisions and Outcomes, 157, 261
Developing programs, goals & objectives, 138
Development, human, 153
Developmental systems for minorities, 258-260
Developmental tasks and career development, 27
Dictionary of Occupational Titles, 46, 62, 63, 183, 184, 262
Differential Aptitude Tests, 58
Career Planning Program, 57
validity of, 58
Domains, career development
educational and occupational knowledge and preparation, 284, 293
knowledge and implementation of life career planning, 285, 301
self-knowledge and inter-personal skills, 284, 286
Dyadic Counseling, 251

E

Education, 12
Educational requirements, 12
Effective Problem Solving, 165-166
Ethnic minorities, 250
Evaluation, in program design, 139
Evaluation, purpose 271-273
Evaluation, summative and formative, 148

F

Family factors, 20
Family (parent) influences on occupational choice, 21
Fantasy, 112, 120
Fantasy stage of occupational choice, 27
Feedback, 71-73
Fixed Role Therapy, 76
Florida State University, 119, 158, 162
Funding counseling programs, 146
Future Group, 119-122

G

Games, 74, 76-78, 80-81, 224
General Aptitude Test Battery, 57

Goal setting, 155, 168, 169
Government, 12
Groups
    attrition, 110, 122
    Career Development, 106-110
    Case-Conference, 115-117
    differentiating, 104-105
    Future, 119-122
    Life-Planning, 117-119
    rationale for, 102
    Vocational Exploration, 110-115
Group Teaching Techniques, 263

H

Homosexual
    Civil Service, 238, 239
    historical references to, 236, 239
    incidence, 234
    literature, 235
    parental response, 244
    stereotype, 238
Human behavior, 11

I

Identifying program constituents, 136-138
Identity, 101
Illinois State University, 115
Indirect services, 155
Individual differences, 155
Industry, 14, 198
Information
    acquisition, 42-44, 48, 181, 194, 195
    counselee needs, 44, 45
    intermix, 263
    man-job links, 110
    occupational, 45, 46
    problems, 38, 39
    purposes, 39-41
    use of, 47-49
    (*see also* Career resource center and
        Career information)
Informational vs instructional materials,
    143
Instructional materials development,
    140-142
Integrating educational/career guidance,
    131-132

Interests, 19
    (*see also* Tests and Assessment)
Internality, 101, 122

J

Job development, 204
Johns Hopkins University, 163
Journal of College Placement, 203

K

Kuder Occupational Survey, 54, 60
Kuder Preference Record, 60, 62

L

Langley High School, 160
Learning thru Discussion, 263
Life/Career Development System, 157
Life Career Game, 76
Life-Planning Workshop, 117-119
Life stages and self-concept theory, 22
Local job information, 198

M

Minority
    career development, 248
    classifications, 249
    counseling, 250, 251
    designations, 250
    testing, 54, 256-258
Modal personality orientation, 23
Modal work environments, 23
Model, Career Development in Univer-
    sity Setting, 283-307
Modeling, 49-75
Models, of occupational decision-mak-
    ing, 18
Multiplier effects, 155
Multipotentiality, 27

N

Needs
    assessment, 133-138, 153-155
    constituent, 137
    and occupational choice, 22
    preventitive, 122-123
    remedial, 122-123
    (*see also* Career development)
Non-Sexist Vocational Card Sort, 61

O

Occupational choice, 30
Occupational classification, 21
Occupational information (*see* Career resource center, Information)
Occupational Outlook Handbook, 46, 63, 183, 184, 185
Occupations, classifications of
  Roe's, 21
  Holland's, 24-25
Optimization, Ginzberg, 27
Outreach in counseling programs, 127, 144

P

Para-professionals, 145-146
Peer influence, 13
Pennsylvania State University, 228
Performance indicators, 273
Personal growth, 264
Personality constructs, 11
Personality theory, of career choice, 21
Phoenix College, 159
Placement service, 197, 198, 203, 227
Police tactics, 236-237
Political activity, 237
Problem identification, 133, 135
Problem solving, 11
  creation, 11
Process
  career development, 18
  occupational choice, 30
  occupational selection, 30
Program model, 128, 283-307

R

Racial understanding, 262
Racism, 250, 252, 262
Realistic period and occupational choice, 27
Referrals in counseling programs, 144
Reinforcement, 71
Religion, 243
Research, 235
  (*see also* Evaluation)
Research designs, 275
Resource Directory, 205

Role conflicts for women, 216-218
Role-models, 14

S

S-R, 71
Self-
  awareness, 155, 156, 160
  concept, 6, 40, 45
    theory of, 27
  deciding, 100, 119
Self-Directed Career Program, 163
Self-Directed Search, 106, 107, 163, 172, 223, 261
Self-evaluation and occupational choice, 26
Self-help techniques
  defined, 152
  described, 161, 172
    Curricular-Career Information Service, 162
    Effective Problem Solving, 165
    Self-Directed Career Program, 172
    Self-Directed Search, 163, 172
    University of California, San Diego, 161
  design of, 172
  goals, 155, 156
Self-knowledge and occupational choice, 26
Sex roles, 13, 216-218
Sex-role stereotyping, 215, 216
Shadowing, 205
Simulation, 70-82
Situation Attitude Scale, 263
Social change, 11-13
Socialization of women, 215-218
Strong-Campbell Interest Inventory, 59
Strong Vocational Interest Blank, 59, 60, 106, 107, 108, 214, 220, 223
Systemic counseling, 264
Systems approaches, 128, 133, 153, 167, 199
Systems approach for program development, 174, 175, 260
  design of program materials, 170
    curricular approaches, 171
    self-help techniques, 172

evaluation of program, 174, 268-279
goal setting, 138, 168
    behavioral objectives, 168-170
implementation of program, 173
modification of program, 175
needs assessment, 133-138, 167
simulate or pilot study, 173
Systems approach model, 133, 167
Systems design of counseling programs, 132, 167

T

Tests
    counselor use of, 52-68
    role of in career guidance, 52
    (*see also* Assessment)
Trait-and-factor, 53
Trait-and-factor theory, 19
Transactional Analysis, 86
Transcendent Counseling, 253, 264
Transfer of learning, 71
Trial and error, 72
Tyler Vocational Card Sort, 62

U

University of California, San Diego, 161
University of Maryland, 165
University of Utah, 158

V

Values, 13, 20, 157, 163, 225
Venereal disease, 244
Vocational decision-making, 213
    (*see also* Decision-making)
Vocational Decision-Making Checklist, 66
Vocational development, 214
Vocational education, 154
Vocational Exploration Group, 110-115, 261
Vocational guidance, 5
    attitudes toward, 6-7
    complexity of, 6, 9-10
    current scene, 5
    history, 5
    in counselor training programs, 8
    movement, success of, 10
    need for, 10
    and personal problems, 11
    routine nature of, 7
    self-concept, 6
    singularity of approach, 9
    therapeutic models of, 6
Vocational implications, 238
Vocational maturity, 28, 65
Vocational models, 245, 246
Vocational planning, 261, 262
Vocational Preference Inventory, 64, 262
Volunteer work, 200

W

Wolfenden Report, 13-14
Women
    aptitudes, 224
    counseling programs for, 228-230
    counselor bias, 219
    interests, 223
    socialization, 215, 220
    values, 225
Work
    demeaning nature of, 15
    dissatisfactions with, 15
    productivity, 14
Work in America, 15, 198
Work Values Inventory, 67

Y

Youth, 11